Voices from around the country

"Vermont welcomes Wal-Mart. But not in a cornfield; not in a big box on a city's outskirts, threatening the vitality of other local communities . . . where cities ringed with suburban malls look for ways to breathe life back into ghost downtowns."
— **Editorial,** *Burlington Free Press*, **August 30, 1997**

"I cherish the lovely times I spend here in Old Saybrook. It would be an absolute shame to allow a commercial development of this sort to forever change our town."
— **Katharine Hepburn, 1995, commenting on Wal-Mart plans in Connecticut**

"Wal-Mart has become a lightning rod for foes of commercialization and bigness. In some communities the arrival of large discount chains has meant the withering and demise of smaller local businesses . . . the beginning of blight in areas which previously enjoyed a rural atmosphere."
— **Editorial,** *The Observer*, **Smithfield, Rhode Island, June 8, 1995**

"Something must be done to help all of the people who are working at Wal-Mart and are being mistreated by this management . . . If everyone who has been treated as I have been would not be so hesitant about speaking out and their families and friends would stop shopping at wonderful Wal-Mart, they would not be so successful."
— **Robert Howell, 59-year-old former Wal-Mart employee, May 3, 1995**

They're just businessmen making money. Culturally it hurts. Economically it really hurts. We're at their mercy. We were dependent on them."
— **Sue Ann Ryan, Director, Chamber of Commerce, Bixby, Oklahoma, March 5, 1995**

"In the ten years before Wal-Mart opened, we had a total of 20 business failures. In the ten years after Wal-Mart was here, we had 185 business failures. You could buy a bicycle in eight locations in this town. Today, if you want to buy a bicycle, you can only buy it at Wal-Mart."
— **Glenn Falgoust, Donaldsonville, Louisiana,** *60 Minutes*, **April 30, 1995**

"Wal-Mart's merchandise has not only homogenized consumption patterns throughout the country, it is homogenizing our experience of the landscape."
— **Ellen Dunham-Jones, *Harvard Design Magazine*, Fall 1997**

"It may be argued that the entry of Wal-Mart should be accepted because it represents free enterprise. This is a reasonable argument when Wal-Mart enters large and growing markets. However, it is not reasonable to assume that when one store dominates a market, that a monopoly can be avoided. In fact, monopoly conditions have been considered inconsistent with the concept of free enterprise for over a century."
— **Tom Muller, economist, August 1997 impact study, Woodstock, Virginia**

"America is absolutely overstored."
— **Kurt Barnard, retail consultant, *US News & World Report*, July 14, 1997**

"One of the sayings that Wal-Mart has is 'Respect for the Individual.' I would really like to know which individual, because I didn't see anyone in the store that I worked at knowing the meaning of the phrase."
— **Lynn Marie Berg, worked at Wal-Mart for 5 years, November 1998**

"I had a heck of a business – four people in sales and two full-time bookkeepers. Now I've got a part-time bookkeeper and a part-time salesman. My business is down 35% since Wal-Mart came to town . . . It's devastating. The merchants downtown are just hanging on, and I don't see it getting better."
— **Rodney Norman, Norman's Hardware, Hazelhurst, Mississippi, June 1988**

"It's just devastated our downtown. The mom and pops are closed up . . . overall I'd have to say it's been a negative for our town."
— **Mayor Harry Hammond, Europa, Mississippi, June 1988**

"What the residents are objecting to is a powerful, monied corporation that is absolutely insensitive to the needs of the neighborhood and only interested in making money trying to use its wealth and legal power to push onto this neighborhood a commercial venture that wasn't ever intended."
— **Sheila Slomski, Mesa, Arizona, January 1999**

"The U.S. is really saturated with retailers in our bigger cities. In the late 1960s there was five square feet of retail space for every person in the U.S. Now there is around twenty."
— **Ken Stone, Professor, Iowa State University, October 7, 1998**

"Seniority and doing a good job mean nothing here. The Wal-Mart Open Door policy means that if you OPEN your mouth, you'll be OUT the door."
— **Dale Stiles, Wal-Mart employee, *Arkansas Times*, September 3, 1992**

"It just isn't the Wal-Mart way to give a rip about the community in which they are doing business. If things go a little sour, they just close up and go some-where else — where the bucks are. It's all business at Wal-Mart . . . they have all the compassion of a sledgehammer."
— **Tom Larimer, Editor, Carroll County, Newspapers Arkansas newspaper, November 7, 1991**

"They claim retail zoning will bring jobs and tax income to our community. These are part-time, minimum wage jobs that produce very little in income taxes."
— **Mayor Ed Boyle, North Olmsted, Ohio, October 25, 1997**

"If superstores would configure themselves in a more environmentally friendly way, they would encounter less resistance."
— **Constance Beaumont, *Land & People*, Fall 1995**

"They destroyed all of their competition and now we can not get anyone to reopen here. We have no place to buy a man's dress shirt, or blue jeans for men . . . They have also pulled out of other towns since then. They are not nearly as stable as they would lead you to believe."
— **Archer Hoyt, Past President, Hearne, Texas Chamber of Commerce, October 1993**

"Growth must come at a pace that a community and its residents can sustain, and in a location and manner that compliments the integrity of a community. If Wal-Mart can conform to these community needs, it is welcome. If not, we are not interested in letting it open its doors."
— **Stan Cox, Simcoe, Ruidoso, Canada, 1995**

"Developers are making huge shopping centers in small towns that are too close to each other. 10 to 12 to 18 miles apart. Somebody is going to be hurt."
— **Mike Noila, Jr., Senior VP, developer Manley-Berenson of Puerto Rico, December, 1994**

"If a community genuinely doesn't want a Wal-Mart store, we won't go there. We will never mistake a vocal minority, however, for the majority."
— **Don Shinkle, Wal-Mart Vice President, Corporate Affairs, November 4, 1995**

"I was in business for 34 years until Wal-Mart came in. Many days the only person that turned the door knob was the mailman and expenses went on as usual and my accountant tried to talk me into quitting business in 1992, but I did not want to. My year 1993 federal tax report showed a loss of $26,000, and that made me see the light."
— **Richard L. Smith, Weston, West Virginia, letter to the editor, May 4, 1995**

"The death knell for any downtown business district is the invasion of regional and large discount retailers which locate outside of the older, established business area. If immediate and effective efforts are not made to breathe life into downtown districts, they can deteriorate into ghost towns within a few years. Just look around at other south Georgia downtowns."
— **Editorial, *The Times-Enterprise*, Thomasville, Georgia, August 21, 1994**

"Wal-Mart in Plainville (CT) will be a disaster for this community and its neighbors. Wal-Mart doesn't contribute to a community, it subtracts from it. The discount department store's predatory philosophy of undercutting local merchants is designed to put them out of business and eliminate alternatives."
— **Editorial, *The Herald*, Plainville, Connecticut, October 19, 1994**

"Let's see — assuming a Wal-Mart-induced commuting delay of 15 minutes a day, 250 days a year, and billing at $20 an hour, that comes to $1,250 per commuter per year. For doctors and lawyers who can charge $200 an hour, it's about $12,500 per year. We'll take it in the form of personal checks, thanks, with a surcharge for air pollution, pain, suffering and ugliness."
— **Donella Meadows, column in the *Valley News*, Plainfield, New Hampshire, June 12, 1993**

"You need to be empathetic to the fact that people are going a little crazy. You're going out, and all you see are these giant Wal-Marts. They are every few blocks, and it is not the kind of environment people want to live in."
— **Republican strategist Christine Matthews, quoted in the *New York Times*, May 4, 1999**

SLAM-DUNKING WAL-MART!

How You Can Stop Superstore Sprawl in Your Hometown

Al Norman

Raphel Marketing
Atlantic City, New Jersey

A town is not land, nor even landscape.
A town is people living on the land.
And whether it will survive or perish
depends not on the land but on the people;
it depends on what the people think they are.
If they think of themselves as living a good
and useful and satisfying life, if they put their
lives first and the real estate business after,
then there is nothing inevitable about the
spreading ruin of the countryside.

- Archibald MacLeish
"Lay Sermon for the Hill Towns"

Acknowledgements

The author would like to thank the following people for their sprawl-busting efforts, especially Jim Vitelli, who was called the "God" of the anti-Wal-Mart effort in New England, and Ben Cassinerio of Diablo Timber, who is Home Depot's "Devil."

Thanks to all the "accidental activists" over the past six years who put me up in the kids' extra bedroom, gave me the tour of their downtown, took me to the airport, held signs at press conferences, fed me sushi or spaghetti, drove me to the high school speech and conspired for hours on the phone: Carol Goodwin of Sturbridge, MA; Dave Koenig and Stephanie Henriksen of Northfield, MN; Art Kreiger of Cambridge, MA; Susy Gibson of Clermont, FL; Maria Tilling of Southport, NC; Peter Roland and Bob Trostle of Lake Placid, NY; John Jarvis of Lancaster, PA; Steve & Linda Bradish of Williston, VT; Maureen Diver of North Olmsted, OH; John Allen of Tucker, GA; Tim Allen and Elizabeth Dissen of Ithaca, NY; Jack Bopp of Henniker, NH; Pam Westgate of Hadley, MA; Russ Onderko of Mansfield, NJ; Jon Hanna of Stratham, NH; Steve Alves, Wendy Sibbison, Bill Forbes and David Bete of Greenfield, MA; Helen Chisolm of Lower Macungie, PA; Elizabeth Michaud of Westford, MA; Bob Gogan of Plymouth, MA; Glenn and Angela Falgoust of Donaldsonville, LA; Sam Mayberry of Des Moines, IA; Jack Drury of Saranac Lake, NY; Sharon Wallace of Yuma, AZ; Ed Russell of Arlington, MA; Nick Gross of North Greenbush, NY; Ken and Brenda Horrocks of Chestertown, MD; Dawn Rapchinski of Ephrata, PA; Mark Reeves of Old Saybrook, CT; Robin Goble of Windsor, CA; Rena and Mort Schlesinger of Nantucket, MA; Susan McElligott of Peekskill, NY; Amy Webber, Marla and Kent Klocke and Colin Murphy of Decorah, IA; Paul Bruhn of Burlington, VT; Steve Burrington of the Conservation Law Foundation; Bud Hudnall of Kilmarnock, VA; Constance Beaumont of the National Trust for Historic Preservation; Tom Morphee of Gig Harbor, WA; Floyd Snyer of Santa Maria, CA; Amy Durland of Saratoga Springs, NY; Ann Leary of East Aurora, NY; Mike Tyler of Lewes, DE; Carol Rettew of Lititz, PA; Peggy Daly-Masternak, Harry Ward and Marie Sienkowski of Toledo, OH; Deanna Zenger of Elmira, Ontario; John Gladysz of Plainville, CT; Bill Pierson of Eureka, CA; Jill Kleiss of Carmel, CA; Dean Cook of Ticonderoga, NY; Kathy Brownley of Paradise, MD; Stephen Shadley of Catskill, NY; David Norden of Warrenton, VA; Peg Larson at Wintergreen.com; Janis Raye for her editing work; Neil Raphel who said I should write a book and made it happen.

For
Lloyd Norman, Donald Morrison,
Dorothy Norman, Edith Morrison,
Anna Morrison,
Winter Miller, Kate Norman, Josie Norman:
three generations of shoppers
who have never spent a penny at Wal-Mart.

Contents

Introduction

Greenfield Slam-Dunks Wal-Mart

"At the end of the day, the only vote that really matters is the consumers'."
— **David Glass, CEO of Wal-Mart stores**

Wal-Mart means nothing to me.

Home Depot and Target mean even less.

So why have I spent the last six years of my life chasing around the country trying to convince people that companies like Wal-Mart and Home Depot are bad neighbors?

Maybe it's because of what happened in my hometown of Greenfield, Massachusetts.

If there is anything remotely close to a normal day in Greenfield, Massachusetts, then October 19, 1993 was normal:

The police received a call reporting a manhole was out of place at the corner of Pleasant and Chapman Streets.

The Solid Waste Management District held a special composting workshop at the Elks Club on Federal Street.

Wilson's Department Store, the 108 year old downtown anchor business, offered free coffee and donut holes during its Harvest Sale.

And two American flags were stolen from a yard on Grinnell Street.

I had lived through sixteen years of such days in Greenfield. But this day in Greenfield was not yet over.

Over the span of twelve hours on this cool, overcast day in October, 5,708 people in this community that describes itself as a "classic American town" and "everybody's home town", went to the polls and voted to reject a Wal-Mart store on the edge of town. The vote was a close call — but we knew it would be.

Our little community of 19,000 people had brought down the Goliath of discounting. By the next morning, people from Berkeley to Bangladesh knew about the town that had slain the world's largest retailer.

*　　　　　*　　　　　*

There were actually two questions on the town ballot. The first question called for the rezoning of 63 acres of industrial land to commercial, so that Wal-Mart could build a 123,000 square foot store plus two out-buildings at the intersection of two major highways.

The second question would allow buildings larger than 40,000 square feet in the general commercial district. Both questions were on the ballot because an anti-Wal-Mart group called Citizens for Responsible Development (CRD) had gone out and collected more than 600 signatures from registered voters, as called for in Greenfield's initiative petition bylaws.

A public referendum was considered a last-ditch effort to stop Wal-Mart's bulldozers. The previous May, in a non-binding vote, townspeople had voted two-to-one in favor of rezoning the Wal-Mart property. Two months later, our twenty-seven member Town Council had also voted two-to-one to rezone. The Citizens for Responsible Development set up tables on the Town Common and collected signatures in the rain. It was an act of desperation — and the mood in town grew hostile. "Who are these people that are responsible for these petitions?" grumbled one Town Councilor. "I want to know who these people are!"

The CRD, in fact, was headed by the owner of one of the largest industrial businesses in town, David Bete. Bete was convinced that rezoning valuable industrial land was a shortsighted mistake that would cost the town financially. Bete's company made fog nozzles. He had nothing to lose financially if Wal-Mart came to Greenfield. Bete wrote a letter to the editor explaining his views:

> Wal-Mart has identified the only sizable piece of land in Greenfield suitable for development. The reasons it is suitable for retail are similar to the reasons it is suitable for industry: good highway access and visibility, access to utilities that Greenfield paid for to service industrial growth, and a

size of more than 50 acres . . . The executives at Wal-Mart must be laughing in glee over the gullible country bumpkins of Greenfield who will turn over one-third of their best industrial land to them for a few hundred thousand dollars so Wal-Mart can annihilate existing business in Greenfield and send the profits to Arkansas.

Bete's efforts helped reach the petition goal, and the referendum was filed in Town Hall. The petition gave the Town Council one last opportunity to rescind its vote in favor of rezoning for Wal-Mart — but everyone knew the Council would never reconsider. Instead, they scheduled a special town election for October.

The Citizens for Responsible Development had an eight-week campaign on their hands — and they needed someone to manage it. One of the Town Councilors, Wendy Sibbison, called me up and asked me if I would be interested in such a campaign, because I had worked on political campaigns from county Sheriff to State Senator. "What's the big deal about Wal-Mart?" I asked. "It's just a store." Today, whenever I think about why most shoppers don't seem to care about Wal-Mart coming to town, I remember that I was exactly in that frame of mind in August of 1993. I couldn't have cared less.

But as I began talking about the project, I realized that a) it would be time-limited and b) it had great campaign potential: Giant corporation pushes around small town. In fact, I saw the proportions of a national story in the making, because I had heard about Wal-Mart's efforts to bust down the door in neighboring Vermont. I had never set foot inside a Wal-Mart, but the corporate bully aspect really appealed to me. I told Wendy I would do it — as long as she promised me it would all be over in eight to ten weeks. Six years and 29 states later, I am still on the campaign trail against Wal-Mart.

Two days after I agreed to submit a proposal to run the anti-Wal-Mart effort, I was interviewed for the job in the corporate offices of Bete Fog Nozzle, David's business, before a committee of half a dozen citizens. I presented an outline for a two-month campaign that combined grass roots organizing, tele-marketing to identify voters who were with us and major print and radio buys. I told the committee that someone else would have to be in charge of raising money, because I could not be designing ads and lining up lawn sign locations as well as fund-raising. David Bete agreed to raise the funds to carry out the plan. Our coordinating group would meet every other week in the upstairs conference room at Bete's. Did we have a shot? I didn't have time to even think about it.

I was hired by the beginning of August, and the first thing I suggested was that we take on a new name, one that was much more direct and to the point. "Let's be very clear about what we're doing here," I said. "Let's call ourselves WE'RE AGAINST THE WAL."

By election day, even those people who were in favor of Wal-Mart were calling it "The WAL". Our goal was to show people in town that there was another side of the WAL — an unattractive, hidden side of this giant conglomerate. That information, I thought, would turn townspeople against the project.

Given the two previous landslide votes in favor of Wal-Mart, everyone thought we had no chance — including Wal-Mart. We caught them with their cash register down. Corporate money from Arkansas was slow to arrive.

*　　　　*　　　　*

I had no clue as to what was going on with the referendum vote until around ten o'clock the night of the election. We knew the wording for the two questions was confusing, so our red, white and blue lawn signs simply read: "STOP THE WAL: Vote No on Questions 1 and 2."

For eight weeks my wife, Anna, and I did nothing but eat, drink and sleep Wal-Mart. We were managing the tail-end of a year-long battle to keep Wal-Mart out. WE'RE AGAINST THE WAL had raised about $17,000 to pay for newspaper ads, telephone polling, and radio spots. David Bete has promised that any money we couldn't raise, he would put up personally.

To do a little reconnaissance, I drove twenty-two miles to the nearest Wal-Mart in Hinsdale, New Hampshire. Inside I wandered through aisles of shoes from Brazil, skirts made in Sri Lanka, and plastic place mats from Korea. There were signs everywhere: MADE IN THE USA. I scribbled down a few prices of grocery items, like Fritos and Wheaties. (When I got back to Greenfield, I found lower prices on the food items.) On my way out I paid for a $1.00 bag of popcorn and a soda. The clerk said I had to wait while they refilled syrup for the soda machine, so I cancelled the drink, and asked for my money back. The frazzled clerk told me I couldn't get my change back until the next customer cashed out, because her register locked after every transaction. I let her keep the change and bolted out. That was only purchase I have ever made at a Wal-Mart.

During the campaign, we built three portable four by six foot "WALs" of our own, that displayed letters from citizens opposed to superstores. These WALs were erected on Town Common every Saturday, and at a circuit of local grocery stores. We wrote to David Glass: "If you want to know why Greenfield doesn't want Wal-Mart here, come on up — the writing's on the WAL."

Wal-Mart eventually spent more than twice what we did, not counting what it cost them to hire a local lawyer to front for them. Every penny they spent came from corporate headquarters in Bentonville, Arkansas. But they hurt their own cause by making some serious campaign mistakes including:

• Mailing out an anonymous flier to every household in town praising Wal-Mart's virtues. The flier had a picture on Town Hall on the cover making it look like an official mailing from the town. Wal-Mart eventually admitted that it was their flier that had gone out unsigned.

• Forming a "front" citizen's group that had very few local citizens in it.

The feeling was pervasive that Wal-Mart was not playing by the rules. On the day after the election, one voter explained to the paper why he was against rezoning: "John Pretto of Chapman Street said he voted 'no' in part because of a flier Wal-Mart paid for that was unsigned. 'I think Wal-Mart is pretty underhanded,' he said."

During the last week of the campaign, Wal-Mart shipped up from Arkansas full page media ads. But their ads were canned, sloppy, unemotional appeals based on "low everyday prices." They failed to address the major campaign issue that appeared on all our ads: "We're not gaining a store — we're losing our community."

Ours was an appeal to the heart, as well as the head: love of town, loss of local control, destruction of the unique character of the community. "There's one thing you can't find on any Wal-Mart shelf," I kept repeating, "and that's small town quality of life. But once you lose it, Wal-Mart can't sell it back to you at any price."

Wal-Mart was only able to relate to pocketbook issues. We were raising issues that they had never encountered before. They started defending themselves very late, perhaps believing that deep down, every voter was fundamentally a bargain shopper. By then, however, scores of letters to the editor had warned about Wal-Mart's economic impact on small towns, including letters from other communities that had been hurt:

To the Editor:

So, Wal-Mart has decided to bless your community with their big, big store and its low, low prices! They have taken it upon themselves to hire your unemployed, attract business from out of town to your community, and just generally impose their formula for making you a better place to live.

They told us that, too! Don't believe it! . . . If you disrupt your local economy with a big injection of Wal-Mart and take out some of the small businesses which have been at the heart of your community in the process, you may find that the true price of all those low, low prices is very high indeed!

Gregory S. Gundy, Rockland, Maine

To the Editor:

Bring Wal-Mart to Greenfield? No way. Not over our dead Main Street! If we vote to rezone scarce industrial land in Greenfield so Wal-Mart can come in and bulldoze existing businesses, we're crazy. So, I say, 'Hey, David Glass. If you think we need you folks from Arkansas to come in and show us how to solve our problems, then I want you to know, I don't think so. We can do it our own way.' Local people generating local jobs, not income for out-of-state fat cat corporations.

Don't back down. Back downtown!

Brian Summer, Greenfield

To the Editor:

People never seem to have enough. They always want more. I have lived here for forty years. I am 73 years old. I think Wal-Mart will only make the town worse, and I think a lot of the older people in town have been around long enough to see a decline in the town's character. Let's not make it worse."

Rose Anderer Miner, Greenfield

We filled up the editorial page of *The Recorder* newspaper with letters. Eventually Wal-Mart caught on and started generating letters of their own, but they were a day late and a dollar short. Their campaign people called me up one afternoon and said: "Al, knock it off with all those letters to the editor. People are getting turned off." I turned back to our Committee and urged people to redouble their letter-writing efforts, because we had obviously hit the other side in a way that hurt.

Despite the visibility of our campaign, I had good reason to be worried. The final eight weeks leading up to the vote had been bitter and ugly. I had been called a Communist. A Judas. An elitist. Some of my "friends" in the neighborhood had written letters to the editor criticizing me personally. The campaign was rapidly descending into the gutter. Pro-Wal-Mart people began circulating a rumor that I was being paid an enormous sum to run the campaign. They followed up with an ad criticizing our group for forcing the taxpayers to spend $12,000 on this special election.

As a deal-sweetener, Wal-Mart offered to pay for road reconstruction near the site, and promised the town $50,000 to help market its downtown. Wal-Mart opened up a candy store of incentives. On the surface, it looked alluring. But underneath there was the $37 million Wal-Mart would pump out of our community, taking several dozen small businesses with it. We published a map showing that the Wal-Mart land parcel was bigger than our entire downtown. New England Yankees are not flamboyant: this building was simply out of scale.

Greenfield had insisted that Wal-Mart pay for an "independent" economic study that would quantify the retailer's impact on the town. Wal-Mart came up with $35,000, and a firm from New Hampshire was hired. We found out later that this firm had already done direct contract work for Wal-Mart. But even this study, which understated the negative side of the WAL, gave us enough ammunition to sink a dozen Wal-Marts.

When Wal-Mart first showed up in town in October of 1992, they boasted that they would create 270 new jobs and $90,000 annually in added property tax revenue. Local officials jumped in the tank immediately! Jobs and property taxes — every elected official's dream. But when the economic impact statement was released in July of 1993, the gild was off the lily: under the "high impact" scenario, only 29 new jobs would be created, and less than $30,000 in property taxes. By not counting jobs it would kill at other businesses, Wal-Mart had inflated its job claims ten times over. The revenue gain was negligible: it amounted to $1.58 in savings per resident per year. One of my neighbors said: "I'd pay Wal-Mart $1.58 a year just to keep their traffic and congestion out of our town!"

Only a handful of citizens in town ever read the Wal-Mart economic impact report. It was 80 pages long and filled with charts and graphs in ten point type. It became our job to translate this dry report into facts people could understand:

• By the fifth year after Wal-Mart was built, they would control 80% of the town's department store sales.

• Existing Greenfield stores would lose $34.8 million in sales transferred to Wal-Mart.

• More than $60,000 in property taxes would be lost from reduction in property value caused by sales transfers from existing stores.

Even loaded with all this data against the development and despite all the political blunders Wal-Mart had made, I still had good reason to be nervous about the vote.

After all, no one had ever beaten Wal-Mart at the polls.

*   *   *

The polls in nine precincts had closed at 8:00 P.M., but there was no visible activity in the Town Clerk's front office until well into the evening. Several staff were huddled in the back room. That meant it was a close vote. They were probably doing a recount. I felt we were going to lose.

All that afternoon I sat by the voting registrars in Precinct 7 with my ruler and red pencil, lining through the names of voters that we had identified as anti-Wal-Mart. Too many of our people had not turned out to vote. One reporter described the scene at the ballot box:

> Inside, a steady stream of voters flowed in. A cross-section of Greenfield, they wore suits and ties, t-shirts and jeans, a Boy Scout leader uniform, a Friendly's Restaurant uniform, a baseball jacket, a dress and high heels, a blue blazer and loafers.

At 5:00 P.M. our volunteers drove around to each precinct and collected all our poll-watchers' lists. We hurried them back to Bete Fog Nozzle. Inside, we had half a dozen people ready to call everyone whom our poll-watching indicated had not yet turned out to vote. There were at least 400 names on the dog-eared sheets.

We gathered our callers in the narrow hallway. "Wendy," I yelled, "you and Steve take these Precinct 2's and give David the rest of Precinct 3. If people say they're eating dinner, tell them to get up from the table and get down to vote. Remember: the polls close at eight!"

We filled up six phone lines for the next three hours. One of my friends asked me: "How's it look?"

"Our polling says we're strong in Precincts 2, 4, 5 and 6," I replied. "But I was over in Precinct 7 most of the day, and it felt like we were getting clobbered. It's just a feeling, but everyone who came in looked like they had just come from Wal-Mart."

*   *   *

As we paced up and down the dim corridor in Town Hall, we could hear the voices of the Clerk's staff. The phone rang inside the office several times. I knew that Town Clerk Maureen Winseck was calling her brother, who was a selectman in town and very pro-Wal-Mart.

"Don't ask for a recount," she shushed him over the phone (I found out later). "We counted it two times by hand."

Standing next to me at the entrance to the Clerk's office was the editorial page editor of our local newspaper. He wouldn't say a word to me, or even look at me. He had editorialized in favor of Wal-Mart at every opportunity. His dislike for me and the "antis" was like a dark air hanging on the first floor of Town Hall. I didn't understand why he wanted Wal-Mart in town. His newspaper stood to lose substantial ad revenues when local businesses shut down.

We had already taken down our tallies off the "tear sheets" from the automatic voting machines. The pale blue numbers on those enormous sheets showed us virtually in a dead heat. "It must be the absentee ballots," I thought. "The absentee ballots are going to kill us." Those ballots were from people who had left town early before the election or voters in nursing homes. Would they end up being the margin of difference?

Two young reporters wandered vacantly up and down the hallway. A television crew from Springfield went down to our headquarters at the Knapp Sack deli on Main Street. The vote was coming in too late to put on the 11 o'clock news.

Finally, around ten o'clock, Maureen came into the front office. She didn't seem pleased with the numbers in her hands.

"OK, she began, "here are the numbers:
Question 1: 2,845 Yes, 2,854 No.
Question 2: 2,811 Yes, 2,897 No."

*   *   *

I stumbled out past the pale editorial page editor without a glance, and pushed through the double doors of Town Hall and out into the street. I let out a loud HOO-WHEEE! several times, which echoed across the Town Common, bounced off the empty buildings on Bank Row, and leapt back towards me off the walls of Town Hall.

This was a 60% voter turnout! It was the largest turnout in recent history, double the turnout for most local elections, and higher than the 1992 Presidential election. We had taken both measures — by narrow votes to be sure. But this was not a game of retail horseshoes. It was winner take all.

We had slam-dunked Wal-Mart!

*   *   *

Over at the Knapp Sack, a crowd of WE'RE AGAINST THE WAL supporters paced around the empty delicatessen, grabbing nervously at potato chips and ginger ale. They were tuned into local radio station WHAI to get the latest count. A large red,white and blue cake with the words VOTE NO ON QUESTIONS ONE AND TWO decorated the empty window. A few limp balloons hung from the ceiling.

I ran into the room holding the Town Clerk's numbers in my hand. I don't remember what I told the group, but here is how the newspapers described it the next morning:

The Recorder

While Wal-Mart may be the nation's leading retailer, it will not be Greenfield's leading retailer.

"We're two for two, we got 'em!" WE'RE AGAINST THE WAL campaign manager Albert Norman exclaimed Tuesday night about 10 as he ran in the door of his group's Main Street headquarters in the former Knapp Sack deli.

Norman hugged group chairman David Bete Sr. and the gathering of about 35 cheered the narrow defeat of Wal-Mart for almost a minute.

"Somewhere in Bentonville (Ark.) there's a family a little less rich, because they are not going to be taking our money," Norman said.

The Springfield Union-News

Goodbye, Wal-Mart!

That was the message an extremely slim majority of voters sent from behind election curtains yesterday, a difference of nine - count them - nine votes.

"I declare Greenfield a Wal-Mart-free zone," said Albert Norman, an organizer for We're Against the WAL, while munching on a piece of cake with "Vote NO on Questions One and Two" frosted on it. Norman could barely contain his excitement. Around him about 40 anti-Wal-Mart campaigners mingled, hugging one another and exclaiming joy over the narrow victory.

When asked what he thought Greenfield will look like in the next five years, Norman grinned. "Beautiful, green and Wal-Mart free," Norman said.

*   *   *

By the time I reached home, it was well past midnight. I let the cats out, emptied out my pockets on the kitchen counter: all the phone numbers and street addresses, paper clips and precinct tally sheets.

And one other thing.

I had been carrying around with me all day a symbol of defeat, just in case. The symbol of the next phase of our fight against megastores.

I had prepared myself for defeat by printing up the following bumper sticker:

IF THEY BUILD IT
WE WON'T COME!

There was no speech that went along with it, I would just ad-lib something about this being the official beginning of a boycott of the Greenfield Wal-Mart.

I took the folded bumper sticker from my pocket, which was now crumpled and full of notes on the back. I threw it in the fireplace. Some other community might need to start a boycott, but not us, not now.

"At the end of the day," David Glass would later tell *Fortune* Magazine, "the only vote that really matters is the consumers'."

Tonight, at the end of this long day, the voters had rejected Wal-Mart! I was probably as surprised as Wal-Mart that we had won. I didn't think we could pull it off. But we did.

The following morning was like a retail obituary for the folks in Bentonville. "Wal-Mart is, of course, very disappointed," the company's local attorney was quoted as saying. The October 21 edition of the *New York Times* carried this typically terse and bitter comment from Jane Arend, a Wal-Mart spokeswoman: "That was the only site we were interested in in Greenfield. There are thousands of other communities in the Northeast where we can continue our expansion."

Continue to expand they did — but with a band of Sprawl-Busters following right behind.

Part One

Store Wars: The Evil Empire

"You are attempting to advance the agenda of an intelligent network of individuals who view corporate development as evil. Attacking Wal-Mart is the easy way to gather attention for this crusade, but the issue is much larger than Wal-Mart."
— Don E. Shinkle, Wal-Mart Vice President, Corporate Affairs, letter to Lake Placid, New York residents, November 14, 1994

1

Wal-to-Wal Wal-Marts

*"Becoming the world's largest retailer was never
considered. And being big has never been the goal."*
— **Wal-Mart's 1996 Annual Report**

America is drowning in retail glut — and we wouldn't have it any other way. As the *Discount Store News* proclaimed in 1994: "Welcome to the United States of Wal-Mart." Despite what they say, being big has always been the goal at Wal-Mart. In 1989, David Glass had caused a sensation when he forecast that 50% of the nation's existing retail operations would be out of business by the year 2000.

Wal-Mart claims that more than 93 million Americans shop at Wal-Mart every week. Sales at Wal-Mart for the year ending February 1999 totalled $137 billion. According to economist Tom Muller, the average American household spends around $1,100 a year at a Wal-Mart. Wal-Mart says in 1996 that the average American spent $360 at their stores.

Wal-Mart is the largest seller of cheap underwear in the world. The company boasts that in 1996, it sold 1.13 pairs of underwear for every man, woman and child in America. My family of five did not shop at Wal-Mart in 1996, so I figure that some family out there bought an extra 5.65 pairs of underwear, and my guess is that those underwear are sitting unwrapped in someone's drawer — because they are too embarrassed to admit that they purchased more than their fair share.

As of February 1999, Wal-Mart operated more than 3,562 "units" in seven countries. Wal-Mart is the largest private employer in America, having surpassed General Motors. The company had 910,000 employees as of the start of 1999. Last year, a new Wal-Mart discount store opened every three days, and anou.. / 200 stores are planned for this year. Other big box retailers are also metasticizing. It took Home Depot twenty years to open 500 stores, but they plan to open another 500 stores over the next three years.

All across America, consumers are making decisions every day that impact the environment they care the most about: that ten or fifteen mile radius that circumscribes most of our daily living. This is our "personal environment." It has more immediacy and relevance to most of us than any other environmental movement today. The personal environment is, after all, where we spend 90% or more of our time. It is the well-worn path to and from work, back and forth from the grocery store or to the shops downtown. Home to mall and back again. We are acutely sensitive to changes in this environment, and to its degradation. It has more meaning for us than any "checkbook" environmental cause. We can "think globally" about ozone depletion, but there are few causes in our own hometown that allow us to "act locally."

Yes, we want to save the whales. Yes, we want to save the rain forests. But attack our "personal environment" and watch out! We are the most protective when it comes to defending our home territory. The construction of land-devouring, windowless hulks of dead architecture in our hometown is like insulting our mother! How else can you explain hundreds of citizens showing up to testify at a Zoning Board hearing? From Kanawha City, West Virginia to Tijeras, New Mexico, we sit through hour after hour of dry testimony from traffic engineers and hydrologists —all because our home is being attacked, our personal environment is on the line.

In many cases, citizen activists have derailed big corporations, or held them at bay for years. The key factor in these confrontations is that we sense that the future of our personal environment, and that of our children, depends on us. It's a matter of home rule. This is one battle where we can make a difference.

The massive invasion of overstuffed retail stores is a hands-on environmental, economic and social issue, which has provoked a widespread citizen response. Retail redundancy, which accelerated in the 1980s and became grotesque in the 1990s, has created thousands of accidental activists. These people never planned on fighting off a multinational corporation but are determined to stop a problem too swollen to hide anymore. We can hear the sound of land being chewed up by the yellow corporate caterpillars.

There, squatting on the edge of our community, we can see the problem. We pass it on our way to and from work. This is not the distantly understood destruction of an "old growth" forest. This hits us where we live. As one woman from Ohio told me: "The first thing we smelled was the burning of trees."

Environmental and land use issues have moved to the forefront of this debate, as citizens pore through zoning by-laws and wetland commission regulations looking for obscure tripwires that could bring down a project. In 1998, Home Depot and Wal-Mart alone built more than 250 stores, or more than 33 million new square feet of retail space in a nation that is already saturated to the bone with plazas and malls. Assuming that each store represents a trade area of at least 40,000 people, more than ten million Americans will find themselves reading headlines about Home Depot or Wal-Mart in their local newspaper. The massive glut of capricious construction raises serious environmental and economic issues such as:

- the impact of traffic on air quality standards
- the threat to water quality and aquifers
- the mismanagement of storm water and sewage
- the reduction of wildlife habitat
- the loss of open space and unique natural areas
- the homogenization of rural landscapes
- the expense of costly new infrastructure: water lines and road
- the deterioration of historic commercial centers
- the overdependence on the automobile and superhighways

"Sprawl" is defined by the National Trust for Historic Preservation as "poorly planned, low-density, auto-oriented development that spreads out from the center of communities." It creates that doughnut effect in some cities where acrylic and asphalt suburban shopping malls form a ring around the dead center, where the old downtown sits decaying. Between 1960 and 1975, the state of Pennsylvania lost a total of 3,600,000 acres of farmland. That's like losing a geographic area the size of Pittsburgh every six months. At the opening of the Wal-Mart store in Rutland, Vermont, a man dressed in a business suit carried a doomsday sign that simply read: THIS IS STUPID!

Here is how the Bank of America, California's largest financial institution, described the impact of sprawl in that state:

> Urban job centers have decentralized to the suburbs. New housing tracts have moved even deeper into agricultural and environmentally sensitive areas. Private auto use continues to rise. This acceleration of sprawl has surfaced enormous social, environmental and economic costs, which until now have been hidden, ignored, or quietly borne by society. The burden of these costs is becoming very clear. Businesses suffer from higher costs, a loss in worker productivity, and underutilized investments in older communities. California's business climate becomes less attractive than surrounding states. Suburban residents pay a heavy price in taxation and automobile expenses, while residents of older cities and suburbs lose access to jobs, social stability, and political power. Agriculture and ecosystems also suffer . . . We can no longer afford the luxury of sprawl.

According to Brian Ketcham, a traffic and environmental engineer in New York City, there are many "hidden costs" of sprawl that we don't traditionally consider. Ketcham argues that these hidden costs exceed the potential profits from a megastore on the order of four to one. In 1995 he explained the costly side effects of retail sprawl in the "Metro Planner" newsletter of the American Planning Association:

> A 150,000 square foot big box store will attract from 5,000 to 10,000 shoppers a day. If 90% drive, as is likely, then a big box store can attract from 2,700 to 5,600 auto trips a day; 1 to 2 million auto trips per year. Assuming an average round-trip distance of 8 miles, this means an additional 8 to 16 million vehicle miles of travel per year . . . A 150,000 square foot big box store will directly increase (traffic) congestion costs by $5 million per year, increase the number of traffic incidents each year by about 190 property damage incidents and 55 personal injuries, with one additional death every three years, at a total added cost burden to New York of nearly $7 million a year. Air pollution and noise will likewise increase: by more

than $700,000 for air pollution and $80,000 in damages for traffic noise. Of even greater consequence is the impact of big box-generated traffic on other traffic. Those motorists already on the road will suffer an additional $30 million in wasted time and lost productivity as a result of one 150,000 square foot big box store.

Part of the mythology about Sam Walton is that he located stores in smaller towns because his wife Helen did not like the big cities. But I believe that Walton did not want to wrestle with big city developers and saturated urban markets. Besides, land was cheap in rural America. There were fewer zoning restrictions —sometimes no zoning at all. Walton sensed that Americans were moving out of the urban core and heading to suburbia. "Our key strategy," Walton wrote, "was simply to put good-sized discount stores into little one-horse towns which everybody else was ignoring . . . It turned out that the first big lesson we learned was that there was much, much more business out there in small town America than anybody, including me, had ever dreamed of."

But small town America started learning a "big lesson" also, one that took years to sink in: saturated retail markets bring deterioration and decay. With retail sprawl development comes a series of economic and social problems for host communities. Sprawl is often mistaken for economic development, and the people it affects the most are least likely to understand it.

The 10 sins of retail sprawl

1. It destroys the economic and environmental value of land.
2. It encourages an inefficient land-use pattern that is very expensive to serve.
3. It fosters redundant competition between local governments, an economic war of tax incentives.
4. It forces costly public infrastructure to extend out to the edge of town.
5. It causes disinvestment from established core commercial areas.
6. It requires the use of public tax support for revitalizing rundown core areas.
7. It degrades the visual, aesthetic character of local communities.

8. It lowers the value of other commercial and residential property, reducing public revenues.
9. It weakens the sense of place and community cohesiveness.
10. It masquerades as a form of economic development.

The violation of our personal environment by sprawling retail development leads to an alienation from community, a sense of isolation and disconnected-ness. When mall developers created interior spaces to shop, they gave them names like "Village Square," or "The Main Street Shops," hoping to console us for the loss of the real commercial centers they were destroying. In Disney World artisans have created an acrylic Main Street facade, where they hand out pins that celebrate "Main Street, USA." These pins have a picture of Mickey Mouse on the front, riding an old-fashioned big-wheel bicycle, tipping his straw boater hat. But stamped on the back of the pin it says: "©Disney Taiwan."

The sprawl corporations are waging a war of indoctrination. They need us as accomplices in the destruction of our own hometowns. In 1997 Home Depot spent $178 million on self-congratulatory advertising. What we ultimately have to do is convince our friends and neighbors that there is a politics of shopping. That is *does* matter to your hometown where you shop.

The big box corporations lay the blame at our feet. First, Wal-Mart says it needs bigger stores because its customers demand wider aisles. Then it says it needs smaller stores because its supercenters are "too busy and not convenient." Most of what we buy at Wal-Mart are unplanned purchases, and many of these items end up in the landfill anyway. A psychologist might argue that as our lives become emptier, our shelves become fuller. This "shop till your community drops" mentality is imploding our own hometowns. We see the results, but apparently are not moved by them, even when the evidence is all around us, as *60 Minutes* noted:

> In Iowa, ten years after Wal-Mart came to the state, nearly half of the men's and boys' clothing stores, and grocery stores . . . closed. That's an enormous impact on a state in only ten years.

When Iowa State University Professor Ken Stone examined the sales changes in Iowa small towns from 1983 to 1993, he discovered "a huge shift of sales to larger towns and cities, with substantial amounts captured by mass merchandise stores." Stone estimates that the total number of businesses lost in small towns and rural areas was 7,326 in the decade studied. Iowans spent $425 million more at discount stores, but $153 million less at variety stores, $129 million less at grocery stores, $94 million less at hardware stores, $47 million less at men's and boys' apparel stores, and so on. In the eleven store types studied, businesses lost more than $603 million in sales. In this ten year period, Iowa lost:

555 Grocery stores
298 Hardware stores
293 Building supply stores
161 Variety stores
158 Women's apparel stores
153 Shoe stores
116 Drug stores
111 Men's and boys' apparel stores

People have said to me: "When Wal-Mart arrives, they hit the town with the force of 100 new businesses opening at once." The demise of smaller, independent businesses in Iowa suggests that the "retail hurricane" theory is true. Stone reaches a similar conclusion:

The shopping habits of consumers fundamentally change after the introduction of discount mass merchandisers. They purchase much more of their merchandise at mass merchandisers and less at local merchants. The result is the loss of many stores across the state.

According to the International Council of Shopping Centers:
• Discount department stores, conventional department stores, and toy stores are store types where three or fewer companies capture 50% or more of sales.
• The top three building materials and supply stores now control 31% of the market ($32 billion in sales).

• The same with the top three drug stores: 33% of the market ($30 billion in sales).

• Between 1987 and 1992, the number of discount department stores increased annually by an average of 3%, while men's and women's shoe stores dropped an average of 6%, household appliance stores fell by 3%, and grocery stores, radio and television stores, drugstores, building materials stores, apparel stores all were in the negative column.

The impact of big stores has also been felt in the manufacturing sector. For example, in the apparel industry, America has literally lost its shirt. Between 1973 and 1996, America lost nearly half of its apparel manufacturing jobs. A total of 597,000 jobs were lost during this 23 year period. The same can be said for the shoe industry, or for the pharmacy industry. Ninety percent of the shoes sold in America today are imported. During this same period, discount super-stores rose dramatically.

Wal-Mart likes to underplay its market share by using the nation as its trade area. Here's what David Glass, Wal-Mart's President, said in the company's 1997 Annual Report:

In the United States, Wal-Mart only holds 7% of a $1.4 trillion retail market. That leaves a tremendous opportunity for future growth. The super market industry, amounting to $425 billion a year, is a great opportunity for continued growth. It's almost three times the size of the discount store industry, where Wal-Mart is one of the three retailers that, combined, hold almost 85% of the market. Yet in the grocery segment, the top five players constitute less than 25%

.

When Glass says Wal-Mart has a 7% share of the retail pie in America, he's talking about ALL retail sales of any kind, from gasoline to tomatoes, from paper clips to lip balm. But in the discount store wars, three companies own the field. At the local level, where a retail trade area might span only a twenty-square-mile radius, the impact of one or two big box stores can be devastating to the rest of the retailers. Consider the study done by the *San Diego Union-Tribune* of the home improvement market in San Diego County. The survey asked consumers where they made their most recent purchase of common items.

The results showed Home Depot had an astonishing hold over the county marketplace:

Product Most Recently Purchased	Home Depot's Share of the Market		
	Jan-June '94	Jan-June '95	Jan-June '96
Garden Care Products	41.5%	46%	51.1%
Hand/Power Tools	42.4%	49.6%	45%
Building Materials	72.2%	70.9%	75%
Interior Paint	43.1%	50%	48%
Exterior Paint	41.8%	43.6%	50%

Economist Tom Muller estimates that in 1994 Wal-Mart in Arkansas had captured $1.2 billion out of a $4 billion market in department store merchandise sales. "Thus, Wal-Mart had captured 30% of all department store sales."

When Wal-Mart says "one stop shopping," you should read that statement very literally. These big corporations want to be the ONLY place you and I shop. It's the Tennessee Ernie Ford theory of retailing: "You will owe your soul to the company store." In 1994, a retail analyst at Management Horizons made this tongue-in-cheek prediction about Wal-Mart:

> If Wal-Mart grows in the next eight years as it has in the previous eight, it will control 100% of general merchandise sales in the United States; if it grows in the next 16 years as it has in the previous 16 years, it will control all of the non-auto retailing volume in the United States; if the same growth pattern for the next 24 years is like the previous 24 years, Wal-Mart will control all of the country's Gross Domestic Product.

That may have seemed like a joke in 1994, but Wal-Mart now has more sales than the gross domestic product of Israel, Greece, Ireland and Egypt. A Price Waterhouse report says that by the year 2005 just ten companies, including Wal-Mart, will control 50% of food store sales.

What's happening here? More money is passing through fewer hands. This suggests that stores like Wal-Mart and Home Depot are not the beginning of competition but the end of competition. According to an International Council of Shopping Centers report in 1998:

> Numerous store types that are key elements in U.S. shopping centers are dominated by a small group of retailers in each category that register a third or more of their respective category's total U.S. sales . . . as fewer firms exercise increasing sales dominance within their respective store types . . . the pricing power that will accrue to the largest retailers will likely make it difficult for large numbers of new, small operators to take root and thrive.

The fact remains, we are over-built and over-stored. The attitude among the development community is that land is superabundant, and the municipal officials who make the key decisions are all Village Idiots. One of the most prolific Wal-Mart developers in New England calls his limited partnerships "Infinity Properties." Every time these developers come before a Planning or Zoning Board, they make their projects sound like they were written in Lake Wobegon, where all the site plans are good-looking, and the economic impacts above average.

The symptoms of retail saturation are everywhere:
• We have more than 4,000 abandoned shopping malls in America.
• We have more shopping centers than high schools.
• We have 20 square feet of retail space for every man, woman and child in America, up from 14.7 square feet per person in 1986, compared with 2 square feet per person in Britain.

If you phone City Hall in Toledo, Ohio, they answer by saying: "Toledo, Ohio, An All-American City." The effects of suburban sprawl in Toledo are certainly all-American. When I went for a walk in downtown Toledo, I passed the old Lamson dry goods store: nine stories of empty retail space. Each floor is the size of a football field. The building served as the home of a Macy's Department store from 1924 to 1984. For the past fourteen years, the store has been empty. The city now owns it, which means the taxpayers of Toledo are paying the freight for its upkeep.

Meanwhile, on the edge of the city, Home Depot is building its second huge warehouse store, each only five miles apart. The city actually let Home Depot demolish dozens of apartments to make way for its second warehouse. A stone's throw away from the Home Depot construction site sits an empty Builder's Square, and across the road, an empty Handy Andy. These are all monuments to the inefficiency of retail sprawl. The strip malls of Toledo have literally stripped downtown Toledo of its people and its character at the expense of the all-American taxpayers.

Even the people who produce all this sprawl admit that we have more retail stores than our disposable income can absorb. Here's Wal-Mart's confession in 1996 taken from a court deposition in North Carolina of Tom Seay, at the time Wal-Mart's vice president for real estate:"We have more shopping center space in the U.S. than is needed. We're in an over-built situation."

It's not as if we haven't been warned about the impacts of sprawl. Nearly 80 years ago, Sinclair Lewis in "Main Street" warned us about the homogenization of our culture:

> Nine-tenths of the American towns are so alike that is it the completest boredom to wander from one to another . . . The shops show the same standardized, nationally advertised wares; the newspapers of sections three thousand miles apart have the same 'syndicated features'; the boy in Arkansas displays just such a flamboyant ready-made suit as is found on just such a boy in Delaware, both of them iterate the same slang phrases from the same sporting-pages, and if one of them is in college, and the other is a barber, no one may surmise which is which.

In her 1961 book, *The Death and Life of Great American Cities*, Jane Jacobs wrote: "Everyplace becomes more like every other place, all adding up to Noplace."

Big box retailers are turning America into a continuous landscape of one-story, pre-engineered, windowless metal frame buildings sitting on concrete slab foundations. Such buildings can simply be described as "dead architecture." Wal- Mart stores are a form of architectural graffitti. The company even writes all over its walls with slogans like "we sell for less", as if we didn't get the message.

The Portable Wal-Mart

As quietly as Wal-Mart tries to slip into a town, sometimes they try to leave just as noiselessly.

"Quite frankly," said Wal-Mart's Tom Seay, "I think the fact that we relocate stores — and we relocate a lot of them— is a well-known fact in the development community." Just how portable Wal-Mart is, however, is not well known by the shopping public. In their 1998 Annual Report, Wal-Mart featured a short profile of their Real Estate division, under the title: "The Wal-Mart nobody knows." According to the company, Wal-Mart is the "largest owner and manager of retail space in the country."

Like a reptile crawling out of its skin, Wal-Mart has shed hundreds of stores to move on to bigger facilities. Most of these relocations have been in towns where Wal-Mart shuts down a discount store to open up a larger supercenter a few miles, or even blocks, away. "As (Wal-Mart) rolls out new supercenter prototypes," the company explains, "it must also find uses for existing relocated stores after they are closed." But often they sit like empty wind-tunnels by the roadside.

Although the company claims that in 1998 it sold or leased ten million square feet of what it calls "once-occupied" stores, the February 1999 list of "available buildings" from Wal-Mart Realty reveals that the amount of buildings on the market at that time was closer to twenty million square feet of empty stores. Based on the company's own list, here are some statistics on these empty stores that you won't see on any Wal-Mart TV ads:

- Wal-Mart had 333 empty buildings as of February 1999.
- These buildings are spread across 31 states.
- A total of 20.66 million square feet of empty stores were on the market.
- Only 17% (58) of these stores are owned by Wal-Mart; 83% (275) are leased.
- Estimating that Wal-Mart has roughly 2,850 stores open in the United States, these additional 333 empty stores meant that 10.5% of the units Wal-Mart owns or leases were "available."

- Fifteen states had ten or more empty Wal-Mart stores:

Alabama 22	Kentucky 16	No. Carolina 10
Arkansas 17	Louisiana 16	Oklahoma 12
Florida 30	Mississippi 15	So. Carolina 13
Georgia 26	Missouri 13	Tennessee 30
Illinois 11	New Mexico 10	Texas 40

- The average size of empty Wal-Marts was 62,057 square feet — larger than most other retail buildings in a small community.
- 52 of the empty stores (16%) were larger than 100,000 square feet, with some as large as 134,000 square feet.
- 54 stores (16%) on the February list were marked "new to the market."

This is the portable Wal-Mart company. This is Wal-Mart's moveable feast. Although the company says very few of its stores have failed, many are unprofitable or marginal performers, and dozens of others are simply shut down to make way for supercenters with wider aisles. This makes Wal-Mart the largest producer of empty retail stores in America, if not the world.

Don't expect a long-term relationship with any superstore in your town. Wal-Mart arrives with its bags already packed.

2

The Case Against Retail Sprawl

"If you could go back, we would have been better off if Wal-Mart had never come to the area . . . My personal opinion is the community would be more quaint, have a greater variety of products, if we never had a Wal-Mart."
— **Robert Donaldson, Ruidoso, New Mexico Village Councilor, September 1, 1997**

Citizens opposed to sprawl generally cite two major reasons for fighting companies like Wal-Mart or Kmart:
1. Negative impact on the local economy
2. Negative impact on their quality of life

1. Voodoo Economics: The Wal-Mart Dust Machine

Sam Walton liked to claim that Wal-Mart was the savior of small town America, that his company was creating jobs every place it touched. Here's how he described it in his autobiography:

> Wal-Mart has actually kept quite a number of small towns from becoming practically extinct by offering low prices and saving literally billions of dollars for the people who live there, as well as creating hundreds of thousand of jobs in our stores.

But such claims are a form of voodoo economics. Former developer Townsend Anderson of Vermont has been quoted as saying, "Sprawl rarely brings about a net increase in economic growth. If there is not real growth, there is simply displacement of economic activity. This triggers a whole cycle of deterioration in older communities."

Companies like Wal-Mart and Home Depot utilize a form of "sprawl-math," which only looks at gross impacts on a community — never at the net effect of their stores. Sprawl-math is not taught in local school systems. On the developer's calculator there is no minus pad to subtract out jobs lost or revenues diverted. The real truth about Wal-Mart and Home Depot, and the rest of the sprawl-mathematicians, is that they represent a form of economic displacement, not economic development. I know that Wal-Mart understands their fiscal impact claims are one-dimensional. The best proof I have of that I found in a most unlikely place: Volume 26, Issue 10 of *Wal-Mart Today*, from October of 1996. This is an internal "associate" newsletter that Wal-Mart says is "your window into our Wal-Mart world." There, in a column called "Wal-Mart Culture," is a quote that should be written on the side of every Wal-Mart superstore in the nation:

"At Wal-Mart, we make dust. Our competitors eat dust."
— Tom Coughlin, Executive Vice President, Operations
Wal-Mart Stores Division

Since 1962, the Wal-Mart Dust Machine has done damage in every state in the country. Companies like Wal-Mart have cannibalized the retail food chain from the Mom and Pops on the bottom, to the mid-level regional chains, to the very top national chains. A recent illustration:

In February of 1999, New England lost another major regional retail chain store. Caldor, the company founded by Cal and Dorothy Bennett in 1951, turned into dust. This was the end of the sales cycle for the fourth largest retail chain in America. 22,000 workers took home pink slips for their trouble. 145 stores in nine states were put up for lease. After 48 years, and annual sales of $2.49 billion, the "going-out-of-business" sales at Caldor began. Bargain hunters who long ago moved to other venues, returned one more time to pick over the bones, looking for that last three-pack of cheap underwear.

The lesson in sprawl-math is inevitable. When you oversupply an area with retail glut, you don't create jobs, you destroy them. Caldor imploded in 1999. Industry analysts say it was expected: Caldor was losing money to Wal-Mart, had fallen into Chapter 11 territory since 1995, and never recovered. As one news story said: "Wal-Mart and other rivals had choked off Caldor's ability to open stores outside its traditional Northeast territory."

The next time some Mayor or Town Councilor starts talking about the jobs that a Wal-Mart or Home Depot will bring to town, remember the jobs lost at Caldor's or Rich's, or the building supply stores Grossman's and Payless Cashways. It would take more than 100 Wal-Mart Supercenters just to break even with the 22,000 jobs that went down with Caldor.

Or consider the case of the small town of Nowata, Oklahoma, (pop. 3,900), hobbled by the closing of a large Wal-Mart retail store. The store closed down to move to a larger supercenter thirty miles away. "They were not playing fair," said the President of the local First National Bank. "They came in and ravaged all the small businesses. And when it came to the point where they were not satisfied, they left." The Mayor of Nowata who welcomed the megastore to town, now says: "Wal-Mart has proven this: They're big and they're greedy. They have no compassion for the community or the individual."

The operating principle is that retail sales are tied to income and population. If you look at the level of retail activity in most communities, retail sales are linked statistically to changes in average per capita income. If income and population are increasing, retail sales can increase. In a number of communities I have studied, retail sales were around 35% to 40% of average per capita income. When companies like Wal-Mart talk about the "new" sales they will generate, the question to pursue with them is: Where are the "new" consumers coming from? When I reviewed the retail sales figures and income figures for Humboldt County, California, I found that the two trend lines over the past twenty years were closely linked:

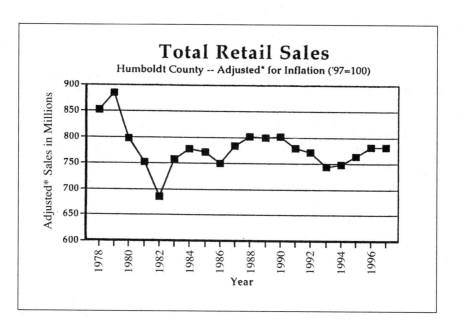

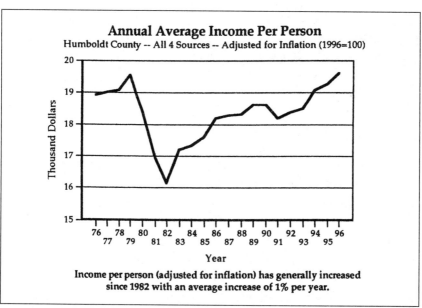

Income per person (adjusted for inflation) has generally increased
since 1982 with an average increase of 1% per year.

Communities around the country have put together economic impact reports that show how Wal-Mart affects their existing businesses. A summary of fifteen such reports is found in Appendix II.

The Saturation Effect

Along with the catalogue of economic impact reports about the real effect of Sprawl-Marts on hometown America, it's important to understand the related concept of saturation.

Wal-Mart's strategy of blanketing America with stores every few miles has confused many local citizens groups. "Why," they ask, "would Wal-Mart want to locate its stores so close to each other?"

On the surface, it appears that Wal-Mart is simply stealing sales from itself. But saturation of stores is actually a defensive strategy, that serves much the same purpose that a dog attributes to a fire hydrant: it's a way to mark your territory.

This defense strategy is revealed in Bob Ortega's book, *In Sam We Trust*:

> Walton . . . raced to open stores as fast as possible and aimed to saturate markets to keep rivals out — even if that meant that, say, his six clubs in Houston or five clubs in Dallas wound up cannibalizing each other's sales. Better to lose sales to his own stores than to somebody else's, Walton figured.

Sam Walton was very transparent on the issue of saturation. When he was deciding whether or not to locate one of his early stores in Bentonville, Arkansas, which eventually would become the empire's headquarters, Walton drove into town with his wife's father in the car, and had a look around the small Bentonville town square. "It was the smallest of the towns we considered," Walton said, "and it already had three variety stores, when one would have been enough."

Three stores, when one would have been enough: that pretty much describes the state of retailing over-storing in America today. Instead of moving on, Walton decided to open a fourth variety store in Bentonville, and put the other guys out of business. There was no need for Walton's 5 & 10 to open in Bentonville.

Walton said his goal, as stated in his autobiography, was to end up competing with himself:

> We figured we had to build our stores so that our distribution centers could take care of them. . . . Each store had to be within a day's drive of a distribution center . . . Then we could fill in the map of that territory, state by state, county seat by county seat, until we had saturated that market area. . . . (W)hat we did was build our stores in a ring around a city —pretty far out — and wait for the growth to come to us ...We became our own competition. In the Springfield, Missouri area, for example, we had 40 stores within 100 miles.

This same perspective has permeated companies like Home Depot. Here's how Bernie Marcus described his saturation philosophy to industry insiders:

> We think that there are markets in the United States that are so badly undersaturated that they need to have lots of Home Depots . . . Here in Atlanta, for instance, we have 22 stores. We'll be going on to 30 stores very shortly . . If you look at the growth factor that we have, to way beyond the foreseeable future, this company is going to grow and grow and grow.

Don Harris, a Home Depot spokesman, told the *Atlanta Journal* in May of 1998 that his company had enormous expansion plans. "We're doubling the size of this company. It took us 18 years to build the first 500 stores, and we plan to build the next 500 stores in the next three years. That is a growth path."

The president of Home Depot, Arthur Blank, says that when people ask him where they are going to add new stores, he says: "We still have room to add a ton of stores . . . We still have to fill in existing markets — a fill-in store is the most profitable you can open."

Home Depot's major rival, Lowe's, hopes to have 700 to 800 of its larger stores open within the next five years, a number, according to the *National*

Home Center News, that "includes a store in every US market of 50,000 house-holds or more." Lowe's is reportedly opening a new store every five days, and hopes to push that pace to every three days.

In Costa Mesa, California, when citizens were fighting a proposed Home Depot store, the irony to local residents was the fact that Home Depot already had another store in neighboring Santa Ana, only three miles away! When asked by a reporter why Home Depot would want to locate a store so close to an existing one, the developer said: "It could be that they want to protect their turf."

In a 1999 report, economist Tom Muller says that Wal-Mart is now filling in the map with "gap" stores:

> Wal-Mart's interest (in Kilmarnock, Virginia) is likely due to two factors: there is no sizeable general merchandise store in the market, and Wal-Mart has exhausted the most obvious sites. Because of this, Wal-Mart now has a policy to 'backfill' gaps on a map where there are no Wal-Marts . . .The company is now closing gaps to assure that no one is more than 30 minutes from one of its stores.

The success of companies like Home Depot and Wal-Mart to saturate an area can be measured by their rising market share. According to a 1994 Congressional Research Service report:

> Saturation in the retail industry also has had implications for competitive strategy in markets with many players . . . At this point, new entrants can succeed only at the expense of existing retailers, in which case there is no real growth, but a zero-sum game in the retail market. In these "overstored" areas, the financially strong and more efficient firms will gain market share at the expense of less competitive businesses, a particular concern of retailers in slow growth areas anticipating the arrival of a large discount chain.
>
> The fundamental question to be answered is what happens to retail sales after Wal-Mart comes to town? . . . Wal-Mart spokesmen have argued that the retail giant provides a net economic gain to small towns …The retail market studies suggest, however, that effect not only can

vary, but may also have some detrimental implications for certain businesses and communities . . . Few would dispute that the local rural retail industry may face significant disruptive restructuring under these circumstances, which may be particularly difficult in communities experiencing slow economic growth.

Tom Muller also testified before the United States House Committee on Small Business about the nature of Wal-Mart saturation:

> The market share of Wal-Mart in the less urbanized states may well be unprecedented. For example, Wal-Mart has captured 28% of all department store type merchandise in Mississippi . . .When Wal-Marts are spatially close to each other, we find that most sales come from merchants located in the same community or county as Wal-Mart. These findings should not be surprising. Wal-Mart and other megastores do not increase the dollar volume of sales, but redistribute such sales.

When 145 Caldor chain stores closed in February of 1999, Wal-Mart bid on some of their stores. In Hadley, Massachusetts, for example, a Wal-Mart developer was already doing site preparation work for a new store, when the company announced it was seeking rights to a Caldor store located six miles away. A Wal-Mart spokesman said: "We put stores where there are customers. Having two stores within ten miles of each other is not unique."

2. Quality of Life

You will not find small town quality of life for sale at a Wal-Mart. They don't stock it on any shelf. But once they steal it from you, you can't buy it back from them at any price.

In Windsor, California, when a consultant's impact study for a Wal-Mart mall was presented to the town, the report highlighted the following issue: "The impacts most frequently mentioned (at public hearings) dealt with quality of life issues for the people already in Windsor, and the overwhelming desire to maintain and enhance the unique character and quality of the Windsor community."

In an appendix to its Windsor report, the consultant, Bay Area Economics, presented notes from an August 15, 1995 public hearing of the Economic Development Committee meeting. Here are excerpts from the actual list of issues raised at the public hearing by citizens in Windsor. They are typical of communities everywhere:

- Windsor should not be lost in freeway madness.
- Wal-Mart lends itself to negative uses, such as fast food, minimarts and other big box retailers.
- Concern that when Wal-Mart outgrows a site, they abandon the building and leave an eyesore.
- If Wal-Mart were a quality development there would be no opposition.
- The proposed center is just too large.
- Have you ever seen a beautiful Wal-Mart?
- Thriving suburbs can't retain charm with big box retailers.
- Windsor will not be as attractive.
- Downtown, formerly predominant, will be depleted of any uses.
- Ownership of small business by locals is key to success of community, and Wal-Mart threatens this.
- Local businesses address local concerns. Wal-Mart will destroy neighborhoods.
- Home values are already less today than six years ago, and this trend will continue.
- Community is the issue.
- Community spirit does not equal big box retail.
- Windsor is unique.
- Wal-Mart represents a quick fix and a slow death.
- Desire to keep Windsor small, bedroom community; keep local.
- Wal-Mart will make Windsor a city and not a town.
- Wal-Mart is not community-supportive.
- The 24 hour open store brings certain crime elements.
- How will Wal-Mart impact immediate homeowners? Noise, smell, walls, graffiti will result in a decrease in home values.
- Windsor equals community ties because it is built on backs of local businesses. Want to raise children with this ideal.

• Let a community that's growing be allowed to continue to thrive.

These are comments that I have heard again and again over the past six years, as I have traveled to twenty-nine different states: Loss of community, loss of that unique sense of place. I remember driving into the town of Henniker, New Hampshire one snowy evening to meet with a new group forming to oppose construction of a Rite Aid store on the edge of town. Henniker is a town that describes itself as a "tranquil 200 year old village, nestled in the foothills of the White Mountains." I was told to watch for a corner acre lot on my right as I came into town. That was where Rite Aid wanted to build its 11,000 square foot store.

As I passed the Rite Aid site, I noticed it was completely wooded. But in my headlights I saw something more significant. There was a wooden sign on footings, maybe four-by-five-feet in size, with an oval top and gold lettering, that read:

WELCOME TO

HENNIKER

Incorporated 1768

The Only Henniker on Earth

I told the residents that night that they should call their group "The Only Henniker on Earth Committee," and they did. According to a Henniker Master Plan Review survey, 86% of town residents said they live in Henniker for the "rural country living." In the survey, 68% of town residents said they live in Henniker because it is located away from high density areas. 72% said they live here because Henniker is a small New England village.

In December of 1996, I testified before the Henniker Planning Board. Part of my remarks touched on the issue of quality of life in Henniker:

> If what people in Henniker wanted was more convenience stores to serve what Rite Aid calls active, time-pressed women, then they would live in Concord, New Hampshire. What many people in Henniker value, is not sold on any Rite Aid shelf. If you approve "format development" in this case, you will generate additional requests in ever-increasing size. This community will change from being the Only Henniker on Earth to simply the 'What on Earth?'

It took the residents of Henniker about a year and a half to beat Rite Aid, with an appearance on *Nightline* along the way, but they fought to maintain their unique sense of place. Even though Rite Aid vowed on national television that "we will not lose in Henniker," there is today no Rite Aid on that one acre lot in the Only Henniker on Earth.

Another community that impressed me with its unique sense of place was Lewes, Delaware. I was invited by the Citizen's Coalition to speak at the Henlopen Grange on September 23, 1995 to oppose a 149,000 square foot Wal-Mart. This community of roughly 2,300 people describes itself as a "jewel among Delaware's coastal towns." Mike Tyler, who is the innkeeper at the Wild Swan Inn just blocks from the Delaware Bay, told me that his community had undertaken the task of developing a Master Plan for the town. But first, they did something unusual. They articulated a set of what they called "Core Values." These Core Values were meant to guide the town as it considered future land use proposals. Three of the Lewes' Core Values struck me as universal:

- We value face to face intimacy.
- We value "busy days and quiet nights."
- We value maintaining our historic connection to the sea.

Quality of life was a key issue also in the decision of the Planning Board in New Paltz, New York in March of 1996. "The Town of New Paltz places high value on its small town feeling and wishes to retain the character of the Town while enabling responsible growth." That statement came right out of their Comprehensive Plan mission statement. The objective of the Comprehensive Plan was equally clear: "To preserve and enhance the natural beauty and rural quality of the community and protect the small town character of the village core."

New Paltz was prepared for Wal-Mart, because these statements were put in the Comprehensive Plan two years before Wal-Mart applied for a special permit. But even ten years before being confronted by a Wal-Mart, New Paltz had formed a Master Plan Committee, which conducted a community-wide survey in 1986 which said:

New Paltz's beauty and small town quality were the two major reasons that people chose to live in the community . . . growth is necessary for the tax base, but development must be carefully planned to avoid compromising the character of the town.

This kind of language in key town documents gave planners the ability to insist that their goal was "to preserve the community's small town character through responsible growth which must be on a scale compatible with the existing Village core, and of a style that would enhance rather than detract from the natural beauty of the area . . . the rural, small town atmosphere which makes New Paltz so desirable should not be compromised for the sake of short term gain."

The town even went so far as to state that "shopping centers on the outside of town . . . serve no social purpose," and that the downtown should be "the major concentration of retail and commercial businesses."

What is Wal-Mart's response to this kind of pride of place? A spokesman for the company said: "One thing Mr. Norman doesn't always remember to relate is that our headquarters is in a small town . . . and we're in a lot of small towns where people said we couldn't make a go of it."

When we were fighting Wal-Mart in my hometown of Greenfield, Massachusetts, I designed a final ad in our ballot campaign that tried to set aside all the economic arguments, and instead focus on hometown pride. Our campaign theme that ran across the bottom of each ad said: "We're not gaining a store, we're losing our community." Here's the text from our display ad in *The Recorder* that we ran on election day, October 19, 1993:

AN ACT OF LOVE

Those of us who have worked over the past year to stop Wal-Mart have done so out of a deep sense of love for this town. It has been an act of hope and optimism about Greenfield's future — not an act of desperation or despair. This is, after all, our home that Wal-Mart wants to enter. We take great pride in our home, and the value of honesty our families believe in. . . . In saying that we are *against* sprawl, we are saying we are *for* Greenfield. By resisting Wal-Mart, we are expressing our deep respect for the generations of Greenfield citizens who built Factory Hollow, and those future generations who will inherit what we do at the polls. We are proud of the way Greenfield citizens have responded to our efforts. We feel we live in a very special town, with much to recommend it — even if it never has a Wal-Mart.

Later that evening, it became clear that the voters of Greenfield had defeated Wal-Mart at the polls. The quality of life issue had been a major factor in the campaign. All Wal-Mart wanted to talk about was cheap prices.

3

Busting Sprawl Myths

"There's misinformation being spewed about Wal-Mart left and right. I don't care if it's Al Norman or a 13 year old, I hear it so often it just grates on you."
— **Keith Morris, Wal-Mart Director of Community Affairs, Hadley, Massachusetts, February 11, 1998, responding to a high school student's criticisms of Wal-Mart**

When companies like Wal-Mart, Home Depot or Target enter a small town, they often flood the community with "disinformation" about the beneficial impacts of their stores. This is sometimes distributed directly by company public relations people, sometimes by hired local PR firms, or even "astro-roots" citizen's groups (fake grass roots groups created by the PR firms). Much of the disinformation is in the form of company myths. Using actual Wal-Mart propaganda disseminated in a San Leandro, California campaign, here are ten common Sprawl-Myths that are part of the disinformation campaign: Creating Jobs; Good Wages; Quality Job Benefits; Stock Ownership/Profit Sharing; Crime; Helping Other Businesses; Buy American; Charitable Contributions; Taxes; Supporting Suppliers.

Many of these myths have nothing to do with zoning, but Wal-Mart and other companies use these arguments when they come into town to convince local officials that these projects are a positive addition to any community. In many communities, local officials jump right in the tank. As Sandra Vance and Roy Scott have described Wal-Mart's early years in the South:

> To these people Wal-Mart was more than a store; it was a symbol of progress and hope. It's founder was a genuine hero, a retail Elvis Presley, a southerner who had made it to the top while remaining faith-

ful to his roots. 'We've got a Wal-Mart, you know,' town fathers across the South proudly proclaimed, as though the store's very presence suggested better days to come.

Ten Sprawl Myths

1. Creating Jobs

"Wal-Mart would generate hundreds of new jobs for local residents . . . "
They don't teach "Wal-Math" in your local school system, but here is an example of how this form of retail mathematics works:

> 1 job created by Wal-Mart
> - 1 job destroyed at another business
> = 1 job created.

This is a wonderful form of new math, especially suited for developers and real estate interests. They never discuss job losses. One half of the ledger is entirely omitted for the purposes of community discussion.

Wal-Mart says its has "created one out of every 16 U.S. jobs over the last five years." But what about the other side of the ledger? How many jobs has Wal-Mart destroyed? Wal-Mart will prominently feature "new jobs" in its pitch to local communities. "We hire our store employees locally," they told the citizens of San Leandro, "with the exception of the store manager and some assistant managers, who are generally transferred from another store to train new staff." The people Wal-Mart puts out of work are also local.

Economist Tom Muller, in his testimony before Congress in August of 1994, undercut the notion that Wal-Mart was an engine of economic growth:

> Wal-Mart has become one of the leading employers in the nation, with over half a million workers, a seven-fold rise in a decade. However, it would be a serious mistake to conclude that these jobs are net additions to the workforce. The presence of Wal-Mart results in fewer retail jobs than would be available in their absence. This is attributable to the fact that sales per employee at Wal-Mart are substantially above the industry average.

In a 1996 economic impact study conducted in Easton, Maryland, researchers concluded that Wal-Mart was not a job generator:

> While representatives of Wal-Mart claim to bring jobs and prosperi-
> ty to localities, a closer look at the larger picture shows that, in the case
> of Talbot County, there has been a net loss of jobs, despite small gains
> in income for the Town of Easton . . . There is some difficulty in deter-
> mining if the chain, in a more symbolic sense, is exactly a chain of bur-
> den, or a chain of strength to the communities involved.

In his 1999 study of Kilmarnock, Virginia, Tom Muller calculates that Wal-
Mart would create 246 mostly part-time jobs, and would destroy 248 jobs at
other businesses. "Thus the gains from Wal-Mart are wiped out by losses from
existing merchants," Muller says.

In Sonoma County, California, a 1995 study of the impact of a Wal-Mart in
the city of Windsor concluded:

> Retail sales in Sonoma County have only been shifted around
> geographically by the new big box centers, with no real net increase in
> sales, despite population increases in the county; job impacts for the
> proposed (Windsor mall) may also follow the same pattern, with no
> total gain in retail jobs in the county, but merely a shift from elsewhere
> in the regional trade area of the center. Thus at the regional level, there
> may be little or no gain in retail employment, and a negligible resulting
> multiplier effect.

According to the Congressional Research Service (CRS), municipal officials
can easily exaggerate the job impact from big box retailers. The CRS warned
Congress in 1994:

> For the community to evaluate the significance of these job gains,
> they must be balanced against any loss of jobs due to reduced business
> at competing retailers. Further, for those considering the quality of jobs
> that might be created, U.S. census data point out that retail jobs, by and
> large, provide a significantly lower wage than jobs in many industries,

and are often only part-time positions, seasonal opportunities, or subject to extensive turnover. In short, it would be easy to overestimate the true benefit to would-be workers and the local economy.

When the Wal-Mart representative tells your local newspaper that they will create 250 new jobs at their superstore, ask them: "Is that gross, or net?"

2. Good Wages

"Our Associates are offered an extremely competitive compensation package . . . (W)ages are market-based and all Associates, including part-time, or 'peak' associates, earn salaries above the minimum wage."

I have seen hundreds of Wal-Mart ads that brag about "everyday low prices," but I have never seen an ad that says: "We pay our people better than anyone." Being number one in compensation does not appear to be a corporate priority at Wal-Mart.

I have heard Wal-Mart say at public forums that they pay the prevailing wage in a given area, or "market-based" wages. They don't like to translate that into an actual hourly wage, however. What they mean is that they look at what their major competitors in an area are paying, and try to at least match that. In North Reading, Massachusetts, in a tight labor market, Wal-Mart ran an ad offering to "negotiate" wages with prospective employees. One Wal-Mart employee from Alabama wrote me recently and said that after six years with the company he was only making $6.50 an hour. "Wages are market-based," the company says, "and all Associates, including part-time, or 'peak associates,' earn salaries above the minimum wage." Wal-Mart tells its workers that its wages "are competitive within the industry and geographic region."

When Wal-Mart was opening up a new distribution center in Tomah, Wisconsin, in 1999, the company described its wages as follows in the *LaCrosse Tribune:* "When we get closer to starting the hiring process, we'll go into the area and conduct a wage survey, looking at what a prevailing wage would be for this type of industry," Wal-Mart spokesman Keith Morris said. Wages will be set after that and will be competitive, he said.

As Bob Ortega has pointed out in his book, *In Sam We Trust,* the typical Wal-wage is not much to write home about: "At 40 hours a week (which would be on the high end for most Wal-Mart workers), that $7.50 average hourly wage worked out to $15,000 a year — coincidentally, the government's poverty level for a family of four."

When Dale Stiles retired after working twenty-five years in management for a telephone company, he took an entry level job at Wal-Mart to get a better look at how the corporate giant made its money. What Stiles found is neither surprising, nor attractive. He wrote about his work in *The Arkansas Times*:

> In October of 1991 I officially became a Wal-Mart associate at $4.25 an hour. It is Wal-Mart policy to schedule associates only 35 hours in order to never, ever have to pay anyone overtime. I am told that if you work more than your scheduled 35 hours you will be summoned into the office and counseled.

According to Stiles, even adding in overhead costs like Social Security withholding, and profit sharing, the average Wal-Mart worker in 1991 was earning only $10,950 a year. "A ten year employee tells me wage increases average about 25 cents per hour per year," Stiles wrote. "The company doesn't seem to have any idea how its employees feel about the organization. After 25 years of working with and against a union, I never thought the day would come that I would recommend union representation for anyone. Seniority and doing a good job means nothing here. The Wal-Mart open door policy means that if you OPEN your mouth, you'll be OUT the door."

In San Leandro, Wal-Mart distributed a list of FAQ's (frequently asked questions) about the company's policies. "We have heard that Wal-Mart is anti-union," the company asked itself. "Is this true?" The company replied:

> No. Wal-Mart stores are non-union, not anti-union. Wal-Mart is pro-associate and is considered one of the top 100 companies to work for in America . . . The company also offers a work environment that encourages the freedom to communicate openly and share ideas. Wal-Mart Associates like what the company has to offer and have chosen not to unionize.

"I have always believed strongly," wrote Sam Walton, "that we don't need unions at Wal-Mart." Although the company doesn't feel it needs a union — a little organizing has crept in nonetheless. A Canadian Court in Ontario has ruled that Wal-Mart broke the law during a Steelworker's organizing campaign. Wal-Mart applied to the Ontario Labor Relations Board for a review of its decision, which allowed the United Steelworkers of America to represent the 209 employees at the Wal-Mart store in Windsor, Ontario.

Upon review, the Ontario court upheld the Labor Board's decision, and concluded that Wal-Mart intimidated workers by failing to answer their questions about whether the store would remain open if it were unionized. "Wal-Mart interfered with the employees' free choice," the union said. "Wal-Mart's actions tainted the vote in such a way that instead of asking whether the employees wanted a union, they were being asked if they wanted a job." Employees at the Windsor store at that time earned about $6.14 an hour in U.S. dollars. A "full-time" worker at 28 hours would make less than $9,000 a year. The Windsor unionization was the first out of 3,050 stores worldwide to be unionized. Wal-Mart had no comment on the adverse court ruling.

Meanwhile, workers at the Wal-Mart in Merrill, Wisconsin voted 54-27 in 1997 not to join the United Steelworkers Union. The vote drew national attention because it was the first time Wal-Mart employees in the United States had voted on unionization. Similar votes have taken place at Sam's Clubs, Wal-Mart's discount warehouse club stores. The Steelworkers promised to continue to try and unionize Wal-Mart. "We are going against their tradition," said Merrill Wal-Mart employee Becky Hehling, "because what they say and what they do don't coincide."

Union supporters said representation would have helped win higher wages and fairer treatment in getting raises, scheduling-by-seniority, and a procedure for settling grievances.

Wal-Mart says it's non-union, not anti-union. By the same argument, I guess that means citizen's groups fighting Wal-Mart are not anti-Wal-Mart, just non-Wal-Mart.

3. Quality Job Benefits
"Full-time associates are those who work at least 28 hours per week (70% of all associates); they receive benefits such as health insurance, life insurance, dental care, and paid vacations."

In their standard community handout, Wal-Mart lists 22 "benefits" that their "full-time" employees receive: everything from medical insurance to bereavement leave and jury duty pay. Wal-Mart says their their workers "are truly 'associates' because it is their work and ideas that will determine the success of the company." The company then describes their "extremely competitive" benefit package:

> Full-time Associates are those who work at least 28 hours per week (70% of all associates); they receive benefits such as health insurance, life insurance, dental care, and paid vacations. Part-time associates are eligible for benefits as well, and all associates are eligible to participate in our profit-sharing plan, making them shareholders in the company.

What can you say about a company that fudges on the definition of "full-time" to make it shrink to only 28 hours a week? In the rest of America, full-time is 40 hours a week, or perhaps 37.5 hours a week, but Wal-Mart says that full-time is really 70% of full-time. In fact, if someone was hired before September 1, 1979, full-time was defined by the company as 20 hours per week.

What can you say about a company that tells its workers they have no guarantees of job continuation, no commitment for a specific length of employment, no commitment to a specific type of work, and that your hours and work may be terminated whenever the company sees fit? When new employees are hired at Wal-Mart, they are asked to sign a statement that acknowledges they "understand" the following employment conditions:

1. All new associates are on a 90 day New-Hire period. This means your performance, attitude, and adherence to Company policies and procedures will be closely observed, and that either you or the company may terminate your employment with or without notice. If, and when you have passed your 90 days, this should not be construed as a guarantee of employment for any specific length of time, or any specific type of work. Continued employment and job assignments are based on your performance and the store's (and/or Company's) needs.

2. A reduction in the number of hourly associates may be necessary once a new store has been opened, or after peak business seasons. The size of the

workforce will be based upon the store's performance (sales volume). From time to time it may also be necessary to change the associate's schedules or numbers of hours worked, depending on the store's business needs at the time. If you are terminated during a reduction in work force, and are rated "Satisfactory, eligible for rehire," you must reapply if and when you want to be considered for re-employment when vacancies occur which the store needs to fill. The Company assumes no obligation to contact you for possible rehire. Remember, applications are only good for 60 days, and must be kept current for consideration.

3. Due to the nature of our business, associates' working hours must remain flexible. Full-time associates will work 28 or more hours a week, and peak-time associates will work less than 28 hours per week. Schedules will be posted well in advance of the work week. Note: if you are a new associate in a new store, you may work full-time and all days during the setup, however, this does not mean you will remain full-time or on days after setup.

4. Most associates will be required to work some nights and some weekend hours. There will be a few exceptions to this due to different job requirements.

Wal-Mart says such employment is "jobs with a future." Based on the contract that employees must sign, the future is viewed at Wal-Mart one day at a time. Here's a story a Wal-Mart employee recently shared with me:

> The company has a habit of laying off and/or sending employees home on short notice. Example: a young man scheduled to work, arrived, then was told his hours were insufficient for him to stay the day, so: go home young man! The heck with your expectations for a full day's work, as you anticipated when you were hired. Wal-Mart didn't let on that when a department's hours were reduced, so were the employee's income hours. You can imagine how this wreaks havoc with family budgets, and the domino effect on local creditors.

Home Depot, which really is little more than Wal-Mart with a hammer, also provides its workers with the same "jobs with a future" rhetoric. But the reality is quite different. Here's a similar excerpt from the Home Depot Associate's Guide: "As an associate of Home Depot, your employment is guaranteed for no set definite term, and you have the right to terminate your employment at any time, at your convenience, with out without cause or reason. Understand that Home Depot also has this right."

"Full-time" workers at Wal-Mart get vacation benefits, holiday pay (after three months), health, dental and life insurance. But when you look behind the benefits, there is not much there. Take the health and life insurance policies for example:

Wal-Mart Health Insurance

Wal-Mart makes a medical insurance plan available to all "full-time" employees who have worked at least three months full-time. Wal-Mart says its health plan comes with a "wide range of deductibles." The employee can choose from a $250 deductible, up to a $3,000 deductible. For example, a worker wanting to lower his monthly health insurance payroll deduction could choose a family plan with a $3,000 deductible, but that would represent nearly one-third of his gross annual pay. That same family plan also could require him to pay as much as $10,000 for medical expenses before the out-of-pocket maximum is reached. Because the payroll deductions and the deductibles are high, many workers at Wal-Mart can't afford to buy into the plan. According to *Wall Street Journal* reporter Bob Ortega, over the years Wal-Mart employees have seen their out-of-pocket health expenses rising:

> By 1994, the average Wal-Mart worker paid $1,900 a year to provide his or her family with health insurance. Wal-Mart workers paid 35% of their insurance premiums (compared to a national average of 20%), plus deductibles and 20% of any medical costs that were covered. Less than half the company's workers opted for health insurance coverage; after all, for a typical worker making between $12,000 and $20,000 a year before taxes, that premium took a big bite out of every paycheck. And nearly a third weren't eligible anyway, because they were part-timers.

Here's how one Wal-Mart employee in Alabama described his benefits to me in a recent e-mail:

I have worked for the company close to six years, and all I get paid is $6.80, what a joke! Lucky for me I am about to finish school and hopefully wander off the Wally World hype. The benefits that most employees of Wal-Mart brag about are what I call semi-welfare. Most doctors in this area will be quick to ask you for a second insurance to cover your bills. It took me two and a half years to pay my doctor bill. Wal-Mart paid some of my bill — $20. I footed the rest of my $2,500 bill. I am angry, because the whole company lies to its employees about how much they care. All we are to them are the slaves that feed their wallets.

Life Insurance, Wal-Mart Style

Life insurance for Wal-Mart employees is actually a tax shelter for the company. Wal-Mart offers its employees something called "company paid life insurance." Employees are told that it is "paid in full by company." The benefit is defined as "equal to your annual pay . . . to a maximum of $50,000." If the associate dies, Wal-Mart says "your designated beneficiary will receive this benefit."

But how does Wal-Mart paid life insurance really work?

In October of 1995, *Newsweek* magazine described the Wal-Mart life insurance scheme:

> Wal-Mart has recently taken to spending around $1 billion a year to buy about $20 billion of life insurance on some 325,000 of its employees. Not only doesn't Wal-Mart charge employees a single cent for this coverage; it actually gives them free benefits to encourage them to sign up. The benefits continue even if an employee leaves the company . . . Wal-Mart actually comes out millions of dollars ahead by buying this insurance, thanks to its clever use of a loophole in the federal tax code. The insurance program saved Wal-Mart about $36 million in income tax last year, and the company expects to save more than $80 million this year. And the real beauty is that this whole thing works . . . because Wal-Mart is the policy's beneficiary. If you croak, Wal-Mart gets the

money, even if you're no longer working there.

Wal-Mart says it offers about $60,000 of corporate-owned life insurance to every employee who signs up for the company's benefit program. Their survivors don't get any of the policy's proceeds, but Wal-Mart agrees to pay $5,000 to the family of anyone who dies while employed by Wal-Mart, $10,000 for an accidental death. Families of former employees get $1,000. This isn't a fortune, but it's free, which gives Wal-Mart employees a reason to sign up. Wal-Mart, of course, gets tax deductions that are worth much more than the death benefit it pays.

This so-called "corporate-owned life insurance" (COLI) is basically a form of corporate welfare subsidized by the American taxpayer:

1. Wal-Mart takes out a life insurance policy on hundreds of thousands of its workers. The catch is — when the worker dies, the money goes to Wal-Mart, not to the employee's family.

2. To pay for all these policy premiums, Wal-Mart borrows money from the insurance company. Even the money needed to pay interest on the loans is borrowed from the insurance company.

3. Wal-Mart is able to deduct the interest on the loans from its federal taxes, thus avoiding payment of millions of dollars to the United States Treasury.

4. When the worker dies, Wal-Mart gets the proceeds from the insurance policy tax free. It uses the death benefit to repay the loan to the insurance company. Wal-Mart wins, the American taxpayer loses.

Newsweek estimates that corporations taking advantage of this "tax gimmick" have cost the American taxpayer $1.5 billion a year in tax revenue, or what amounts to a "raid on the Treasury by giant corporations."

Stock Ownership Plans

Companies like Wal-Mart and Home Depot heavily tout their employee stock ownership plans. Home Depot, for example, offers its employees a traditional 401(k) savings plan, and an employee stock purchase plan (ESPP). But the ESPP is predominately paid for by the worker, not the company. "You decide how much money you wish to have deducted from each paycheck," the

Associates handbook says. "At the end of each plan year, your payroll deduction will stop for that Plan and Home Depot will issue you as many shares as the money deducted from your pay will allow." The only "contribution" Home Depot makes to the ESPP is a 15% discount off the price of their stock. The discount is taken off the closing market price on the first or last day of the Plan year, whichever price is lower. If the closing price of Home Depot stock is $69, employees can buy it for $58.65. Employees are allowed to contribute up to 20% of their gross pay into the stock plan.

Unlike a 401(k) plan, any employee wages that are contributed to the Stock Plan are after federal income taxes are deducted. In other words, a worker's contributions are taxed as part of their pay. The sole incentive to buy the stock is a slightly discounted rate. But the ESPP contribution level itself is financed wholly out of the worker's paycheck, and many Home Depot employees are in no position financially to be able to afford investing 10% or 20% of their gross pay in a stock fund.

Peak Employees

For those "peak" employees at Wal-Mart (at least 219,000 workers) who are working less than 28 hours, there is no vacation time, and no medical, dental or life insurance coverage. Yet Wal-Mart says that "part-time associates have one of the most generous benefit plans in the industry for part-time workers." After two years on the job, part-timers are eligible for health insurance (if they can afford it), and vacation time "based on their length of service." A 20 hour per week peak employee at Wal-Mart makes roughly $7,830 a year, or $150 a week.

4. Crime

"Safety is a top priority ...We have begun discussions with the San Leandro Chief of Police to ensure a safe shopping experience for our valued customers and a safe work environment for our sales associates."

Crime at Wal-Mart is not that different than crime at any other mall. Most malls attract criminals. When towns are considering the cost impact of a mall on their local budget, they will factor in the added cost of increased police patrols at shopping centers. Typical of such calculations are these comments from Economic and Planning Systems, a Berkeley, California land use consultant:

A recent fiscal analysis conducted by EPS of a major new regional shopping center in the Bay Area indicated that the local police department reported an average of 50 calls for service per month, or about 1.5 calls per 1,000 square foot of retail space annually after the shopping center opened for business.

Because of Wal-Mart's enormous scale, the issue of crime is a very visible concern in many communities. The best symbolic evidence of the growing crime problem at Wal-Mart is their sponsorship of police "substations" inside Wal-Mart stores. When I was speaking recently at an anti-Wal-Mart rally in Stratham, New Hampshire, residents there told me that the Wal-Mart in Somersworth, New Hampshire actually had a police substation inside the store. This is government efficiency at its best: it saves the town wear and tear on police cruisers, and puts police right in the lap of the crime center. It also suggests that there is enough crime activity to warrant a police presence right in the store, although Wal-Mart denies the police substation is there because of crime. Similar police substations have been reported in Tennessee and other states as well. In Somersworth, the substation was explained by Captain Dan Donovan this way:

> When (Wal-Mart) expanded to the grocery division and almost doubled their size, we tried to get as much out of it as we could. Because of the type of work that the officers have to do, it would be nice if we had a room for the Police Department where we could go and talk to the people. They (Wal-Mart) did us one better. They gave us an office in the front of the building. It saves a heck of a lot of time.

When asked about the nature of crime at the Somersworth Wal-Mart, Donovan said it was the same as in other plazas, with shoplifting at the top of the list. "When you get a lot of people in one area," he told *The Exeter News-Letter*, "crime increases…But because of Wal-Mart being there? No. It could be anybody, actually."

The logo doesn't matter. Crime is crime. And large parking lots bring together "a lot of people in one area." Donovan admitted that "we may have no

(Wal-Mart) calls in a given day, and other days we may have four or five calls. With a big place like that, you have a lot of people going in there." He said the Somersworth Wal-Mart does "have a lot of thefts out in the parking lot, kids looking for cash for cigarettes. We had a couple of assaults there, but they were minor."

Just how safe are you when you step out into one of those multi-acre parking lots at the local mall? For that matter, how safe are you inside a Wal-Mart? Unfortunately, malls attract more than just shoppers. Wal-Mart knows that consumers are beginning to pay attention to crime at big malls. Here is what Wal-Mart told the people of San Leandro:

> Wal-Mart stores are safe. The store provides its own in-store security and does not allow loitering in the parking lot. Surveillance cameras deter criminals. Money transported from the store to the bank is guarded by a local security agency. Hundreds of Wal-Mart stores now patrol their parking lots with golf carts that further deter crime. These voluntary measures greatly reduce the burden on the police department.

What could be a clearer admission of the problem of crime at superstores? You don't put golf carts in your parking lots unless enough people have been victimized to require such protection. Unfortunately, crime stories from malls are easy to find:

On September 7, 1990, a 37-year-old woman went shopping at a Wal-Mart in Memphis, Tennessee. As she was returning to her car around noon, she was abducted at gunpoint and forced into her car by a 16-year-old man from Chattanooga. The woman was raped, and later forced into the trunk of her car, where she suffocated. She was found a day later in an Arkansas field by hunters. Her abductor was convicted of kidnapping, rape and murder, and hanged himself with a bed sheet after being sentenced to life in jail.

The victim's husband sued Wal-Mart on behalf of himself and his three children. In his suit, he claimed that Wal-Mart and the shopping center were negligent in failing to provide security measures for the parking lot, and that their negligence resulted in his wife's death.

The Tennessee trial court that first heard the case ruled in favor of Wal-

Mart, because prior court rulings in the state said that shop owners are not responsible for the criminal acts of third parties unless the owner knew, or should have known, that acts were occurring, or were about to occur, that would pose an imminent probability of harm. When the husband appealed to the Tennessee Court of Appeals, the judgment in favor of Wal-Mart was affirmed. The plaintiff then pursued his case to the Tennessee Supreme Court.

In the Supreme Court case, the judge pointed out that "parking lots in particular have provided fertile ground for crime, because customers usually possess money or recently purchased merchandise." She also noted that most courts have ruled that businesses do have a duty to take reasonable precautions to protect customers from foreseeable criminal acts. The judge set a new negligence standard for Tennessee that the "foreseeability of harm and the gravity of harm must be balanced against the commensurate burden imposed on the business to protect against that harm." She said this standard "recognizes the national trend that businesses must justifiably expect to share in the cost of crime attracted to the business."

During the case, the husband presented records from the Memphis Police Department which showed that during a seventeen month period leading up to his wife's abduction, 164 criminal incidents had occurred on or near the defendant's parking lot. The crime reports included a bomb threat, 14 burglaries, 12 reports of malicious mischief, 10 robberies, 36 car thefts, 9 larcenies, and one attempted kidnapping on an adjacent parking lot. One nearby business even posted guards in five watch towers in its parking lot. The manager of the Wal-Mart store testified that he would not hold sidewalk sales at his store, except for "dirt," out of fear the merchandise would be stolen.

Wal-Mart in its defense argued that the parking lot attack was neither foreseeable nor preventable. Wal-Mart added that providing security was prohibitively expensive, and had little impact on preventing crime. However, the plaintiff produced an article written by Dave Gorman, Wal-Mart's vice president of loss prevention, published in *Security Management* magazine in March of 1996, in which Gorman boasted that Wal-Mart's security measures in parking lots had produced "outstanding" results. In another interview in the June 1996 issue of *Parking Security Report*, Gorman admitted that "the biggest issue for us when we first started talking about it was the fact that we were having a lot of crime on the lots. The huge majority of it was crimes against property." After new security measures began, Gorman says that "crime went down dramatically. It just dropped." Gorman further contradicted Wal-Mart's claims in court that security measures were expensive. "The cost of doing it wasn't quite as expensive as what we had been doing. So we saved a little money and did much more effective work."

On October 28, 1996, the Tennessee Supreme Court ruled that the risk of injury to the plaintiff's wife was reasonably foreseeable, and that a jury could conclude that Wal-Mart's negligence was a substantial factor in bringing about the harm. The case was sent back to the Trial Court for a trial by jury. The response from Wal-Mart's lawyer? "Crime is here to stay, unfortunately, and this (ruling) is putting it over on businesses instead of the police department. Are businesses in high crime areas going to be required to put an army outside their door?"

About six months ago, I had coffee with the Chief of Police in Tappahannock, Virginia. I asked him to tell me honestly what he felt about the 24 hour Wal-Mart that had opened a couple of years ago in his small town in the Northern Neck of Virginia. He told me that police records in Tappahannock indicate that the supercenter has been responsible for 21% of all criminal offense records over the past 21 months in that community. "It's been a drain on our resources," he said. The Chief told me he would be happy to see the store close and move to some other location. He said the major mistake was letting the store stay open all night. People gather there at night because there are very few other places to go.

Citizens in Mesa, Arizona who are battling a Wal-Mart sent me a report from the Chandler, Arizona police department. It's a "call type summary" of police reports from one address: 800 West Warner Road, the location of the Wal-Mart store. The police report shows that in 1998 alone there were a total of 434 police calls at Wal-Mart, including the following reports:

Call Description	Call Total
Accident/non-injury/hit and run	11
Disorderly Conduct	11
Forged Checks	63
Shoplifter in custody	101
Shoplifter combative	8
Theft Report	24

The list includes a narcotics report, a sex offense, domestic fights, found juvenile, indecent exposure, mentally disturbed person, missing juvenile – everything from abandoned vehicles to bomb threats. A total of 434 police calls, which means that in Chandler, you not only get low, everyday Wal-Mart prices, but everyday police calls as well. You'll find it all at Wal-Mart.

My analysis of police reports in Rohnert Park, California over a seventeen-month period shows that police had to respond to 614 calls, or more than one call daily to the Wal-Mart plaza. Ninety reports resulted in arrests.

In a similar situation, the Town Administrator in West Boylston, Massachusetts testified before his Zoning Board that the Wal-Mart in town should not be permitted to remain open 24 hours a day — even if only to restock shelves at night. He noted that Wal-Mart generates the most police calls of any retail establishment in town, and that if the company was allowed to stay open all night, they should be required to hire a special police detail during its extended hours.

Wal-Mart may tell residents in towns like San Leandro that "safety is a top priority" precisely because crime has become a top priority at stores like Wal-Mart. Here are some examples of the top priority cases that made it into the newspapers:

• As the 1999 New Year began in Monroe County, Michigan, the sheriff's deputies were busy searching for a man they believe raped an Exeter Township woman last November, and who attempted to rape a Wal-Mart employee just after Christmas. The 26-year-old Wal-Mart employee told police she was sitting on a bench right in front of the store, taking a work break around 8:30 P.M. when a man approached her, grabbed her and lifted her up, and began fondling her. The man attempted to drag the worker into a field just north of the store, but the worker hit him with a box cutter, and drew blood. The woman ran back to the store, and police followed a trail of blood into a nearby apartment building, but found no suspect.

• There was some trouble at a Home Depot parking lot in Clay County, Florida in December of 1998. Investigators from the County Sheriff's department indicate that a woman by the name of Jing Jerky was coming out of a Home Depot to her car when she was approached by two men who hit her, forced her into her car, and then drove off with her. Jerky managed to pull open the front door of the car, and rolled out of the moving car. In the process she broke her pelvis. Ironically, Jing Jerky happens to be a Home Depot employee who was going to her car for some food during a break. The newspaper report stated that the Home Depot "lot is well lit, but has no security guards." According to Home Depot, the manager of the Orange Park store told the media that the company will walk employees to their cars on request. Jerky's car, and the suspects, still have not been located. Jerky was listed in fair condition at the hospital following the abduction.

• On November 12, 1998, two girls, ages ten and eleven, were approached by a man at 2:00 P.M. in the afternoon inside the Home Depot on Shields Boulevard in Oklahoma City, Oklahoma. The man told the girls he was a Home Depot security guard, and he informed them that they were under arrest for shoplifting. He then took the two girls into a Home Depot rest room and molested them. The man was described as being between 30 and 40 years old, white, wearing a black leather jacket and blue jeans. What has authorities concerned even more is that similar attacks have taken place at Wal-Mart locations in Norman and Moore, Oklahoma. On October 16, a ten-year-old girl was reported fondled at the Wal-Mart store in Norman. On the same day, a man attempted to molest a girl at the Wal-Mart in Moore. Two days later, another attempted attack was made in the Moore Wal-Mart. The previous August, a third girl reported being molested at the Moore store. All of these attacks took place inside the Wal-Mart and Home Depot stores, during the middle of the day. The attacker would seem to be hard to miss: he was six feet tall and weighed around 300 pounds.

• At 9:30 P.M. on the night of April 17, 1995, Mitchell Skinner and Patrick

Patterson drove to the Wal-Mart supercenter in Searcy, Arkansas, and parked their vehicle in a space close to the door. For thirty minutes or more, the two sat in their car smoking marijuana and methamphetamine. Later, both men left the car and proceeded to the front of the store, where Skinner watched as Patterson pretended to make a phone call and play a video game. Patterson carried a twelve-inch knife in his pants, which created a huge bulge in his pocket. After the two had pretended to make a phone call and play video games for ten minutes, they sat down on a bench in front of the store. They were there for ten to fifteen minutes, during which time Patterson made comments of a sexual nature about various women as they entered the store. Skinner was shaking due to his consumption of methamphetamine, and he returned to the car. Around 10:15 P.M., Carla Willmon Jones arrived at the Wal-Mart supercenter, parked her car, and entered the store. While she was shopping, Skinner and Patterson moved their car to a parking space near Jones'. When Jones returned from shopping, Patterson approached her and asked her for assistance in starting their car. When Jones refused, Patterson shoved her inside her car, and the two men drove her car to a nearby business and forced her into the trunk. The two men returned to Wal-Mart to pick up their vehicle. Later that evening, Skinner and Patterson raped and murdered Carla Jones. Her father, Roy Willmon, brought a wrongful death action against Wal-Mart for negligently failing to implement feasible precautions and failing to use ordinary care to maintain store premises in a safe condition.

• On July 30, 1993, 46-year-old Larry McDonald and a female friend were returning to their car after shopping in a Wal-Mart store in Jacksonville, Florida. A gunman approached McDonald and shot him in the head. McDonald sued Wal-Mart, and after a five-day jury trial, he was awarded $1.5 million. Wal-Mart was found 75% negligent in the 1995 case.

• In 1994, "Jane Doe" was kidnapped from a Wal-Mart parking lot in Beckley, West Virginia and raped. Her abductor had kidnapped another woman from a Wal-Mart parking lot the year before. Wal-Mart denied they had any responsibility for the parking lot, since they only leased the store, and not the lot itself. The company famous for putting the customer first told the court they owed no "duty to any customer after the customer leaves the building."

• Terri Reinholtz, a Wal-Mart employee, was forcefully and brutally raped by her Wal-Mart supervisor while she was at work in the early morning hours of February 19, 1995. The supervisor who raped Terri had been working for Wal-Mart for more than ten years. Terri was employed as an assistant customer service clerk at the automotive department at a Wal-Mart store in the Tulsa, Oklahoma area. Her duties included opening and closing the automotive store, securing the cash register, and conducting inventory assessments. Her assailant had made sexual advances toward her for more than a year. She was raped in the automotive store at Wal-Mart on a morning when her supervisor knew she was scheduled to open the store, and would be there alone for several hours.

• On November 21, 1998, at the Wal-Mart in Conyers, Georgia, Chris Jernigan and his friend Nick Jones were standing in line, when Russell Jackson and David Hill were apparently overcome with Wal-Rage. Jackson and Hill clipped the shopping cart of Jernigan and Jones, who took offense and suggested that the four men settle their argument out into the parking lot. Once outside, Jones hit Hill with a tire iron, Jackson pulled a gun and shot 20-year-old Jernigan in the face. The police were called in and arrested Jackson, 28, and charged him with aggravated assault and battery.

• Jean Santino of East Haven, Connecticut was shopping in the toy section of Kmart when a hooded robber knocked her over with a cart and ripped the purse from her hand. "It makes me so angry," Santino said. "For that to happen inside the store with so many children around is unbelievable." The expansive parking lot of the new Kmart Super Center has been targeted by thugs since opening in October of 1995. Police were called to the store 54 times in December, and 88 times in just three months.

• Bill Enright, selectman in the town of Avon, Massachusetts, has a new 120,000 square foot Wal-Mart in his town. There was little opposition to the store, but Enright says today: "If we had to do it over again, I don't know." According to Enright, "We've had a lot more than our share of police problems down there." The local police chief says, "We're down there all the time," and estimates they make three or four arrests a week.

• Kidnappings in 1995 from Wal-Mart stores in rural areas, and the subsequent rape of two women and the murder of another have raised questions about the safety of stores. In the fall of 1995, three women and an eleven-year-old girl were abducted from stores in Conway, Morrilton, and Jasper, Alabama.

According to Department of Justice and FBI crime reports, robberies at supermarkets, department stores, and discounters rose 19% from 1989 to 1993 (while robberies at convenience stores dropped 13%). If a Wal-Mart superstore comes before your community, the cost of the additional demand on your local police department should be weighed against any benefits Wal-Mart claims it will produce.

The logical extension of building sprawl and generating crime is explained by the former Mayor of Hailey, Idaho, Keith Roark, as quoted in *Smart States, Better Communities* by Constance Beaumont: "The emphasis is all on getting those jobs, creating that growth. But then later, after you've got all that growth, you also have a lot of sprawl, a stressed infrastructure, things are breaking down everywhere, and you look around and wonder: Why is crime so high? The next response is to build more prisons."

In April, 1999, a District Court Judge in Jefferson County, Texas fined Wal-Mart stores $18 million for a "pattern of false and misleading discovery answers." Discovery is the pre-trial process during which both parties in a lawsuit try to get information out of the other side to promote their case. In the Texas lawsuit, a woman named Donna Meissner sued Wal-Mart for "premises liability" after she was kidnapped in a Wal-Mart parking lot, and then raped. She charged that Wal-Mart had not taken the steps necessary to protect customers in the store's parking lot. During the course of discovery, Meissner's lawyer tried to get Wal-Mart to produce a copy of a company study that had been reportedly conducted in 1993, showing that 80% of crimes at Wal-Mart occur in their parking lots. When the court pressed Wal-Mart to produce the study, the company tried to argue that the study was just a survey. When Wal-Mart failed to produce the report, the Judge said that the company had a "corporate policy" of undermining the discovery process, and he fined Wal-Mart one-thousandth of its net worth ($18 million), saying: "I hope the stockholders do learn about this, and I hope some pressure is applied to Wal-Mart to make it behave as a responsible corporate citizen."

Donna Meissner's lawyer, Alto Watson, told the court that Wal-Mart had "systematically engaged in a conspiracy...to withhold evidence from victims who have been injured at their stores relating to a lack of security nationwide." Watson described Wal-Mart's actions against his client as "simply reprehensible and execrable. There is not an adequate adjective or adverb to describe it other than criminal."

Wal-Mart reportedly has a legal staff of somewhere around thirty in-house lawyers, plus another one hundred law firms that it retains across the nation. These lawyers are managing as many as 10,000 legal cases against the company. The May 1999 issue of the *National Law Journal* quotes another Texas judge as saying of Wal-Mart: "Rarely has this court seen such a pattern of deliberate obfuscation, delay, misrepresentation, and downright lying to another party and to a court."

5. Helping Other Businesses

"We believe the opening of a Wal-Mart will significantly benefit the city of San Leandro and its local businesses . . . This is due to the increased consumer activity and local spending that is generated, not just in Wal-Mart, but throughout the entire retail sector."

Is Wal-Mart a shot in the arm for struggling merchants, or a shot in the head? In August of 1998, a Wal-Mart opened in Ticonderoga, New York. Sprawl-busters had fought the store, but lost. After the store opened, a local writer went around to businesses in the downtown area, to actually see how they were doing. Here is what Phil Gallos found:

Howard Rathbun at Rathbun Jewelers says overall traffic in his store is down 20%. Dick Arthur at Arthur Drugs says that, while his prescription business is holding, his sales tax figures are down, also by 20%, indicating a corresponding fall in taxable sales. Rick Osier, Rite Aid's manager, says traffic in his store is "down quite considerably from last year at this time." Douglas Spaulding says "traffic has definitely decreased" at his Agway store. Fred Vialt, Aubuchon's manager says his traffic is down nearly 20%. Big A Auto Parts owner Glen Moorby says he has seen at least a 25% decrease in his business. Valerie Mullin, whose NeedleWorks and Crafts Plus is one of two she owns, is closing the Ticonderoga store. Her overall sales have fallen 50%, beginning in August. One merchant, who did not want to be identified ("I might want to sell this place"), said she's had her worst Christmas season in thirteen years....The most recent casualty has been the Great American Market.

GAM owner Kaz Licygiewicz first had to cut his operating hours as a direct result, he said, of business lost to Wal-Mart. His payroll dropped correspondingly from 27 people to 17. Then, on January 16, both hours and payroll dropped to zero, and Ticonderoga lost its only centrally located full-service grocery store . . . Even Jay Fortino, whose minimally affected Sunoco station sits at the corner of Montcalm Street and Champlain Avenue, marvels at the impact. "I've been here 25 years," he said. "On the week before Christmas in past years, you couldn't find a parking space on this street. This year, you could've landed a plane on it."

If there is one quote to remember about Wal-Mart's attitude towards other businesses, it is this one from May 1997, spoken by Wal-Mart CEO David Glass during testimony in the Federal Trade Commission hearings on the proposed merger of Staples and Office Depot: "Anyone who sells anything that we do is a competitor."

Although Wal-Mart has promised to help other businesses, they have no corporate policy that says "help thy competitor." To the contrary, the evidence clearly shows that large national chain stores have a negative impact on competitors. This should not be surprising, yet many local public officials base their entire argument for big box retail on its salutary impact on other businesses. But, as Sam Walton wrote: "Nobody owes anybody else a living."

Much has been made in the media of Wal-Mart's decision several years ago to move into a 60,000 square foot recycled store in "downtown" Bennington, Vermont. While most Wal-Marts today range between two and three times this size, the company wanted to plant its flag in Vermont soil, and Bennington was the first pin on the map for Wal-Mart. Was this an attempt by Wal-Mart to help other businesses?

"It was a total surprise," Bennington's Planning Director Steve Juzczyk told a reporter. "We heard a developer was coming in to fix up an abandoned shopping plaza, and the next thing we knew, we had a Wal-Mart." Juzczyk adds: "I sent Wal-Mart a letter in 1993 asking them if they had any plans to build in Bennington, and I got no response. So I sent them another one, and didn't get a reply that time either. Then one day, they were putting up the sign."

Contrary to media reports, the Bennington Wal-Mart is not located downtown. In fact, the store is located more than a mile from the downtown shopping district, making it unlikely that pedestrian shoppers would use the facility. According to a newspaper account, downtown Bennington "supports 20 or 30 businesses. The loss of businesses has accelerated since Wal-Mart's arrival, say some locals."

Although Juzczyk repeats the common wisdom that Bennington stores can survive by selling goods and services not found at Wal-Mart, local art supply and novelty store owner Jay Zwynenburg was skeptical. Zwynenburg has operated his store for 25 years. He says his annual sales rose every year for the ten years leading up to the 1994 opening of Wal-Mart. Since that time, Zwynenburg says his revenues have fallen substantially. He adjusted his inventory, just like the consultants told him to do. But it made little difference. "You don't have to compete with Wal-Mart on a particular item," Zwynenburg explains. "They're just like this big sucking sound taking activity out of the community." Some local businesses claim to have seen sales plummet since Wal-Mart arrived, some by as much as 30%.

This is easily explained by Jay Allen, Wal-Mart's vice president of corporate affairs. "Whenever we come into a town," Allen said, during a tour of a store under construction in Williston, Vermont, "the businesses who want to compete do. They don't like us so much, because we make them work so hard."

In a September, 1994 edition of *Doonesbury*, artist Garry Trudeau depicted the confrontation between a Wal-Mart man and local pharmacist Gilbert Wax:

Gilbert Wax: It's not fair. I'm a third generation druggist. You'll ruin me!
Wal-Mart: Now, Gil, you have nothing to worry about. Wal-Mart will serve as a magnet, creating a boon for all local stores.
Wax: Oh, right . . . Your 20,000 sq.ft. superpharmacy is going to act as a draw for my 600 sq.ft. drug store? I don't think so!
Wal-Mart: Then sell something else. Local crafts! Corn cob pipes.

Companies like Wal-Mart and Home Depot are not in business to help other businesses. That would be a form of corporate charity. Lee Scott, the Vice President for Merchandising at Wal-Mart described the superstore concept very clearly: "It's one stop shopping for the small town." Wal-Mart told the people of San Leandro that "a Wal-Mart store acts as a magnet for out-of-town shoppers" to increase both the large and small business revenue base. But this is not what the record shows.

According to a 1995 study in three Iowa towns commissioned by the National Trust for Historic Preservation, Wal-Mart gave no "bounce" to other area merchants:

> Although five years after Wal-Mart came to the towns, new stores opened in the downtowns of all three communities, there was still a net decline in the number of stores downtown. There was no evidence to support the claim that Wal-Mart had boosted downtown shopping. In all three downtowns there are non-retail businesses in prime first floor space that are typically found on side streets or upper floors in healthy downtowns. Each downtown had vacancies on the upper floors.

Beyond that, the National Trust study found additional damage to the retail base caused by Wal-Mart:

> Wal-Mart appears to have negatively affected some businesses outside of the downtown that existed prior to the store's opening. In all three cases there were general merchandise stores on the highway business corridor that closed after Wal-Mart opened. Other retailers closed as well ...Although some suggest that the presence of Wal-Mart outside of, but near to, the downtown area results in additional activity downtown, both sales data and traffic data do not show this gain. Traffic count data indicate that average daily traffic volumes actually declined or stayed somewhat constant in the downtown areas, while it increased out by the Wal-Mart stores.

In the case of building supply chain stores, Alex Czopke of Tru-Serv knows that companies like Home Depot will not mean more sales in his members' cash registers: "When Home Depot arrives, the disposable dollars in a given market available to other dealers shrink, which sometimes results in independents battling among each other. That leads to fewer retailers."

Wal-Mart likes to tell small businesses that they can "survive, and even thrive" in the shadow of a Wal-Mart. As Wal-Mart spokesman Les Copeland told an audience in North Elba, New York in 1997:

> What we are seeing around the country is that small businesses don't necessarily like Wal-Mart, but they are benefiting from us. Not all small businesses. But the ones that are benefiting are the small businesses taking their own money and reinvesting it in themselves to become more efficient and change with the times, rather than taking their money and using it to fight Wal-Mart.

To understand how one-stop shopping affects other businesses, it is important to understand the difference between a discount store and a superstore. In 1989, there were no Wal-Mart supercenters. By 1998, there were 473 supercenters. These supercenters range in size from 110,000 to 220,000 square feet. The supercenter combines traditional discount goods with a full-line grocery store, including all perishables (meat, bakery, produce, frozen foods, etc.). Wal-Mart supercenters generate three times more sales than a conventional Wal-Mart discount store. I have seen estimates that Wal-Mart gets 25% to 50% of its sales in a supercenter from grocery items. The typical Wal-Mart supercenter in the early 1990s committed about one-third of its selling space to food, two-thirds to non-food items.

A 1995 report from James M. Degen & Company says that the average Wal-Mart supercenter was 170,000 square feet, and sold 100,000 store keeping units (SKUs). Typical superstores, like a Fred Meyer's, Meijer's, SuperKmart contain the following merchandise mix:

Supercenter Departments

Discount Items	Grocery	Services
infant, boys, girls apparel	dry grocery	florist
men's apparel	health & beauty	video rental
women's apparel	frozen foods	photo studio
hosiery	dairy	food service
fashion accessories	bakery	optical
cosmetics	deli	pharmacy

Discount items	Grocery	Services (continued)
jewelry	produce	bank
lawn and garden	fresh meats	
electronics		
sporting goods		
automotive/car care		
hardware		
shoes		
domestics		
crafts/fabrics/home decorating		
furniture/home office		
pet supplies		
greeting cards		
household/personal care appliances		
books		
toys		
seasonal		

"The consumer of the '90s is a value shopper," the Degen report says, "and more motivated by everyday low prices and one-stop convenience of the supercenter than the typical supermarket price specials and couponing." As *Business Week* magazine said in 1993: "Wal-Mart is betting that selling juice, jumper cables and blue jeans in one low price store is the future of retailing."

By 1994, Wal-Mart alone had a 28% share of the supercenter industry, but it was second in market share to the Meijer's company. The three top firms controlled 81% of the superstore market. Wal-Mart's average sales per store were around $38 million a year. Wal-Mart started building supercenters in 1988 in Washington, Missouri, and ten years later had 473 supercenters open. Most supercenters are relocations in towns that already have a Wal-Mart. The company is looking for annual sales of $60 million or more from each "unit."

The rapid increase in supercenters has the grocery supermarket industry worried. As Degen explains: "Not only is the grocery industry facing overall no real growth in sales (up only 1.9% in 1993), but also no inflation."

6. Buy American

"Wal-Mart Stores, Inc. is proud to provide tens of thousands of jobs to California residents, as well as purchasing billions of dollars of produce and merchandise from California growers and manufacturers."

The new employee at Wal-Mart is told that "our company is involved in creating and saving American jobs through our Buy American program . . . We are constantly seeking more items to convert from foreign sources to American manufacturers. We prefer to place American-made products on our shelves."

Wal-Mart actually claims that "millions of dollars in goods once produced overseas have been brought back to the USA." But they add: "It is not a blind commitment to buy American products at any price." On the infamous 1992 NBC *Dateline* show, NBC charged that Wal-Mart directly imported 288 million pounds of goods from Hong Kong and China — 8,000 times more than it did before it began the Buy American campaign.

Of course, even when you can find products that say "Made in the USA," like the Wal-Mart clothes that are made in the Northern Marianas islands, the products may have been produced by child laborers in a "hotbox" sweatshop.

According to an in-store survey in the summer of 1998 carried out by the National Labor Committee, 85% of the 92,000 clothing items reviewed at Wal-Mart stores in a dozen states were made overseas. Wal-Mart spokeswoman Betsy Reithmeyer disputed the 85% figure, and came up with the company's own estimate:

> I don't know how much of our private labels are made offshore . . . I'm not disputing that it's probably 80%, which is probably the same as Target, Kmart, and everybody else…That's just a fact of the global marketplace.

In that international marketplace, Wal-Mart has become the new "Great WAL" of China, importing more foreign goods than any other single American retailer in history. This comes at a time when the United States trade deficit has surged to record highs. Weak economies abroad have hurt American manufacturing efforts to sell United States goods overseas.

The American trade deficit hit $19.4 billion in February of 1999, nearly a

16% increase from the previous record set the month before of $16.8 billion. In 1998, America lost nearly 400,000 manufacturing jobs because of slumping exports. AFL-CIO President John Sweeney called the widening deficit "a low road to nowhere."

Our trade deficit was spurred higher by increasing American demand for foreign-made products, such as imports of clothing, toys, television sets and stereos posted major gains. Cheap imports, carried into the country for Wal-Mart distribution, helped to drive the trade imbalance even higher.

In a 1997 interview in a trade publication, Home Depot's Executive Vice President for Merchandising, Bill Hamlin, was asked if his company — which once emphasized the American products it sold — had any concern today about United States versus global products. Hamlin responded:

> We love to buy the best brand names and sell them at the best prices. That's what our business has been built upon . . . Obviously that's been one of the key successes of the Home Depot since the beginning. It doesn't matter whether it's Made in the USA brands for USA, or Made in Canada brands for Canada, or Made in Chile brands for Chile. With (our new) Savannah distribution center, we'll be buying a lot of products that have been manufactured outside the United States direct, and we can take advantage of the cost savings as well as have better control over the quality aspect.

If "Made in the USA" doesn't matter to Home Depot, it doesn't seem to matter much to Wal-Mart either. One Wal-Mart official told reporters in 1998 that the company was committed to buying American-made goods "whenever pricing and quality are comparable to goods made offshore." In 1993, United States Congressman James Traficant, Jr. of Ohio, went on the House floor and called Wal-Mart "Sam the Sham's Discount." The Congressman said that "many companies improperly bask in the patriotic lights of 'Made in America'."

In that same year, Wal-Mart opened its huge "foreign trade subzone distribution center" in Buckeye, Arizona, a $20 million, 1.2 million square foot warehouse. Wal-Mart became the first United States retailer to have its own foreign trade zone status on a large scale. Wal-Mart uses the zone for imports, storage and distribution of imported goods, and packing of items for its own use and for export. The Arizona plant became the command headquarters for Wal-Mart's growing international empire. With the foreign trade subzone designation, Wal-Mart is able to delay paying import duties for goods shipped to the distribution center until they're moved into United States commerce. According to Lebhar-Friedman, the delay in paying duties is "a float that can be worth millions to the chain – avoid duties on exports, and reduce the duties on goods processed from imported components." Wal-Mart also avoids having to apply for repayment of duties for goods imported to the United States that are then rerouted to foreign countries. The Buckeye center provides direct connection with a major shipping center in Long Beach, California and the Phoenix, Arizona airport.

"The truth is," says the National Labor Committee, "Wal-Mart has moved far more production offshore than the industry average. For example, only 11% of Wal-Mart's famous Kathie Lee line of clothing is made in the US, while 89% is made off-shore. Only 17% of Wal-Mart's men's Faded Glory clothing is made in the US, while 96% of its children's McKids label is made offshore. Wal-Mart has shifted the majority of its Kathie Lee production to Mexico and Indonesia — two countries where the local currencies collapsed, driving real wages through the floor, to 50¢ an hour in Mexico, and 9¢ in Indonesia. It is as if Wal-Mart were chasing misery."

Despite the megastore claims that they are "bringing it back to the USA," our American apparel industry has literally come unstitched. According to a July 1998 report by the United States General Accounting Office, over the past 23 years, United States apparel industry jobs have shrunk by 41%. There were 1,450,000 United States apparel workers in 1973, and only 853,000 similar jobs by 1996. According to the GAO, in 1995 more than half of the $178 billion in apparel sold at the retail level in the United States at companies like Wal-Mart were imported. Between 1987 and 1997, imports from the Caribbean grew from $864 million to $6.4 billion — a sevenfold increase.

Sam Walton admitted that his company at one time had fallen into "a pattern of knee-jerk import buying, without really examining possible alternatives." Wal-Mart would take its best-selling item, like a Nike Air Mada shoe, and send them to the Orient, and say, "See if you can make something like this." In 1997 a United States District Court in Virginia saw the similarities between Nike shoes and the knock-offs Wal-Mart was selling. The court ordered Wal-Mart, and its shoe supplier in Korea, Hawe Yue, to pay Nike a total of $6 million for infringement of Nike's design patent on its Air Mada outdoor shoe. The Court also prohibited Wal-Mart from selling any more infringing shoes.

Sometimes, in trying to bring everyday low prices to you, Wal-Mart has to step on a few toes. In this case, the toes stepped back.

In 1997, a Wal-Mart store in Newburgh, New York was picketed by members of the Professional Workers Association, after 290 workers were laid off at the Hudson Valley Tree Company. Wal-Mart had canceled its contract with the artificial Christmas tree manufacturer. Hudson Valley Tree claims it lost its contract with Wal-Mart because the retailer found a similar product in China. A Wal-Mart representative said it purchases 83% of its trees from a Virginia-based company, and 17% from China.

In 1996, the Kanienkeha Lure Company, owned by the Native American Mohawks, went out of business on the St. Regis Mohawk Reservation in northern New York state when Wal-Mart decided to pull their contract for fishing lures. Eighty workers at the Kanienkeha factory lost their jobs, and the Mohawks urged a boycott of the chain.

According to research by reporter Bob Ortega, Wal-Mart's highly publicized Buy American program had little impact on the company's import activity:

> By 1988, Walton was saying that Wal-Mart had brought back to US manufacturers $1.2 billion in retail goods . . . creating or saving some 17,000 jobs. But Wal-Mart's direct imports, as a percentage of sales, hadn't shrunk at all, because the company was buying more goods directly than before —including more imported goods. Wal-Mart's buying staff in Hong Kong and Taipei alone had grown to 90 people.

As I said at a United Food and Commercial Workers rally in Bentonville, Arkansas in 1998: "The label isn't 'Made in the USA,' it's 'Betrayed in the USA'." Wal-Mart imports alone have done a number on our nation's balance of trade deficit. The bumper sticker that once read: "Think locally, act globally," should be replaced with the new sprawl sticker: "Profit locally, buy globally."

I will give Wal-Mart the last word on this Buy American debate. "The confusion about our Buy American program," Wal-Mart CEO David Glass told a Town Hall Forum in St. Louis in 1993, "is we've never said that we buy everything in America."

7. Charitable Contributions

"We make substantial investments in the communities we serve, and are proud of our history of community involvement and participation."

In my family, we would call people who made a big show of their good works "loud givers." Wal-Mart and Home Depot are loud givers. It seems like at the end of almost every Wal-Mart press release, the company touts their corporate giving programs. "In 1998," says Wal-Mart, "the company raised and donated more than $127 million for charitable organizations." Wal-Mart bought full page ads in national magazines promoting its "Competitive Edge scholarships." The company says it has donated scholarships to more than 900 students since 1992. The tag line at the end of the ad reads: "Because we live here, too. And we believe good works." As my mother used to say: "Be suspicious of people who have to constantly remind you how good they are."

Wal-Mart's public relations people have obviously told management that they have to spend millions on ads like these to counter the image of the "outsider" company, the bullies from Arkansas. The truth is, Wal-Mart doesn't live in your hometown. The cashiers and the stockers who work there were already working at some other store in town. The management, and the money, reside in Bentonville, Arkansas. Your hometown is just a pin on the map, and Wal-Mart assets are often shuffled around based on market decisions made in Bentonville.

In Marietta, Ohio, a Wal-Mart spokesman told *The Athens News* that the company provided a $300 Grandparent's Day Grant to a youth group that delivered meals to seniors. It offered $500 to a Teacher of the year; $5,300 in environmental grants; $3,000 in special donations; $12,000 in matching grants; and $3,000 for miscellaneous causes.

While Wal-Mart was wooing Chandler, Arizona, and other towns in the East Valley in December of 1998, a newspaper article appeared announcing that "a member of the wealthy family that runs Wal-Mart is behind a $2 million scholarship fund to help low-income Valley families pay for private or parochial school tuition." The report said that 500 scholarships would be given to kids from poor families "chosen by a lottery."

The *Arizona Tribune* story said "The Wal-Mart corporation says this money has nothing to do with its controversial efforts to build giant retail stores in the Valley." A Wal-Mart spokeswoman was quoted as saying,"It's something that John Walton is doing as an individual. It's not something we can speak about through Wal-Mart." The story's headline proclaimed: "Wal-Mart Director's Fund to Give Kids Scholarships."

In San Leandro, Wal-Mart's "open letter" to citizens says that Wal-Mart generates "hundreds of thousands of dollars for local community and non-profit organizations through individual store fundraising efforts, volunteer programs, and Wal-Mart Foundation matching grants . . . supporting local schools and education through a variety of grant and scholarship programs. In 1996, Wal-Mart contributed over $8.4 million in national scholarships alone." Sam Walton liked to say that "each year, every Wal-Mart store sponsors one student in its community to a $1,000 scholarship."

On the other hand, Wal-Mart critics have long noted the company's talk of giving may be worth more than the actual giving. In their 1994 book on Wal-Mart, Sandra Vance and Roy Scott looked behind the press releases:

> In comparison with other firms, Wal-Mart was parsimonious when it came to corporate giving. In 1987, for example, according to the standard gauge of corporate philanthropy, the percentage of pre-tax earnings a firm donates to charity, Wal-Mart ranked last among the major discounters. Rival Kmart contributed 3.6 times as much. In that same year, the Wal-Mart Foundation, with total assets of $6.1 million, ranked nowhere near the top 100 corporate foundations in charitable expenditures.

Walton admitted that this kind of criticism "annoyed me considerably." When critics said, "Wal-Mart doesn't do its fair share of giving to charities," here is Walton's response:

I would argue that our relentless effort to improve our business has always been tied to trying to make things better for the folks who live and work in our communities. We have built a company that is so efficient it has enabled us to save our customers billions of dollars, and whether you buy into the argument or not, we believe it. That in itself is giving something back, and it has been the cornerstone philosophy of our company.

Walton made it clear that "beyond that, we feel very strongly that Wal-Mart really is not, and should not be, in the charity business. We don't believe in taking a lot of money out of Wal-Mart's cash registers and giving it to charity for the simple reason that any debit has to be passed along to somebody — either our shareholders or our customers. . . . By not designating a large amount of corporate funds to some charity which the officers of Wal-Mart may happen to like, we feel we give our shareholders more discretion in supporting their own charities."

Ironically, Wal-Mart, which defines charity as saving its customers money, adopted a mechanism to shift "the debit," as Walton called it, from the company onto its workers and its venerated customers. Vance and Scott explain:

> Employees were also expected to contribute directly to charitable causes endorsed by the company and, more important, to raise money for local projects from customers through in-store cash solicitations and through such fund-raising enterprises as car washes, rummage sales, and fried-pie and bake sales. Wal-Mart touted the leadership role its associates assumed in fund-raising activities as a sterling example of its emphasis on employee involvement in community affairs. Also to be considered, however, was the benefit to the company: in using the associates to solicit contributions from Wal-Mart shoppers, the firm was able to garner a significant portion of its philanthropic expenditures from its customers.

At Home Depot, the company gave less than 1% of its pre-tax profits to charity in 1997. It made $10 million in donations, or roughly .0004% of its gross sales that year of $24 billion. Every Home Depot store has a budget for making contributions to local community organizations. Home Depot says its workers "volunteer their time to make our communities better places to live." "We do more than just hand out checks to charities," the company says. "We help make advances in community service, environmental concerns," etc. Home Depot claims it contributed $8.6 million to charity in 1996, a year in which total Home Depot sales exceeded $19.5 billion. By comparison, if a family with $35,000 income gave at the same rate as Home Depot, it would add up to 29¢ per week in the church plate.

Half of many Home Depot gifts come from the workers, not the company. Under the "matching gift" program, the worker's donation is matched fifty cents on the dollar by Home Depot. The "Team Depot" program is a group of employees in a store that offers its time to work on a community project. Workers are reminded that Home Depot does not pay for time spent helping the community: "Participation in Team Depot takes place during your personal time."

Home Depot rules do not allow "non-associate" groups, like the Girl Scouts, church groups, the Boy Scouts, the military, or other local groups to raise funds on Home Depot sidewalks or parking lots.

Sometimes charity begins at home. In 1997, Home Depot gave a group called Christmas in April $265,000 worth of merchandise credit. Christmas in April took that credit to Home Depot and spent $878,000 at their stores — more than three times what Home Depot donated.

The most commonly heard complaint about companies like Wal-Mart and Home Depot is that they rarely get involved in corporate giving for local civic projects. Typical of the stories I receive is this comment from Sharon Wallace of Yuma, Arizona:

> My kids are in Scouts. One boy needed three cans of paint to finish his Eagle Scout. Wal-Mart said no. The girls that sell cookies are allowed to stand outside, but not saying anything, like 'Would you like our cookies?' Unbelievable..

8. Taxes

"California Wal-Marts generated a total of $287 million in state and local sales taxes in 1996, benefiting local schools, police, fire and other important community services."

In the Easton, Maryland study of Wal-Mart impact conducted by the University of Maryland, researchers looked at the fiscal impact on taxes:

In the years following the arrival of Wal-Mart, town tax receipts from personal property and ordinary business corporation taxes grew, but at a declining rate. Real property and income tax receipts rose slightly, however income tax receipts grew much more slowly than would have been predicted. The expected growth in income taxes may have been offset by low-wage jobs offered by the large retailer and by the loss of employment in competing businesses . . . The retail trade sector in Talbot County as a whole experienced business closures and job losses in most sectors that compete directly with Wal-Mart. There are high vacancy rates in some shopping centers distant from Wal-Mart. Many downtown businesses have closed, while others have reported significant declines in sales.

In Toledo, Ohio, Home Depot's real estate manager presented the city in November of 1997 with a breakdown of the project's fiscal impact on the city. "We estimate this project will pay about $248,000 per year in real property tax," said Tim Platt, Home Depot's Midwest Real Estate Manager. Three days later, the City's Commissioner of Economic Development submitted a memo to members of the City Council repeating the tax revenue impact of "$238,000 to $248,000 per year on completion." These figures, however, were then analyzed by the Westgate Neighbors, a citizens group opposed to the construction of a second Home Depot in Toledo. The residents found that the slightly larger Home Depot a few miles away was only paying the city $153,132. Using that tax bill, and subtracting out the property taxes already being paid by an existing commercial tenant on the site, along with the taxes paid by a series of apartment buildings that Home Depot wanted to destroy, the Westgate Neighbors showed that the Home Depot tax bill would net out at only $69,430, or 28% of what Home Depot had estimated, and city officials had parroted. In their exuberance to build, Home Depot had magnified the projected property tax increase three-and-one-half times. The estimated property tax change calculated by the citizens, and based on Lucas County property tax payments, meant that Home Depot's project would translate into a savings of 41cents per year per voter in Toledo.

In the Kilmarnock, Virginia study of a proposed Wal-Mart, the report concludes that Wal-Mart assessed valuation would be around $3.65 million. The assessed value of retail property likely to compete with Wal-Mart was around $8 to $10 million. "If these competitive properties," the study says, "were to lose 45% in value over time compared to what they would have been in the absence of a Wal-Mart, the decline would exceed the property gain from Wal-Mart . . . Often local officials consider only property values based on new construction, and do not consider the effects of new commercial space on already present property values."

In New Paltz, New York, the town did a careful analysis of the public revenues to be derived from a proposed Wal-Mart in Huguenot Plaza. The Planning Board came up with the following fiscal impact on both town and school taxes. Their analysis looks at not just revenue derived from the project, but the offsets, including the impact on other business property, and the likelihood that the developer would ask for a 50% property tax abatement for the project under state property tax law. The Planning Board estimated that the total tax revenue from the project would come to $252,000, of which $100,000 would go to property taxes, and $152,000 to the schools. But before public officials started planning how to spend this new-found wealth, they projected how much this development would cost the public:

Item	Value
Town taxes paid by Wal-Mart	$100,000
Offsets Due to:	
Police, Fire and other town services	-$29,000
Services to three other deteriorated or abandoned malls	-$ 5,000
30% tax reduction for other malls	-$29,000
30% residential tax grievances from 15 nearby households	-$ 5,940
50% tax abatement on Wal Mart's tax bill	-$50,000
Net Town Tax Impact	**-$18,940**

The Planning Board in New Paltz found that the Wal-Mart "would cause a deficit in terms of municipal services and tax dollars received by the town."

Wal-Mart would also pay school taxes to the town. The town also examined these impacts:

School Taxes	$152,000
Cost of six new students in town	-$ 48,000
30% tax reduction three existing malls	-$ 44,000
50% of $150,000 tax abatement	-$ 75,000
Net School Tax Deficit	**-$ 15,000**

The Planning Board also noted that the "state often reduces its aid in the same proportion as the School District gains from its local tax revenue" — so that even if the project raised local revenues, it would be offset by state losses.

The Planning Board concluded that "the Huguenot Plaza would cause a deficit in term of tax dollars received by the School District," and "the Plaza will cause future community costs for community planning, assessment, and community development to counter negative fiscal/social impacts." The Board also warned that taxpayers would bear the costs of highway improvements on Route 299, where the store would be located. The New York Department of Transportation estimated that widening the road from two to four lanes would cost around $2 million per mile. The new Plaza would cost the taxpayers $5.1 million in traffic improvements, the Board noted. "In sum," the town of New Paltz concluded, "it would take years for the Huguenot Plaza to pay more than it costs in town government expenses and reduced assessment and possible highway improvement costs."

An analysis published by the Maine Coast Heritage Trust on the economic impact of mall and other commercial development concluded that "the extensive mall development in South Portland (Maine), championed as growth that would bring in revenue, dramatically raised the state valuation of the area, which caused the state school subsidy to drop significantly...advocates for constant expansion of a community's tax base, particularly in high valued coastal areas, have probably ignored the effects such raised valuations have had on reducing education subsidies and raising taxes."

As Alan Altshuler of the Lincoln Institute of Land Policy has concluded: "The traditional view of the matter which prevailed into the 1970s was that most development pays its way. The emerging view today is that virtually no development does."

Sweetening the Deal

Over and above exaggerated claims of sales and property tax bonanzas, developers will often add in "sweeteners" to their deal, including land improvements that may have no connection to their project. Superstore retailers believe that every town has its price — all they have to do is open up their checkbook and buy their way into town. It turns out that the free market can be very expensive, but if you have deep enough pockets, some communities are for sale. Consider the following five examples of "sweeteners":

• In the city of Lancaster, Pennsylvania, a developer offered the local community a $5 million sweetener to bring their "power center" into town: $1,000,000 towards the development of any industrial site in the city; $750,000 for the local office of Economic Development; $1,000,000 for the Lancaster School District; $375,000 for a job training program; and $1,500,000 in road improvements. Lancaster city officials were struggling with a difficult budget situation, and along comes a developer loaded with off-site goodies.

• In the case of Quincy, Massachusetts, according to the *Boston Globe*, "Some local business people and politicians expressed concerns that (Wal-Mart) would further damage Quincy's already struggling central business district. However, Atlantic Development Corp., developer of the Wal-Mart, won over most of the project's early critics with a lucrative financial package." The sweetener that the developer used to enhance his Wal-Mart proposal included: $150,000 over a three-year period for the Quincy Center Business and Professional Association to promote and advertise the downtown shopping district; a grant to Quincy 2000, a local business group located in a downtown mall, to allow them to hire staff to recruit new businesses downtown; $100,000 to demolish the interiors of an old Child World vacant building downtown and a local clothing store; $100,000 to pay for plans and permits for the city to develop an office building "that local officials want to see built on an underused downtown parking lot; the cost of running a shuttle bus to connect the local elderly housing complexes with downtown and area supermarkets; a $600,000 "mitigation" package for residents of The Falls condominium project, which are across the driveway from Wal-Mart. Since this project will devastate the value of these condos, the Developer offered to buy out the current condo owners at the price they bought in, or, pay them seven percent of the value of their condo if they stay.

• In St. Albans, Vermont, developers offered to form a St. Albans Marketing Association and give this new group $225,000 to be spent over several years. However, the state's Environmental Board dismissed this offer saying: "The structure and goals of this organization, as well as the uses to which funds will be put, are too vague to provide a reasonable assurance that this money will in fact lead to public benefit."

• In Greenfield, Massachusetts, Wal-Mart offered to spend $900,000 on road improvements and $200,000 in water and sewer improvements. They also offered the town $1,400,000 worth of fill dirt to use at the local industrial park. Opponents of the project called this "The Dirty Deal: We get the dirt — Wal-Mart gets the deal."

• In Warrenton, Virginia, Wal-Mart proposed to build a store just over the town line in order to avoid a town ordinance limiting the size of retail buildings. But Wal-Mart still needed to petition the Town Supervisors to extend water and sewer lines to their property, or the company would have been required to install a septic drainfield on property adjacent to their building. Before the town vote over extending utilities to the site, the owners of the Wal-Mart property offered to donate a piece of the land to the town for a new elementary school. Wal-Mart's lawyer then pointed out that if the town didn't extend water and sewer, that Wal-Mart's on-site septic system would require use of the land offered for a school. At the public hearing, one Warrenton resident said: "I feel I'm being held hostage. More important, I feel our kids are being held hostage." According to a local newspaper account, Wal-Mart's lawyer "scoffed at suggestions that Wal-Mart cast a shadow of doubt over the new elementary school merely to squeeze the supervisors for sewer capacity. 'There's a difference between a threat and a consequence,' he said." The Supervisors voted three to two to give Wal-Mart the sewer connection, with one supervisor clearly voting for a new school as the prime motivation. "We need to get our education moving forward," he said, "and to block it is wrong."

9. Prices

"Wal-Mart will provide good products at good prices . . . Wal-Mart prides itself on offering quality products at competitive prices. That's the Wal-Mart tradition our customers have come to know and expect."

When competitors and an advertising industry review group challenged Wal-Mart to justify its slogan "Always the low price, always," Wal-Mart responded by dropping the slogan. Wal-Mart agreed to change its slogan in response to the challenge from the National Advertising Review Board. The review board, which is made up of seventy advertising professionals, told Wal-Mart that they should eliminate any references to "the low price." Instead, the Board recommended that any modified slogan refrain from stating or implying that Wal-Mart prices are "always the lowest." Rob Schafer, owner of a leather store in Marietta, Ohio, says that just because Wal-Mart stocks a product does not mean they're cheaper than anywhere else. Schafer says he can beat Wal-Mart prices, but the impression is that if they have it at Wal-Mart and I have it at my place, it's cheaper at Wal-Mart".

In 1993, three drug stores in Conway, Arkansas charged that Wal-Mart had engaged in predatory pricing of health and beauty care products and over the counter drugs, by selling these items below cost at their Conway supercenter. The drug stores claimed that Wal-Mart had violated a 1937 Arkansas Unfair Practices Act. A Chancery Court agreed with the druggists, but a higher court later ruled in Wal-Mart's favor. But during the trial, in court depositions, Wal-Mart employees said that their company set prices based on how much competition it faced — more competition meant lower prices. During the lower court proceedings, according to the *Economist* newspaper, the judge found evidence that Wal-Mart would "lift its prices as and when competitors disappeared. Nearer to Little Rock, where there are plenty of pharmacies, its drug prices are lower; in more remote towns than Conway, they are higher."

In 1986, Wal-Mart lost a similar suit in Oklahoma. The company had violated a state law requiring retailers to sell goods at least 6.75% above cost, except during a sale or to match competitor's prices. There was an out-of-court settlement in the case, and Wal-Mart raised its prices. The retailer also spent $80,000 to lobby the Oklahoma state legislature to overturn the law. They were unsuccessful.

Several years ago, a house painter in Atlanta sued Home Depot for price discrimination, arguing that the giant home improvement retailer lowered its prices for common household items in Atlanta, where the competition for market share was intense, and raised prices on the same items just outside of Atlanta, where Home Depot had little competition. Home Depot was charging what the market would bear. "When they control the market," said John Connoly, " they gouge their prices." In Atlanta, a study of 35 products at Home Depot showed prices 10% higher than in Greensboro, North Carolina where competition was stiffer.

After decades of being told that Wal-Mart has the lowest prices, it is certain that most consumers believe it. But in Carroll County, Arkansas, the local newspaper decided to explore the "low price" claim of Wal-Mart. The newspaper staff generated a list of nineteen household items, and then went to six stores in Berryville, Eureka Springs, and Green Forest, Arkansas. The shopping survey was conducted over a one month period so as not to give any one store an unfair advantage for the shopping day to coincide with a sale. The Carroll County Newspapers staff said the results "were surprising." Of the nineteen items purchased, Wal-Mart was the cheapest on only two items. "Wal-Mart, which advertises itself as the everyday low price leader, 'Always the low price on the brands you trust — Always', isn't necessarily so. The lowest register receipt total for the nineteen items was $12.91. The highest on the total — the most expensive on the nineteen items, was Wal-Mart, at $15.86."

"At least on these two shopping days," the report concluded, "on these items chosen at random, Wal-Mart isn't necessarily the everyday low price leader . . . Consumers have to decide for themselves where they are getting the best value, but the results of the CCN survey indicate that where we think we're getting the best value might not necessarily be where the best value can be found."

Common sense suggests that retailers — big or small — will price items at what the market will bear. If we care about the free market, remember that Wal-Mart is not the beginning of competition, but the end. As the competition withers away, those everyday low prices don't look so low anymore. In the long term, Wal-Mart's negative impact on the competition in a local market is bound to have a negative impact on what the consumer cares about most: getting a bargain.

10. Supporting Suppliers

"Wal-Mart (supports) the local economy . . . by our commitment to purchase from local and regional vendors and suppliers."

Companies like Wal-Mart and Home Depot have a reputation for being tough on their suppliers, including not just the vendors who supply them with merchandise, but the developers and landlords who rent them space as well. This reputation of being hard on vendors is a self-described attitude in which these companies take great pride.

One of Wal-Mart's "10 Basic Principles" — the last one — is "we control our expenses." "Our vendors resented us for prying the lowest prices out of them," Sam Walton admitted. The rise of Wal-Mart meant the demise of independent sales agents, distributors and jobbers. As Bob Ortega has pointed out:

> Thanks to Wal-Mart's greater size, makers of name-brand goods that had once snubbed Walton now came to Bentonville hat in hand. And as in every other area, Walton made sure his buyers used the company's growing clout to demand special discounts and the lowest possible price from manufacturers.

As one Wal-Mart executive, Claude Harris, has written: "Don't ever feel sorry for a vendor. He knows what he can sell for, and we want his bottom price."

At Home Depot, they boast that the company is "a very difficult customer" for vendors. According to Chairman Bernie Marcus, "We buy so much that they (manufacturers) had to change many of the ways they do business." According to Wall Street analysts at Raymond James, Home Depot is guided in part by "the love/hate of its suppliers." As Marcus told the *National Home Center News* in 1997:

> Every time a vendor tries to raise a price, we say the same thing to

him: "We don't want to accept the price rise" . . . So we try to keep the prices down. Now that makes it tougher for the vendor. Now all of a sudden, in order to sell to us, he's got to go back and he's got to say, "Wow, these guys want to buy it at a lower price. I'd better do something about my business. I'd better be more productive. I'd better figure out ways that I can get the product done cheaper."

Home Depot says it has "changed the whole way that manufacturers sell." As the huge retailers used their size to leverage lower prices out of their suppliers, the suppliers looked to their internal price structure, particularly one major cost center: labor. The globalization of product supply meant that if domestic vendors could not supply companies like Wal-Mart and Home Depot with product at the price they wanted, the retailers would procure their merchandise overseas. When Home Depot opened their Savannah, Georgia distribution center, they boasted: "We'll be buying a lot of products that have been manufactured outside the United States direct, and we can take advantage of the cost savings as well as have better control over the quality aspect."

This race to the bottom placed enormous pressure on manufacturers to cut labor costs, which meant "outsourcing" production jobs to the Caribbean, to Mexico, and to Asia. The superstore retailers developed direct relationships with sweatshop manufacturers around the world, producing such controversial stories as the Kathie Lee Clothes sweatshops, or the Saipan child labor lawsuits in 1998 — stories which played out for months on national television.

A typical example of what has happened to American manufacturers comes from one of the signature products at Wal-Mart: underwear. Wal-Mart featured in its 1996 annual report that it sold 1.13 pairs of underwear annually for every man, woman and child in America. One major Wal-Mart vendor is Fruit of the Loom, which is also the BVD brand. In 1998, Fruit of the Loom announced that it was cutting 2,908 American jobs. The supplier said it had to tighten its belt in order to remain "a low-cost provider of quality family apparel." Wal-Mart is one of Fruit's largest customers. Wal-Mart may be selling lots of cheap underwear, but tell that to workers in towns like Abbeville, Jeanerette and St. Martinville, Louisiana, or Jamestown and Campbellsville, Kentucky — the places where Fruit of the Loom factory jobs were cut.

Fruit of the Loom has 31,000 employees worldwide, and it has moved many of its jobs overseas. Where have all the underwear jobs gone? According to a Bloomberg news report, Fruit of the Loom "began five years ago to move its more labor intensive operations, such as sewing, to Mexico, the Caribbean Islands, and other locations to save money."

Fruit of the Loom and Wal-Mart are sewn together at the hip. Wal-Mart wants to sell cheap underwear to every American. The pressure is on Fruit of the Loom to deliver cheap underwear to its large customers, like Wal-Mart. To cut labor costs, Fruit of the Loom cuts higher-wage United States jobs and ships the work to apparel workers in Third World countries. You and I get cheap underwear, the workers in Jamestown and Campbellsville get pink slips. These are the true Fruits of the Loom.

In April 1999, *Inc.* magazine ran a feature story about GTO, a Florida vendor that made automatic gate openers for Wal-Mart. "Seasoned vendors to the so-called big boxes know that dealing with them requires a constant series of compromises and accommodations," *Inc.* reported. "They believe such slights and injustices are costs of doing business, not the stuff of litigation." But GTO ended up suing Wal-Mart for breach of contract: for sending them back "defective" products that were not defective, for taking cash discounts off its invoices even when Wal-Mart didn't pay on a timely basis, and for other unauthorized credits. At one point, GTO said Wal-Mart owed them nearly $45,000 in "invalid" returns. Wal-Mart had also mistakenly sent the company items that GTO didn't even make, like diapers, car winches, and bicycle chains. GTO sued Wal-Mart in 1996 for more than half a million dollars, and in a court settlement won nearly all of what they were after.

In Tulsa, Oklahoma, the ADDvantage Media company watched a supplier's dream relationship with Wal-Mart turn into a lawsuit. ADDvantage markets a shopper's calculator which is solar powered and mounted on a shopping cart. It allows advertising displays to be inserted on the calculator. In 1993 and 1994, ADDvantage entered into contracts with Wal-Mart to install its calculators in certain Wal-Mart stores. When those contracts were not implemented, the company sued Wal-Mart for breach of contract. They reached a settlement in 1995 for a new contract to install calculators in all Wal-Mart supercenters. The calculator deal added up to some big numbers: $23.5 million in revenue for

ADDvantage. As of the end of March, 1998, ADDvantage had installed shopper's calculators in 336 Wal-Mart supercenters. In 1997 the company submitted a proposal for a new contract with Wal-Mart to go beyond the $23.5 million level.

In the spring of 1998, Wal-Mart told ADDvantage it would not enter into a new agreement or extend the old one. By autumn of 1998, ADDvantage sued Wal-Mart again, this time charging that CEO David Glass had breached contracts and was liable for misrepresentations, deceptive trade practices, and injurious falsehood. The president of ADDvantage told his stockholders that their calculators had been "a huge success for Wal-Mart," and that the company was "shocked and disappointed" when Wal-Mart dropped them. The calculator company said Wal-Mart's decision was "wholly unexplained and unexpected." "Furthermore," they said, "it's a decision we find especially difficult to understand in view of our proven ability to increase Wal-Mart's advertised product movement . . . and the very enthusiastic support voiced in behalf of the program by Wal-Mart's management, their store managers, and their customers." Apparently all these endorsements by Wal-Mart officials didn't add up to enough in the big company's calculations.

Other vendors doing business with Wal-Mart have also found themselves "shocked and disappointed." The United States Circuit Courts of Appeals have seen repeated cases of landlords in Tennessee, Alabama, Louisiana, Oklahoma, and South Carolina, who have leased property to Wal-Mart, only to later sue for breach of contract when Wal-Mart moved out and left its stores empty. Many shoppers don't realize that the Wal-Mart building they drive by on the highway in many cases is not owned by Wal-Mart.

In February 1999, there were 333 empty Wal-Marts up for sale or lease, and nearly 70% of them were leased spaces. When a real estate company in Jefferson County, Texas brought a breach of contract lawsuit against Wal-Mart, they cited five other lawsuits in which "Wal-Mart interfered with contractual relationships."

In Lebanon, Tennessee, a real estate company sued Wal-Mart for $54 million, saying that the retailer moved out of its lease eleven years early, despite the fact that the landlord spent $1 million to increase the store's size. Wal-Mart offered to fill the empty space with a Bud's Discount Center (which has since ceased all operations), but the landlord relied on a lease agreement with Wal-Mart to get a percentage of gross sales each year in addition to rent. The Bud's store would not come close to the estimated $28 million in sales that the Wal-Mart was doing. Wal-Mart had moved out of this site to build a new supercenter several miles away. "There's a lot of tenants in that shopping center depending on Wal-Mart being there whose business will be adversely affected," said the lawyer for the landlord.

In Catoosa, Oklahoma, a United States Bankruptcy Court found that Wal-Mart had breached its lease with Oklahoma Plaza Investors. Wal-Mart left its store with eight years still to go on a twenty-year lease. Wal-Mart removed its inventory and fixtures, locked the doors, and covered the windows with brown paper. The Court ruled "this is a desertion of the premises and a breach of the lease . . . Wal-Mart should be required to keep its promises . . . (Wal-Mart) should not be allowed to break their promise to operate a discount store or to ignore an agreement that desertion of the premises would be a default." Wal-Mart argued that it was still using the premises by holding meetings there on occasion, and for storage. But the Court ruled "the use of the premises for storage or meetings after a complete closing of the store is a mere subterfuge to try to avoid the consequences of an obvious desertion."

Many of the court cases I researched were not so obvious, and often developers and landlords ended up losing their rent on legal technicalities found in their open-ended lease agreements with Wal-Mart. These cases of supplier and landlord grievances illustrate, as *Inc.* has said, that people who do business with giant retailers often must get used to "a constant series of compromises and accommodations."

4

How Wal-Mart Creeps Into Town

*"We agreed to keep quiet until they get things concrete.
What's the point in getting people worked up — there may
not even be an application."*
— **Mayor Ron Webber, Courtenay, British Columbia, April 1999**

Citizen's groups often complain to me that Wal-Mart has tried to conceal its
intentions in their town by working quietly behind the scenes. I remind them:

Q: Why is Wal-Mart like a cheap pair of underwear?

A: Because they keep creeping up on you.

The stealth of a Wal-Mart approach is a carefully designed strategy to limit
public involvement. Wal-Mart says the real reason they hide their activities for
so long is to keep the price of land they want from skyrocketing. But many of
the "secret" dealings Wal-Mart or Home Depot engage in take place long after
they have a buy-sell agreement on property. As Ellen Dunham-Jones, an
architect from MIT has written:

> Typically, Wal-Mart buys the land for new stores as quietly as pos-
> sible, then sells the land and leases the building when construction is
> done. In this way, Wal-Mart uses the common practice of leasing as a
> strategy for abandoning a market once it has damaged the local econo-
> my and begun to compete mainly with its own neighboring Wal-Marts.
> . . . Often Wal-Mart will retain the lease on the vacant store simply to
> keep competition away.

In Courtenay, British Columbia, Wal-Mart's developer, a company called First Professional, did the early stalking. First Professional held at least two private meetings with city councilors. One of the meetings was brokered by the Comox Valley Chamber of Commerce, which arranged a meeting in the Chamber's Board Room with the Mayor of Courtenay, developers, a realtor, and the land owner attending.

A conference call was placed to Toronto to First Professional. Another participant at the meeting was Norm McLaren, manager of the local government created Economic Development Society. According to *The Voice* newspaper, when McLaren was asked about the secret Chamber meeting, he said: "I am sworn to confidence. The meeting was in a confidential capacity. I will make no comment whatsoever."

Courtenay Mayor Ron Webber, who also sat through the presentation, likewise remained silent about the project. "We agreed to keep quiet until they get things concrete," he told the press. "What's the point in getting people worked up — there may not even be an application."

Wal-Mart customarily will screen itself from the public by working through developers or newly-formed corporations that are affiliates of Wal-Mart's real estate division. In Manhattan, Kansas, for example, Wal-Mart was in the middle of a land deal to build a supercenter on the west side of the city, when the newspapers got wind of the fact that Wal-Mart was purchasing land on the east side next to its existing discount store. In fact, Wal-Mart had become the owner of Frank's mobile home park, and proceeded to evict as many as 50 homeowners, including some elderly residents. All of this was done through an affiliate, Broadstreet Investment Company. Here is how *The Manhattan Mercury* described the deal:

> Broadstreet Investment Co. is a Tulsa affiliate that works on the real estate side of Wal-Mart, said Keith Morris, director of community affairs for Wal-Mart's corporate office. "The timing of the land purchase," he said, "was coincidence, and it was simply a business decision. Wal-Mart often buys land near existing facilities," he said.

In the same article, Wal-Mart revealed that its current store in Manhattan was not actually owned by Wal-Mart, but was leased from "a Kansas City individual." Wal-Mart had a "long-term lease of 10 to 15 more years there."

Wal-Mart often will construct a store, and then lease it to a third party, sometimes a company Wal-Mart has created just for this purpose. In Decorah, Iowa, Wal-Mart Properties, Inc. sold its discount store a few years after it was built for the sum of ten dollars to a company called Decorah Associates Limited Partnership, a New Jersey company. But the city was instructed to send the property tax bills in the name of Decorah Associates "c/o of Wal-Mart Stores, Inc., Bentonville, Arkansas." The real estate holding company was created to take ownership of the store, which separates the financial liability of the store from the parent company, Wal-Mart.

From the citizen's perspective, all this concealment and dealing through surrogate companies means community groups often have to telescope their opposition into a smaller window of time. It also means that Wal-Mart or Target is allowed to meet discretely with public officials without citizen knowledge. In Gilbert, Arizona, when the local newspaper revealed the fact that Wal-Mart had plans for a 161,500 square foot superstore, it ended "weeks of secrecy and speculation about the store's identity." It turns out that a "small group of town officials said they knew Wal-Mart was the retailer," but they were "sworn to secrecy by the company." This is a traditional ploy of developers. Wal-Mart quietly enters a town, begins chatting up local officials, usually one at a time (to avoid violating open meeting laws), while the real estate people line up their land, and talk to state officials about permitting issues . . . all under the table. In the case of Gilbert, Arizona, all this was going on, but worse. Town officials later admitted that "Wal-Mart threatened to pull out of Gilbert if their confidentiality was broken." Town officials essentially provided Wal-Mart with cover while the company set up its lobbying operation to woo Gilbert residents.

In Oakland, Maryland, radio station WKHJ broke the story that Wal-Mart had an option to purchase land near Weber Road. The landowner, Russell Sines, was mum about the project. "I have an oath of confidentiality," the told the local newspaper, "that my client, a developer — not Wal-Mart itself — has required me to sign regarding that property."

When reporters went to Wal-Mart for comment, a Wal-Mart spokesman gave the usual ambiguous response: "I've checked into your area. We don't have any plans for an Oakland area store that I can locate at this point." But then she went on to say: "There's a lot of preplanning and study that goes into the process before we can announce that we're bringing a Wal-Mart store to serve your community."

So just what does this preplanning and study process consist of?

By the time Wal-Mart unveiled plans for a 142,000 square foot Wal-Mart in Potsdam, New York, they had already been operating behind the scenes in the community for many months. In fact, Wal-Mart Real Estate manager Gene Borsattino apologized to the community for having taken so long to become visible. "One mistake we made here," Borsattino told the *Daily Courier-Observer* in February 1999, "is that much too much time went by. We apologize for that."

Here, according to Borsattino, is how Wal-Mart spends that "much too much time" getting ready to target a store for a given community:

1) Identify the Trade Area: Wal-Mart specialists in Bentonville, Arkansas devote all their energies to the task of identifying trade centers that would be amenable to a Wal-Mart facility.

2) Watch the Market: An identified site is watched for a period of about four years until it is "at a point where, in fact, it could serve or be served by a Wal-Mart unit."

3) Local Fact-Finding: Wal-Mart consultants are brought into the community to identify issues relative to land, competition, environmental and traffic, and then report their findings back to Wal-Mart headquarters.

4) Real Estate Visit: Next, the real estate manager for the area visits the locations with the consultants.

5) The Committee Visit: A Wal-Mart committee comes "driving the community." They visit every store and every neighborhood attempting to identify problems the corporation will not be able to control.

Borsattino said that all of the process thus far is done with the hope that the news will not leak that the giant retailer is targeting the location. "We're not trying to be secretive," he says, "we're just trying to maintain some confidentiality."

Lining Up the Ducks: Wal-Mart's Local Campaign

Once Wal-Mart has set its sights on a community, it will begin an elaborate process of building its nest. This intricate ritual of building community support was not always necessary in the past, but since the mid-1990s, when Wal-Mart began to run into more than just occasional community opposition, the corporation has had to beef up its public relations capacity and approach a community as if it were launching a run for public office.

Here are the first ten things that companies like Wal-Mart, Home Depot or Target will do in your community. Many of these strategies are imitations of tactics Wal-Mart has learned from the community groups who opposed them:

1) Create A "Citizens" Group. The United Food and Commercial Workers has called such company creations "astro-roots" groups, as opposed to the real "grass roots" groups that organize to stop sprawl. Sometimes the leader of these groups will be a lawyer or public relations person who is already part of the Wal-Mart local payroll; sometimes they will be "locals" who are recruited to lead the charge. In Greenfield, Massachusetts the "Citizens for Economic Growth" was coordinated by Wal-Mart's attorney. In Northfield, Minnesota, the "Citizens for Target" actually ran newspaper ads using the official Target bulls-eye logo.

2) Hire a local land use attorney. Wal-Mart will try to locate an attorney from a prominent local or regional law firm that a) has good connections in town hall and b) is aggressive and has a good reputation in the community.

3) Hire a local public relations firm. Wal-Mart will look for a company that can put out a decent press release, line up a community polling survey, a direct mail campaign, and design display ads for the newspapers. Companies like Wal-Mart and Home Depot are extremely sensitive to media coverage. According to Don E. Shinkle, a Wal-Mart vice president who has been with the company since 1985, Wal-Mart tracks, measures and analyzes, on a monthly basis, all electronic and print media stories, by specific market area. An article Shinkle wrote in the *Public Relations Quarterly* boasts: "We know precisely where to focus special attention next month, based on last month's report." When Wal-Mart says "special attention," they mean right down to the level of individual reporters. "We also know, through this data base," Shinkle says, "which reporters are more balanced, and which ones need special stroking based on previous reporting."

Wal-Mart's "service" identifies each clip as a letter to the editor, editorial, or opinion piece. It lists the media outlet and the reporter's name, "So we can see exactly how our company is being portrayed in each (market area) — for that reporting period and year-to-date," Shinkle notes. Wal-Mart overlays these reports with 435 Congressional districts and 50 states, so they can track "earned media" by state, congressional district, even by congressional subcommittees. "We know if our negative press is coming from a ruling on a legal case or on a new market entry," Shinkle explains. "We know if it comes from a mistake in something we said."

With this intricate media tracking and stroking system, Wal-Mart can ensure that in "the court of public opinion," the readers "get the whole story." If you see a particularly single-sided story about the attributes of a Wal-Mart in your local paper, assume that Wal-Mart has been busy tracking your local media. With all the negative media Wal-Mart has been getting over the several years, their arms must be worn out from special stroking.

Since the early 1990s, Wal-Mart has added several new staff just to handle public relations at the community level and to respond to citizen organizing.

4) Set up a Local Office. The local office may be a storefront to give the company some visibility, and to serve as a mailing address for postcard campaigns, etc.

5) Set up a Wal-Mart hotline. The company will begin urging people to contact Wal-Mart if they want a new store to come to their town. They will also leave out petitions in their neighboring stores asking their customers to sign the form to bring a new store to the area. These petitions are often used to counterbalance any similar petitions circulated by local citizen's groups. In Clermont, Florida, teenagers were paid $6 dollars an hour to circulate a pro-Wal-Mart petition that appeared to come from the Mayor's office, but was actually engineered by Wal-Mart's local real estate lawyer. The Mayor claimed he knew nothing about the "citizen's" petition.

6) Generate a Postcard Campaign: "Yes, I want a Wal-Mart in (your town). Complete this card and drop it off at the Wal-Mart table, or mail it to the address on the back, and we'll add you to our mailing list." The return address will be the storefront office in town they have rented.

7) Release a Public Opinion Survey: Wal-Mart will hire a polling firm from the general region to conduct a survey, usually employing a very small sample of several hundred people, and asking very leading questions about a proposed Wal-Mart. The company will then put out a press release touting the survey results, which generically show that Wal-Mart is as popular as Viagra.

In Eureka, California, for example, Wal-Mart hired a company from Seattle to survey 500 registered voters in Humboldt County. The poll showed that "Wal-Mart is well known and well liked in Humboldt County, with a 58% favorable rating and 63% of voters wanting a new store to be built. The same poll showed that less than half those surveyed said they were "very likely" to shop at Wal-Mart, and 41% either gave Wal-Mart an unfavorable rating or couldn't rate them at all. Wal-Mart usually only releases the results of these surveys, but does not reveal the actual questions used in the survey.

Sometimes polls can be used against Wal-Mart. Consider the survey conducted in one town in Pennsylvania:

Kelly Cochran, 11, and Blake Williams, 12, are students at the Charles F. Patton Middle School in East Marlborough township in Pennsylvania. Kelly and Blake are not retailing experts, but they learned a lot from a survey they conducted during the last presidential elections. The Discovery Team at the Middle School completed a survey of 1,330 township residents at the polls. The focus of the survey? To study attitudes towards a proposed Wal-Mart store on Route 1 at Schoolhouse Road. The proposed store was the subject of heated controversy in East Marlborough for several years.

The students wrote the survey, conducted it and tabulated the results. They presented their findings to the East Marlborough Board of Supervisors. "The students hope to demonstrate to the Board that, as fledgling citizens, they have an investment in the future of this area," said their teacher Kathie Gregory. "They will do this by letting these community representatives know the unbiased results of a wide sampling of the citizens of the school's home township."

To help the student's understand local community issues, four teachers and 74 students explored the issue of a Wal-Mart in their town. Before designing their survey, the students heard from speakers on both sides of the issue. The survey reflected the arguments the students heard during those discussions.

As people waited in line to vote on election day, students administered the twenty-question Wal-Mart survey. The first question asked whether or not the person wanted a Wal-Mart built in in East Marlborough. Residents were then asked to check any of twenty statements about their opinions on the issue, such as: "will provide one stop shopping," "will create a safety hazard," "will provide new jobs," or "existing local businesses will suffer from competition."

The results of the Patton School survey: 61% of those polled voted NO on Wal-Mart. 29% voted YES, and 10% were undecided or didn't care. For every one person who wanted a Wal-Mart, two voters did not. Gender did not seem to play a major role. 61% of women of all ages opposed Wal-Mart, and 62% of men. People over the age of 40 were somewhat more negatively disposed towards Wal-Mart, especially women, who voted two-thirds against Wal-Mart. Most people who voted "yes" for Wal-Mart cited convenience and low prices as their motivation. Most people who voted "no" on Wal-Mart cited changing the area's culture as the main reason for their opposition.

The final "lesson" of the student poll came on the evening they delivered it to their town supervisors. "You have produced for us some scholarly research," said Supervisor's Chairman Richard Hannum. "Unfortunately, we will not be able to consider your work in our decision, since it was not submitted as official testimony."

But the message from East Marlborough is clear, and it's a message being replayed all across the country. The "unbiased results" are in — and Wal-Mart is out. Wal-Mart, by the way, had no comment on the student's poll. But don't expect an unadulterated dose of public opinion to mean very much in Bentonville, Arkansas---even if it's delivered by eleven- and twelve-year old children.

8) Speak on the Rubber Chicken Circuit: Wal-Mart representatives will begin showing up at the breakfast or lunch gatherings of local Chamber of Commerce, Rotary and Kiwanis clubs. They will already have solicited the support of the leadership of these groups, so they can display endorsements from the Director of the Chamber of Commerce, etc. They will also try to hold informal discussions with Planning and Zoning Boards to review the general outline of their plans for their store. Chamber of Commerce will be encouraged to hire consultants to train local merchants how to "thrive and survive" with a Wal-

Mart in town.

9) Send You A Video: Wal-Mart has recently begun producing video tapes to use in their campaigns. In Arizona, Wal-Mart produced an eight-minute video called "Here to Serve," which was mailed to every voter in targeted Arizona towns. The video features a circle of Wal-Martians doing their morning corporate cheer:

> **The Wal-Mart Cheer** (reprinted from the "Wal-Mart Culture Corner"):
> Give me a W!
> Give me an A!
> Give me a L!
> Give me a Squiggly!
> Give me a M!
> Give me an A!
> Give me a R!
> Give me a T!
> What's that spell?
> Wal-Mart!
> Who's number one?
> The Customer!

(I have been told by Wal-Mart employees that if you refuse to recite the cheer, you will be fired.)

10) Distribute a Community Resource Guide: Wal-Mart has produced a twenty-two page, spiral-bound Community Resource Guide that features endorsements from community leaders from several states, the background story of Wal-Mart ("It all started with an understanding of what consumers want from a retailer"), charts on Wal-Mart sales and employee growth, impact on the local economy, and Wal-Mart's philanthropic and community involvement.

When I am asked what community groups should do in response to this multi-level activity by Wal-Mart, I say: Do everything on this list, because they are all ideas stolen from community organizers.

5

The Top Banana

*"The handwriting is on the wall: Thousands of U.S.
supermarkets will be forced out of business over the next
few years."*
— *Forbes* **Magazine, January 22, 1996**

The latest permutation in the Wal-Mart game plan has been the creation of smaller stores targeted at the traditional grocery store market share.

Wal-Mart has always worked hard to create the image of a family-friendly atmosphere at its stores and to counter the big corporate stereotype. Wal-Mart has hyped their stores as "a personal place where people don't just shop. They visit. They help one another. Aisle to aisle. Store by store." In fact, the company refers to its stores as "the friendly Wal-Mart or Sam's Club that's just down the street or around the corner." Wal-Mart is the giant company with small town roots. That's what is says in the Wal-Mart Culture book.

In March of 1998, the *Wall Street Journal* reported that Wal-Mart was planning to roll out new 40,500 square foot stores in the towns of Springdale, Sherwood, Fort Smith, Fayetteville and Bentonville, Arkansas. These stores would be only one-third of the size of most supercenters. "In building smaller stores," the article said, "Wal-Mart is also acknowledging that giant stores require a commitment of time and energy that shoppers don't always have."

"We lose a lot of customers because the supercenter is too busy and not convenient," said one Wal-Mart senior vice president. "Where we're losing sales is to the grocery stores." The idea of a Wal-Mart executive calling a supercenter "not convenient" sounds like retail heresy — but actually the company is just continuing a long pattern of trying to work both sides of the aisle. The company that justifies huge stores by saying its customers want wider aisles, also claims that the supercenters are "too busy" for some shoppers. Wal-Mart sounds like an advertisement against itself. Price Waterhouse described the supercenter dilemma this way:

> The supercenter format is proving a very powerful consumer draw.
> They shop the format frequently due to the grocery section, and then
> they move onto the general merchandise areas and shop some more . . .
> A supercenter can go wherever a traditional discounter is today, except
> where the real estate isn't big enough.

The reality is that Wal-Mart is confronting a dwindling supply of 20+ acre lots on which to place superstores. Some small towns and even urban areas where Wal-Mart smells market pie, just don't have enough room for a supercenter. So the inconvenience, in fact, is to Wal-Mart, not its customers. "We want to address those markets where we couldn't get a supercenter in," explains Wal-Mart's Jay Fitzsimmons.

Wal-Mart later named these smaller stores "Neighborhood Marts," despite the fact that most convenience stores are not much larger than 3,000 square feet. In Wal-Mart's neighborhood, a 40,500 square foot store is sized just right. The Neighborhood Marts are designed to function like traditional grocery stores. They have twelve check out stands, carry a full line of groceries, including produce, meat and deli departments with no service counters, a photo lab, as well as a flower shop and drugstore merchandise. The stores also feature a drive-through pharmacy, but there is no bakery department. These Neighborhood Marts are expected to generate as much as $15 million in sales annually, and lead Wal-Mart in the direction of taking over existing grocery stores in urban areas. "Left unchecked," the United Food and Commercial Workers Union warns, "Wal-Mart's move into the retail food industry will be the demise of good paying union jobs held by tens of thousands of UFCW members." Or, as one industry analyst put it: "The danger for supermarkets is that Wal-Mart is turning their business virtually into a loss leader."

At about the same retail moment, Home Depot announced that it too was going to experiment with "Villager" stores — prototypes much smaller than their warehouse stores. The Depot announced that it was going to build four prototype 35,000 square foot stores in New Jersey to make a play for the small do-it-yourself homeowner, what the company calls the "home improvement convenience market." Home Depot said such stores would be built in "densely populated areas." In other words, the huge megastores would still go into rural areas, where land is cheap, but the smaller "convenience stores" would be located in larger markets. Home Depot later announced that the new stores would be called "Villager Hardware" stores. Like Wal-Mart, they are appealing to the charm and quaintness of small-town life — minus the charm and quaintness. A 35,000 square foot building supply store is nowhere to be found in the villages of America. If there were no history of superstores, the idea of using labels like "neighborhood" or "villager" for stores of this size would seem absurd. But Wal-Mart and Home Depot have changed forever our sense of scale and perspective in America.

Wal-Mart's shift into the traditional grocery store market sparked a strong response from the United Food and Commercial Workers. In December of 1998, the UFCW sponsored a rally in Bentonville, Arkansas in which more than 2,000 union members marched on the town square of Bentonville. The marcher's chant of "Wal-Mart, Not in My Neighborhood" could be heard from blocks away, as I stood on the podium waiting for the rally to start. "The true legacy of Wal-Mart isn't lower prices," explained UFCW President Doug Dority. "The true legacy of Wal-Mart is lower living standards for hard working Americans. Wal-Mart has dishonored our flag and deceived consumers with its phony 'Buy America' program; has destroyed more small businesses and more small towns than any company in America; and has exported more manufacturing jobs to sweatshops across the world than any company in America."

At the Bentonville rally, AFL-CIO president John Sweeney told supporters that he would direct all labor credit unions to stop distributing Sam's Club membership cards, and urge all union joint employer benefit funds to stop using Wal-Mart pharmacies. He implored all union members to sign the following good neighbor pledge:

I will use my voice, my vote and my consumer dollars to promote good jobs with living wages and family health benefits for my community. I pledge to buy my groceries at supermarkets that support these community values with fair pay and affordable health benefits for workers. I will NOT buy groceries from Wal-Mart or other stores that destroy existing jobs, pay poverty-level wages, and do not provide employees with adequate health benefits. I am a good neighbor. My shopping dollars will go to responsible supermarkets that support my community.

According to the UFCW, by 1997 Wal-Mart supercenters had become the sixth largest grocery company in America, with total sales of $11.3 billion:

Rank	Company	1997 Sales ($billion)
1	Kroger	$41.5
2	Albertson's	$33.8
3	Safeway	$25.7
4	Royal Ahold	$18.5
5	Winn-Dixie	$13.2
6	**Wal-Mart**	**$11.3**
7	Publix	$11.2
8	A&P	$10.3
9	Food Lion	$10.2
10	H.E. Butt	$ 8.5

"As profits from its supercenters continue to soar," says the UFCW, "Wal-Mart has begun attacking traditional supermarket competitors in order to take over and control the U.S. grocery business." The UFCW warns that the Neighborhood market stores could generate as much as $15 million each per year, and that Wal-Mart could produce 50 to 100 of these smaller formats stores in a year, creating a new billion dollar plus division for Wal-Mart. "Wal-Mart can now easily take over established grocery stores located in urban areas as well as in small towns," the union explains. "Left unchecked, the next chapter in Wal-Mart's move into the retail food industry will be the demise of good paying union jobs held by tens of thousands of UFCW members."

None of the retail analysts or reporters ever thought to connect the new "smaller marts" with the growing citizen opposition movement in this country.

Although the *New York Times* proclaimed in 1999 that in New England "Wal-Mart is no longer treated as an invader," in almost every venue they select, their mere shadow over a town spawns another opposition group. What used to be a four to six month permitting process now can take two or three years, especially if a legal challenge arises.

I believe that Wal-Mart and Home Depot are looking at smaller stores as a way of circumventing sprawl-buster opposition at the community level. These companies hate the negative press these community battles engender, but more importantly, a one year delay in opening up a supercenter can cost Wal-Mart $40 million in lost sales. For a company driven to expand just to keep up its sales growth, this kind of delay is intolerable.

Villager stores and Neighborhood Markets will only intensify the battle over sprawl at the local level. Community groups will find these stores still to be on the large end of development, and since their intended effect is merely to grab more market share for corporate headquarters, citizen's groups are likely to end up "villager-busting" such projects.

It turns out that stopping such sprawl is not that difficult – if you know how to go about it.

Part Two

How You Can Stop Superstore Sprawl

"To value community is not to deny economic growth. It is to determine what kind of growth is best for the community ... There will always be those who don't care about community, and don't think about its future, who will shop wherever the stores are ...Our values are what we have. We have what we believe in ... (and) most of us will admit that we believe in more than dollars."
— **Editorial,** *Daily Herald*, **Rutland, Vermont,   August 1, 1993**

6

Letters From Home

"One, two, three, four, we don't want your lousy store."
— **Citizens protesting Wal-Mart in Tijeras, New Mexico,**
  September 1997

The very first question I am asked by citizens who are up against Wal-Mart is always: "Can we win?"

In my travels to twenty-nine states over the past six years, one of the most pervasive attitudes I have encountered is the sense that sprawl is inevitable. As one Wal-Mart employee admonished me: "Just go with the flow." Superstores are seen as a natural consequence of "progress."

Over the years I have written letters from many of the communities I have visited, in part to report back that sprawl is not unstoppable. Here are a few letters from hometown America.

A Letter From Buster: September, 1997
"Your Lousy Store"

Dear Sprawl-Busters,

I had to squeeze through the crowded doorway to the Tijeras, New Mexico City Hall to get into the hearing room. By the time I entered, every seat was taken, and the standing room crowd of 150 people spilled out into the hallway. The Mayor of this small town of 320 people, Juan Griego, was listening to the engineer from Wal-Mart describe his plans for a 155,000 square foot superstore. Mayor Griego nervously tapped his pencil, while outside, another 100 or more residents of the East Mountain communities stood in the light rain, chanting: "One, two, three, four, we don't want your lousy store!" Here's how the *Albuquerque Tribune* described the scene:

When Mayor Griego allowed time for public comment, he restricted speakers to people living in the village, who constituted a minority in the room filled with people from other East Mountain communities. A Tijeras resident appointed Norman to speak on her behalf, but Norman was silenced by Griego. "I only want to hear from Tijeras residents," he said.

Arsenio Lovato, who lives next door to the proposed site, expressed his worries about the development's probably impact on property values, water, and the East Mountain lifestyle. "I moved out here for the quietness. Now they're coming in and bringing that stress out here," he said. "If Wal-Mart comes in, I'm moving out." Other Tijeras residents echoed Lovato's concerns and cited other potential problems, including increased crime, homeless populations, grime, visual distraction, noise and general irritation. Norman got a few moments to speak at the end of the meeting. He said that a Wal-Mart store is not consistent with Tijeras' zoning requirements, which specify that developments must harmonize with rural atmosphere. He finished by telling Griego, "You have all the evidence you need to reject this project."

Right in the middle of the hearing, Mayor Griego dramatically stopped the proceedings and read from a document he had just been handed. "I want to inform everyone here that the Bernalillo County Commissioners have passed a resolution tonight four to nothing opposing the construction of this store." The room burst out into sustained applause. "I also want to remind people that we are a municipality," Griego continued, "and we are not bound by the decisions made by the County."

But the damage had been done. One of the members of the Tijeras Planning and Zoning Commission made a motion that the vote on Wal-Mart be tabled, and the residents of Tijeras be polled for their opinion on the store. The Mayor accepted the motion and gaveled it through, as the meeting dissolved into noise.

Wal-Mart's Director of Community Affairs, Keith Morris, who sat quietly listening to the "lousy store" chants echoing down the short hallway, later told reporters he was not concerned about the residents who were against his store. "We're not going to cater to a few people in the community," Morris told reporters."This is our second meeting with Tijeras, and essentially nothing has happened yet."

But County Commissioner Les Houston, who represents the East Mountains, saw it differently. "I think (Wal-Mart) is inappropriate and will be extremely detrimental to the overall rural climate that you have in the East Mountains." When asked if the County Commissioners would reconsider their negative vote on the store, Houston said: "The other commissioners and I knew what we were doing."

Does Wal-Mart know what it is doing? There are already six Wal-Marts within 30 miles of Tijeras, and two of them are located less than 10 miles away. The market area is already saturated with Wal-Marts — but that is the point. As Sam Walton wrote: "We became our own competitors." The fact is the Tijeras zoning ordinances says that shopping centers should be "in harmony with the small village character of the area." Wal-Mart has not yet found a way to construct a small village superstore. For Tijeras to support this store, it must do violence not just to the intent of its own ordinances and land use plan, but to the quality of life on the Turquoise Trail which climbs all the way to Santa Fe.

I can still hear in my ears the chanting from outside the Tijeras City Hall. More importantly, I know that Keith Morris can still hear it too. Morris says Wal-Mart won't cater to a few people in the community, but he will be happy to hear that a few people in Tijeras want to control the destiny of an entire region. The protesters were right: this is a lousy store.

Keep on bustin',

Buster

Postscript: In April of 1999, citizens from Tijeras told me that Wal-Mart has not been heard from in months. They felt that the Wal-Mart project was dead, and asked me what they should do. I told them they should all dress up in black, hold a press conference at the Wal-Mart site, and conduct a funeral service for the deceased Wal-Mart store.

Letter from Buster: September, 1998

"A Storybook Place"

Dear Sprawl-Busters,

Edenton, North Carolina is a coastal community of just under 6,000 people. It describes itself as a "storybook place . . . a remarkable small southern town with an unsurpassed feeling of romance, charm and warmth." "Most people," says the guidebook, "can only dream about living in a place like Edenton." It sits right on the Albemarle Sound, and has a beautiful working downtown with local businesses that elsewhere have disappeared: independent drug stores, a hardware store, etc. Its residential homes are graced by broad lawns and blooming crape myrtles. It has all the ingredients of classic small town American life — but it has no Wal-Mart.

Within thirty miles of Edenton there are three Wal-Marts. Recently the citizens of Edenton inadvertently found out that Wal-Mart wants to build a 110,000 square foot supercenter on residentially zoned land on the edge of town — in fact, on land that first must be annexed into the town from Chowan County. Wal-Mart, of course, has denied it has any interest in Edenton. "I'm looking at projects five years out," Wal-Mart spokesman Laura Pope told the local papers, "and Edenton is not on that list."

Mayor Roland Vaughn does not believe that. He and six other members of the Town Council will have to decide whether or not to rezone the residential farmland for Wal-Mart. The Mayor is concerned about his downtown, and what will happen to the vision of Edenton if the downtown goes down. "The savings you enjoy today," the Mayor warned shoppers, "will come back and take a bigger bite out of you later."

The financials support Mayor Vaughn's concerns: The population projections for all of Chowan County show that over the next 20 years only 1,471 more people will live in the county than reside there today. That is hardly enough to absorb the $37 million in sales the new Wal-Mart needs to generate. By comparison, in 1992, thirty stores in Edenton had total sales of $36 million in food, general merchandise, apparel and drug store sales — the sales that compete directly with Wal-Mart. In other words, Wal-Mart will suddenly double the market capacity of Chowan County.

Because Edenton is already ringed by Wal-Mart stores, most sales at Wal-Mart will be transferred from existing local businesses. That means businesses like the Peebles department store, Food Lion, IGA and Winn-Dixie grocery stores, and Byrom's Hardware. Ten local investors, calling themselves the "Ten Ways of Edenton," bought an empty double-storefront building downtown and then spent months convincing the regional chain store Peebles, to locate downtown. These local citizens even help pay the rent. If Wal-Mart comes, that Peebles will likely be one of the first businesses to go.

Wal-Mart also disavows any negative impact it has on local businesses. "Wal-Mart doesn't go in with a goal of putting mom and pop stores out of business," spokesman Pope says. That's their public line. But privately, Wal-Mart has a very different goal. With one stop shopping the goal is to help one company, not many.

Edenton is aggressively trying to promote tourism, attract manufacturing jobs and bring in retirees. The town is also committed to preserving and promoting its downtown business district — or at least that's what the Land Use Plan says. "Edenton residents wish to enjoy prosperity," it says in the Plan, "but not at the expense of the community's historic charm and sensitive environment." No one ever accused a Wal-Mart of being long on charm and romance.

"Summertime in Edenton is a celebration of American life." This is the image presented to the tourist. Broad lawns and deep shade. A sailboat in the dock. But this storybook town could have its last chapter written by Wal-Mart. Four members of the Council must vote against rezoning land for Wal-Mart. If they don't, Edenton could become a most unremarkable southern town in no time at all. Such treasures have been lost before.

Keep on bustin',

Buster

Postscript: As of the spring of 1999, there is no Wal-Mart in Edenton, North Carolina. No plans have been filed with town officials.

Letter from Buster: February, 1998
"Making Developers Do Better"

Dear Sprawl-Busters,

The citizens of Fenton, Michigan are justifiably confused. On the one hand, a developer from Alabama wants to build a 265,000 square foot mall (reportedly with a Wal-Mart) on 32 acres at the edge of this community. On the other hand, the city says it wants to reinvent its downtown into an "active, vibrant" commercial center. A glut of malls on the edge of town, or a compact, commercial center in the heart of the community: which will it be? Fenton's dilemma is that of Everytown, U.S.A.

Over the years, Fenton has frustrated its own best intentions, by doing things like rerouting traffic around its downtown. Downtown Fenton is a confusing jigsaw puzzle of dead end streets and grab-bag architecture. Recently, a 113 year old retailer named Dancer's moved its store from the downtown to a strip mall — only to announce just before Christmas that it was closing for good. "It's difficult to be competitive with the larger chain stores," admitted owner Doug Dancer. "Our families have shopped at Dancer's forever," lamented Fenton's Mayor, Patricia Lockwood. "It's going to be strange not having them as part of the community."

Stranger still are the plans for the new Wal-Mart plaza. Behind the property sit homes worth a quarter of a million dollars. Right across Silver Parkway is a gleaming strip mall anchored by a 128,000 square foot Big Kmart, a VGs grocery, and a Sears. The Kmart transplanted itself from a smaller store in downtown Fenton. The Rite Aid pharmacy in the downtown also closed. The retail disinvestment in the downtown is painfully clear. Yet the community's Master Plan has as its primary commercial goal to "improve the image, design, cohesiveness and vitality of Downtown Fenton."

Fenton has a population of less than 10,000 people. Like many other communities across the country, Fenton has had trouble holding onto industrial jobs. In Genesee County, more than 18,000 manufacturing jobs were lost between 1987 and 1992. During the same period, the county's retail employment jumped by 8,000. The city of Fenton's retail activity jumped 32% during this period. Fenton knows it will never be a regional retail center, because it is located just outside of larger Flint. According to Wal-Mart, there are already four Wal-Marts within 18 miles of Fenton.

As industrial jobs leave the Fenton area, and are replaced by retail sales clerks, the potential sales capacity of the community drops, but actual sales have been increasing. The last thing Fenton needs is a Wal-Mart that must consume $66 million in sales annually, taking most of that from other existing businesses. If the Silver Lake Village loses its Big Kmart, what has the community really gained from a Wal-Mart on Owen Road?

Fenton's Master Plan says that the downtown is "arguably one of Fenton's most valuable assets." The Plan also says that Fenton wants to maintain its "small town sense of community." It should be obvious that allowing sprawl on the edge of the city is the worst case scenario for Fenton. Yet Fenton is being advised by planning consultants who assert that commercial development on commercial land is permitted by right. The Mayor of Fenton knows this Wal-Mart project is not right for her city. "This type of development would not have been my choice at this time."

This struggle of downtown versus mall has become the prototypical economic battleground in small town America. In Vermont, the legislature is considering the Downtown Community Development Act, which offers new tax credits for the rehab of older buildings, planning funds, employment tax credits, and other economic incentives. Vermont found that its 10,500 downtown businesses account for nearly 18% of all businesses in the state, and $21 million in sales tax collections. Twenty percent of Vermont's jobs are in the downtown, generating $1.6 billion a year in wages, and $46 million in income tax revenues. Fifty-five percent of the tourists who come to Vermont say they are interested in historic sites and museums found downtown. The people of Fenton know instinctively that their downtown is a "valuable asset," but their advisors tell them that sprawl is inevitable.

As one Fenton resident said: "The developers here have not been pressed to do something exceptional. They know how to do a much better job, but they only do what they're asked to do."

It's time for all of us to not only ask developers to do more — but to force them to do more.

Keep on bustin',

Buster

Postscript: Five months after my visit to Fenton, I received word that developers had withdrawn their plans for a Wal-Mart after their plans were tabled by the city's Planning Commission. But Wal-Mart pushed the project ahead on their own, got town approval, and now face a lawsuit from Fenton residents.

Letter From Buster: December, 1998
"Beggar Thy Neighbor"

Dear Sprawl-Busters,

All the big retail chain stores do it. They not only compete with their retail rivals, but they shamelessly pit one town against another in their bid to develop property. What developers will do is say: "Fine, if you don't take us, we'll just go down the road a mile or two."

When Wal-Mart couldn't get into Warrenton, Virginia, they went just over the line into Fauquier County. After they jumped ship in Plainville, Connnecticut, Wal-Mart applied next door in Bristol. Target must have watched in amusement as Northfield and Dundas, Minnesota tried to one-up each other to get the "prize." A newspaper editor in Northfield wrote: "Losing Target to Dundas would not be a victory. It just doesn't make sense to derail the project and let it go to Dundas. Dundas, not Northfield would receive the tax benefits."

On September 18, 1998, real estate owner Phil Thayer of Lake Placid wrote an "I told you so" letter to the North Elba Town Board, which had blocked Thayer's effort to bring a Wal-Mart to their town. "So that there is no misunderstanding as to what the likely outcome will be," Thayer wrote, "I have reason to believe that (Wal-Mart) will try and locate a store in the Saranac Lake Region . . . It seems inevitable that the Town will now miss out on a project which would have helped to expand our tax base and contribute to relieving some of the school and town tax burden on our citizens." Thayer predicted that if Wal-Mart built in neighboring Saranac Lake, "it seems logical that additional retail stores will locate to take advantage of traffic generated by Wal-Mart shoppers, and thus Saranac Lake could become the regional shopping center for the Tri-Lakes."

True, Mr. Thayer lost a "financial opportunity" (as Wal-Mart called it) to develop his property, but his threat is that North Elba will very soon regret its decision. Thayer's motivation is pretty transparent. He was making one last attempt to convince the town — after five years of law suits and controversy — that Wal-Mart should be allowed to build in their town. He ends his letter with this hopeful thought: "It is still conceivable that Wal-Mart would come to Lake Placid if they were assured that a permit would be issued to them, provided they complied with reasonable conditions the town may wish to impose." Ever the optimist, Thayer will still not see a Wal-Mart in North Elba. And the citizens in Saranac Lake have already geared up to block any Wal-Mart project there.

The Wal-Mart real estate manager who handled the North Elba project, Robert Stoker, was similarly embittered by the process. He wrote a letter to

Thayer in which he said Wal-Mart was "obviously disappointed with the political motivations responsible for the demise of our proposal to build on your property." Stoker notes that many towns like North Elba have "survived and thrived" with a Wal-Mart in town "through solid planning (not blocking economic growth and investment) which has not only allowed, but encouraged retailers, including Wal-Mart, to build in their towns." Stoker blames town planners who "turned up their noses and covered their eyes and ears" to the positive impacts of Wal-Mart.

Lake Placid resident Peter Roland fought Wal-Mart for five years. He calls Thayer's letter "just another example of the 'beggar thy neighbor' policy that Wal-Mart has used so well to their advantage in pitting neighboring municipalities/counties against each other."

The solution to this town versus town strategy by the developers and chain stores is obvious. Towns and counties have to start working together to do regional land use planning. It may be hard for some towns to drop their weapons and begin working together, but these megastores are by definition regional projects, and they deserve a regional approach. Several alternative strategies are possible: 1) creation of a regional land use commission, such as the Cape Cod Commission, Adirondack Parks Administration, or Vermont's Act 250 Board, which covers the entire state; 2) creation of revenue sharing projects, like the Fiscal Disparities Act in Minnesota, in which 88 communities, including the Twin Cities, plan for projects on a regional basis, and share the revenues that are generated from such development. If communities have the will to work together, and call off the economic warfare over which exit on the interstate can dominate the trade area, they will find the way to cooperatively plan for growth.

In the meantime, companies like Wal-Mart continue to deceive local officials with "Wal-Math" calculations of job creation and property/sales tax bonanzas. When I was in Tappahannock, Virginia recently, I visited the Wal-Mart superstore, surrounded by two large dead malls. Wal-Math job figures ignore such dead malls, and lost jobs. Local officials forget the devastation too. But the malls are still dead. They became dead because local officials refused to work with their neighbors to determine their retail market capacity, and plan for growth. As the Mayor of Northfield, Minnesota said: "It's not how big you grow, but how you grow big."

If towns don't learn how to hang together, they will surely hang separately. And Wal-Mart will be holding the noose.

Keep on Bustin',

Buster

Postscript: After Wal-Mart lost in Lake Placid, New York, they moved their plans to neighboring Saranac Lake. The company's plans there were destroyed in March of 1999 when a local resident purchased part of the land Wal-Mart wanted for $850,000.

A Letter from Buster: February, 1996
"Journey's End for Home Depot"

Dear Sprawl-Busters,

On a warm afternoon in early June, 1995, Lola Strom, a senior citizen who lives in the Journey's End Mobile Park in Santa Rosa, California, opened her mail to find a letter from a company called Crossroads R/W. It says on their letterhead that they are "Governmental Acquisition & Relocation Specialists."

The letter informed Lola that the owners of her Mobile Park were planning to change the zoning of her park and close it down. "They have found a buyer," the letter continued, "the Home Depot company, who plans to build a new retail store on the property after the park closes and after all the residents are properly relocated into new housing situations." Lola learned that Home Depot would prepare a Relocation Plan for all the elders in the park. They will receive information, counseling, moving assistance and other benefits which "will ease the burden and costs of moving."

"We fully understand the effects of relocating from a place that has been 'home' for many years," the company assured Lola. "Please do not feel compelled to move out," the letter added, "until the new store and the Relocation Plan are approved" by the Santa Rosa City Council. Lola was told she would be given six months notice of the park's closing. The 200 elderly residents would have to move so that Home Depot could lease the land to build a 154,000 square foot store on the north end of Mendocino Avenue. "It'll break our hearts when we have to leave here," one elderly resident told the media.

But Lola and her neighbors never had to move. They began gathering petitions asking city officials to reject Home Depot. The City Manager came out against converting 13 acres of residential land into retail. After all, Santa Rosa's General Plan for land use called for "preserving existing mobile homes, and preventing conversion of mobile home parks to other uses." Home Depot was undeterred. "We're confident that the opposition will recede," a Home Depot lawyer said, calling conversion of the park "inevitable." Home Depot had recently converted 39 mobile homes in Seattle, Washington into a new store — so why not here too?

"They have a great tiger by the tail," warned the mobile park residents. The elders began appearing weekly at City Council meetings wearing STOP HOME DEPOT t-shirts, and plans were underway for a five-hour picketing session at a nearby Home Depot.

The picketing never happened, because Home Depot decided to "relocate" their proposal instead of relocating the elders. "They said it was generating more heat than they wanted to endure," said Mayor Jim Pedgrift. For Home Depot, it was the journey's end. But it was a journey that never should have begun. Home Depot was defeated by a group of less than 200 senior citizens. Home Depot tried to take away the homes of the elderly, just to add one more "home" to their chain. But seniors broke the chain.

Keep on bustin',

Buster

Postscript: Home Depot tried to locate in one other location in Santa Rosa, but faced with mounting opposition, gave up on the second site as well. Ultimately they were able to locate a store in the next community over, Windsor, California, a community that lost a bitter referendum battle against Wal-Mart by just a handful of votes.

A Letter From Buster: December, 1998
"Nazi America"

Dear Sprawl-Busters,

"We won't lose in Henniker." Those were the last words spoken by Rite Aid's spokesman on the "Nightline" show on January 24, 1997. But less than four months later, the Planning Board in Henniker, New Hampshire, by a majority vote, had denied Rite Aid's application for a site plan review. The Board ruled that the Rite Aid plan was "too intensive for the site" because the building and parking combined left inadequate buffers to neighboring residences, and that the building itself "due to a combination of size, single level, flat roof . . . is neither harmonious nor compatible with the long term use and enjoyment of the adjacent residential area." The Board further stated that there was "an unacceptable level of conflict" with pedestrians versus drive through and delivery vehicles. Also on the list of seventeen objections was the fact that the plan "provides an inadequate buffer to protect Henniker Village's eligibility for the National Historic Register."

This decision was immediately praised by the Only Henniker On Earth committee, the citizens group that had fought Rite Aid from day one. It was also immediately appealed by Rite Aid and their real estate company, the Rared Company. Rite Aid sued the town, claiming that its denial of their site plan exceeded its legal authority, was unreasonable and that members of the Board had demonstrated bias and prejudgment against the project.

All through the hearing process, Rite Aid's position was that the town of Henniker had no legal authority to deny the use of this commercial property for their use. Rite Aid argued that a drive-through convenience store was a use "as of right," and therefore could not be denied. It is a line of reasoning that I have heard more times than there are Rite Aid stores. Municipal officials repeat this developer's mantra: "You can't tell someone what to do with their property. They can build anything they want."

Under New Hampshire law, Rite Aid had to show the courts that the town's decision was unreasonable. Not only were they unable to do that, the court found that "Rite Aid was substantially inflexible regarding the size of its building and the configuration of its site plan." The company was entitled to come into town with a "cookie cutter plan," Judge Arthur Brennan said, "but the Board is not required to accept a plan solely because it can be shoe-horned onto a lot." Even though Rite Aid's lawyers said that the Board had exceeded its legal authority, the Court ruled that issues like open space, harmonious and aesthetically pleasing development were proper concerns during site plan review applications. Even though all of Rite Aid's "experts" told the Board that their project met all the guidelines, the Court said the Planning Board was "not compelled to accept any provision of a site plan simply because the 'experts' agree that the provision is reasonable or legal. Board members are entitled to use their own common sense and judgment."

Finally, Rite Aid complained that the town had violated its equal protection rights by giving their application greater scrutiny that other proposals in the past. The Court agreed that Rite Aid had been subjected to a "more rigorous application process," but added: "equal protection does not require that the Board exercise a foolish consistency in carrying out its duties under the law." Henniker had allowed a post office to be built across the street from the Rite Aid parcel, but the Court said earlier mistakes had resulted in "an overdeveloped parcel," and Henniker was not bound to make the same mistake over and over.

Several weeks ago in Menomonee Falls, Wisconsin, a developer named Harvey Neu presented plans for a 112,000 square foot Home Depot – ten times larger than the Rite Aid proposal in Henniker — on land that isn't even zoned commercial. At the Home Depot hearing, the Village President got up and told residents: "How do you stop Mr. Neu from developing? This is America, folks, this is not Nazi Germany." If anybody has been goose-stepping across America, it's the developers and their lawyers who have intimidated local officials into believing that you can't tell somebody what to do with their property. But here's the truth: This is America, and you can.

The Henniker case is legal proof of that, and its not the only similar story on earth.

Keep on bustin,

Buster

Postscript: There is no Rite Aid in Henniker, New Hampshire. The landmark court ruling in the Henniker case has been used by other communities to demonstrate that just because property is zoned commercial does not mean that anything commercial can be built there.

A Letter From Buster: August, 1997
"Home Depot's Sour Grapes"

Dear Sprawl-Busters,

Home Depot must have really wanted to locate a store in Yarmouth, Massachusetts. They would have been the only big box home improvement store on Cape Cod. On April 8, 1996, a non-binding ballot question was put before voters on whether they wanted a Home Depot store located in a former warehouse. Home Depot won that vote 3,353 to 2,735 (53% of the voters stayed home). This vote reversed an earlier Town Meeting vote in which citizens voted 547 to 342 to keep Home Depot out.

The day after the election, the citizens opposed to Home Depot cried foul. They claimed that Home Depot had "bought" the election with an enormous outpouring of campaign spending. Home Depot had reportedly spent $25,000 on a local attorney, who was the former chairman of the town's Planning Board, to head the Home Depot campaign. Voters were sent several first class mailings signed by a group called "Yarmouth for Jobs and the Economy." A telephone campaign was paid for by Home Depot, a breakfast was held, signs were print-ed, etc. "It is unfortunate that a billion dollar corporation . . . could launch an expensive campaign to interfere with a Cape Cod town's normal voting proce-dures," said a leader of the citizen's group, the Yarmouth Neighborhood Coalition.

It wasn't until more than a year later that citizens in Yarmouth found out just how expensive that election was for Home Depot.

The headline in the July 3, 1997 *Cape Cod Times* read: "Home Depot to Pay $10,000: The payment will settle claims of campaign violations during a 1996 referendum in Yarmouth." According to the Massachusetts Office of Campaign and Political Finance, the world's largest home improvement compa-ny failed to report $63,407 it spent on the Yarmouth election until state officials began asking questions. According to the agreement Home Depot signed with the Finance office, the company had filed a spending report three days before the election listing $25,000 in expenditures, all of which went to the group Yarmouth for Jobs and the Economy. Months later, Home Depot reported anoth-er $14,000 contribution it made to the group, plus $49,407 that Home Depot spent directly on its own, including the hiring of a Washington, D.C.-based pub-lic relations company that organized the "get out the vote" campaign of letters and phone calls. Home Depot also failed to file reports between April and October of 1996.

Home Depot spent $88,407, and reported only 28% of what it lavished on the election. The orange giant spent $26.37 per vote--undoubtedly the most expensive vote in Yarmouth's history! "We knew they spent a tremendous amount of money," said one resident, "Everybody got mailings. Everybody got phone calls. There was a lot of stuff going on." Ironically, Home Depot might never have been caught if it were not for the actions of one citizen in Yarmouth who wrote to state officials in September of 1996, five months after the campaign was over.

The citizen's letter informed campaign officials that "a week before the election, Home Depot, or someone on its behalf, employed a voter-targeted polling firm with phone banks in Maryland and Virginia to conduct a massive telephone campaign . . . there has been no accounting of who paid for them, although it is reasonable to assume that Home Depot was responsible." Months after sending the letter, the citizen told me: "I had pretty much given up on this when, unexpectedly, I had a call from (Campaign Finance) to say that their office had completed its investigation (and) determined that Home Depot had in fact violated the campaign finance law and had agreed to a payment to the Commonwealth of $10,000." State officials told the citizen that "it was a precedent-setting case and will send a strong signal to other huge, mega-store, retail corporations that they had better respect and observe the laws of the Commonwealth, or else pay the price of not doing so."

So what "strong signal" did Home Depot get? The local lawyer Home Depot hired to run their campaign shrugged off the affair. He said the worst Home Depot could be accused of was being tardy in filing its reports. "It's like a library fine," the lawyer explained. "The book was due, but they didn't get it back on time."

Fortunately, this closes the "book" on Home Depot's short romance with Yarmouth. Last March the company withdrew on its own from Yarmouth, citing conflicts with the landowner. But the citizens against Home Depot believe it was because the company was facing tough grilling about the economic impact of its store on the Cape and the adverse impact on the character of the community.

When the citizens of Yarmouth first raised their concerns about Home Depot's massive spending to influence the outcome of this local election, the local newspaper editorialized: "To say the votes were bought, smells of sour grapes." Now that Home Depot has paid its $10,000 settlement, and revealed the true extent of its "tardy" campaign spending, it is something else that smells.

Keep on bustin',

Buster

Postscript: There is no Home Depot in Yarmouth. The company moved its plans just off the Cape to the town of Plymouth, Massachusetts. Home Depot unveiled plans for a store in Cedarville, a small Plymouth neighborhood. In February of 1998, the Plymouth Planning Board voted 3-1 to reject their application. Home Depot is now in the midst of pushing for a third location in the Plymouth area.

7

When the Fat Company Sings

"Why all the anger? We're a retail store, not a nuclear waste dump."
– **Bob Cheyne, Wal-Mart Director of Community Relations, 1995**

Wal-Mart is not a government mandate. A tightly organized group of home-owners and taxpayers – a slingshot coalition – can topple Goliath. You can make the fat company sing.

The fundamental fallibility of these big stores has been proven repeatedly across the United States: citizen's groups can slam-dunk even the biggest retail corporations. Some people will tell you that Wal-Mart has no Achilles' heel.

Wal-Mart is the premium retailer in the world. It is literally an industry unto itself, and it terms of its growth, it is unstoppable," says Kurt Barnard of *Retail Trend Report.*

Unstoppable? We've proved that wrong. Even though companies like Home Depot and Wal-Mart may act like they are entitled to land in your hometown– they have to play by the same zoning rules as everyone else.

On November 21, 1998, this was the headline on the front page of Section B in the *St. Petersburg Times* in Florida:

Wal-Mart drops quest to build store
Wal-Mart has surrendered to Lakewood residents who had fought an impassioned battle to keep the world's No. 1 retailer from moving into their community.

Wal-Mart attempted to build a 222,230 square foot superstore in St. Petersburg, but an overflow crowd of angry residents — organized by the Lakewood Civic Association — filled the Planning Commission hearing room for more than four hours. After the Commission voted not to rezone land for Wal-Mart, the lawyer for the property owner emerged from the hearing room and told reporters, "What happened here is that the Planning Commission slam-dunked the world's largest retailer."

In Brookfield, Wisconsin, the Town Board set a Guinness Book World Record by rejecting Home Depot in less than five minutes time. According to local media:

> With almost no discussion, the Town Board Tuesday night unanimously rejected a rezoning proposal that would have helped clear the way for a $15 billion Home Depot store just off Blue Mound Road. "It was a deaf ear," Jim McPhail, the site development manager for Home Depot, said after the vote. "When they don't want you, they don't want you."

In Walpole, New Hampshire, the end came so fast for Wal-Mart that the executives in Bentonville were left in the dark. The company had planned to put a 109,000 square foot store along a Route 12 strip, but the developer pulled out of the deal in the face of growing citizen opposition, and the story hit the newspapers before Wal-Mart even heard about it. One of the owners of the parcel Wal-Mart wanted remarked, "The folks in Walpole must have done their job. I don't know what's behind this — I assume it was the opposition in Walpole." Instead of buying the land for Wal-Mart, the developer withdrew from Walpole saying, "Ever try to roll a snowball uphill? Walpole's a lovely town. I have no interest in putting in something the people don't want."

This developer's comment closely echoes a statement made by Sam Walton himself in his autobiography, *Made In America: My Story:*

> Today, though, we have almost adopted the position that if some community, for whatever reason, doesn't want us in there, we aren't interested in going in and creating a fuss. I encourage us to walk away from this kind of trouble, because there are just too many other good towns out there

who do want us . . . Wal-Mart wants to go where it is wanted.

The easy victories in places like Walpole, Brookfield and St. Petersburg are in stark contrast to communities like Keene, New Hampshire, Plainville, Connecticut or North Elba, New York, where the battle raged on for years. In North Elba, Wal-Mart spent five years and nearly $3,000,000 trying to locate a store on Whiteface Inn Road, only to go down to defeat at the hands of the Residents for Responsible Growth. Company officials began by presenting a 102,000 square foot store in October of 1994, but by 1998 they were pleading for a 58,000 square foot store. After fighting a losing battle in court, Wal-Mart finally took a walk in October of 1998. Their real estate manager took one parting shot at the community:

> It is too bad that the political community (of North Elba) has allowed the opinions of a few to disproportionately influence and suppress retail and economic development . . . We will proceed to spend our capital and invest in communities where economic growth is not looked at as "the plague," and where the common sense of the many can still direct the outcome of such development...

Wal-Mart spokesman Les Copeland admitted that he walked unannounced into the office of Town Supervisor Shirley Seney a week before Christmas of 1997 and talked to her for 45 minutes. Seney refused to speak with Copeland. She said: "When somebody is suing you, you don't sit down and talk it over with them."

North Elba spent more than $30,000 in legal fees to keep Wal-Mart out. W later told reporters: "No question, it's been ugly. This project has been dragging on and on for a long time. We need to move ahead. The only people getting wealthy off this have been the attorneys."

From Puerto Rico to Alaska, from Maine to California, the message from hometown America is clearly written on the WAL: "We don't want you, Sprawl-Marts!"

8

How to Slam-Dunk Sprawl-Mart

"They just said they had spent enough money up here.
They were just kind of fed up with the situation."
— **Paul Poquette, developer, announcing Wal-Mart withdrawal**
from St. Albans, Vermont, October 20, 1997

The best place to slam-dunk a superstore is in your hometown. But be forewarned: the playing field is not level.

Developers and their corporate anchors have enormous advantages. Beating a company like Wal-Mart is a three step process:

Step One: Educate
Step Two: Activate
Step Three: Coordinate

The first step is educating your neighbors about the sins of sprawl. In the political consulting world, this information is known as "opposition research." What do we know about these companies that can — and should — be used against them?

Once educated, consumers may be more intelligent, but not necessarily any more motivated to act. When I hold strategy sessions with local groups fighting sprawl, I tell them when it comes to community organizing, there is no such thing as spontaneous combustion. Everything — from the placement of the spark to the fanning of the flames — must be done carefully and repeatedly. The people who usually find themselves fighting Home Depot or Wal-Mart are "accidental activists." They had not planned on defending their own personal environment — but the issue inserted itself onto their "short list" of things to do. When Morley Safer asked me on *60 Minutes* how I got pulled into the Wal-Mart campaign, I said: "All of a sudden, there was this huge 300 pound gorilla sitting on my sofa, you know, smoking a cigarette and kicking my cat, and saying, 'we want to be in your community on our terms'."

Some of the best activists I have met in my travels are people who had no formal background in community organizing. They will say "I'm just a housewife," or "I just own a small business in town." And then they will go out and blow the opposition away. But sheer energy is not sufficient. Even a savvy activist needs to know something about the opponent he or she is facing, what the rules of engagement are at the local level, what kinds of expertise you may need to present your case, what tactics work the best, and where to get the money to keep the whole effort financed.

Educated and activated consumers will remain a dispersed force without the final step in the process: coordination. I often tell people what songwriter Jeff Cain used to say: "You've got to keep on winning every battle that you've won." Fighting Target or Rite Aid is a campaign. In campaigns, everyday is a new day. You may have had a great hearing, or public rally yesterday — but today you have to build momentum all over again. This philosophy is even more useful after lousy days: a bad newspaper story can ruin your whole week. But a campaign lives to fight another day.

Most local groups want these battles to be over as soon as possible, but it is actually better to have them drag out as long as possible, because the longer your group is in the public eye, the more powerful the message becomes, the more educated the consumer gets. Home Depot and Wal-Mart hire public relations companies who understand this as well, and their goal is to get decision-makers to move quickly before the public opposition has time to form and strengthen.

There is no one "right way" to stop a Wal-Mart or a Home Depot, but there are common strategies that if employed will give you the best shot you have at making the fat company sing.

Sometimes the odds seem daunting: the little town versus the big corporation. Having participated in these battles over the past six years, I think it's amazing that developers ever lose.

Constance Beaumont, in her book *Smart States, Better Communities,* points out that there is an "imbalance of power between volunteer citizens operating on shoestring budgets who are not professionally involved in zoning or real estate matters, and large corporations or deep-pocketed developers whose attorneys are not only well-versed in land-use arcana but also backed up by significant financial resources."

A woman from Montreal recently phoned me to ask if there was any difference between fighting a Wal-Mart in Canada versus the United States. "I don't see any difference," I told her. "The rules of community organizing are pretty much universally the same — and Wal-Mart seems to operate the same north of the border too."

When I am invited into a community to help citizens organize an anti-sprawl campaign, I perform an "audit" of the community's capacity to respond to the challenge facing it. Based on that strategy check list (see Appendix I), a citizens' group needs only four things to wage a successful campaign against big box retail. If these ingredients are present, a community has at least a fighting chance to slam-dunk Sprawl-Mart:

1) A broad-based citizens' coalition
2) A land use attorney and related expert witnesses
3) Constant visibility
4) A source of money

1. The Citizen's Coalition

Membership: The Bank of America in California, in a 1997 report called "Beyond Sprawl," suggested that citizens pursue the following goal:"To build a broad-based constituency to combat sprawl that includes environmentalists, community organizations, businesses, farmers, government leaders, and others."

When I sat down with a gas station owner recently who wanted to prevent a major chain store from putting in a discount gas station in their parking lot, I asked him who he knew locally that could spearhead a citizen's group against the project. He looked back at me like I was asking him to recall his high school chemistry teacher's name. A couple of customers came to mind, but mostly cold leads. It turns out he didn't live in the town where his station was located, but after digging for a while, he came up with a few possible contacts.

In building a local slingshot coalition that is going to take on Goliath, you should aim for an "all-walks-of-life" group. This is no time to reject people because they are Republican, Democrat or Libertarian. Restrain any party politics. A successful group must have environmentalists, religious leaders (a parish priest makes a great witness at the Zoning Board), heads of civic groups like the Rotary, the Chamber of Commerce, local and state politicians, small business people and just plain "mom and pop" citizens.

The most effective leaders or spokespersons for such groups are the "mom and pop" citizens. Asking a merchant to lead a group makes little sense, because they are seen as having a "special interest." The high school principal, the head of a local gardening club, a retiree from a local manufacturing company — what you are looking for is an opinion leader or someone with an attractive public image who can appear before local boards and present well.

In our campaign in Greenfield, Massachusetts, the chairman of our Citizens Against the WAL was David Bete. His family name in Greenfield was as old as the water, and the family was associated with industrial and commercial success. Bete himself was the CEO of a company that employed nearly 200 people. David had never gathered signatures before, never spoken before a town board and never chaired a campaign committee. The fact that he could do all of these things well, and actually have fun doing them, is very typical. Some of the best campaign leaders are what I call "accidental activists." People like Dawn Rapchinski of Ephrata, Pennsylvania, or Carol Goodwin of Sturbridge, Massachusetts, Kathy Thompson of Tijeras, New Mexico or Amy Webber of Decorah, Iowa. These people had no plans to become community organizers, but they excelled at it in the defense of their hometown.

Size: You don't need an army to overcome Wal-Mart. The core group of a campaign committee can be anywhere from a dozen to thirty people. The core group only needs to be large enough to divide into committees, and it must be willing to meet regularly, every other week, during the campaign.

Delegating Labor: A key factor in running a campaign is being able to prevent two or three people from doing all the work. The Coalition should divide itself into 5 subcommittees:

• **Steering Committee:** The Chairman of your group, and four or five other people who are empowered to make decisions for the whole group when such decisions have to be made in a hurry. The Steering Committee should represent any major interests in the group, or include some of the "natural leaders" that come forward wanting to play a leadership role. This committee should definitely not be larger than a dozen people, and it must be flexible enough to be hastily called together, or networked by phone to quickly respond to a situation. If Wal-Mart announces that it is taking its campaign to a referendum, you need to be able to get a response to the media within a few hours of such watershed events in the campaign. In such a situation, the Steering Committee is polled and then contacts your organization's media committee to put out a press release on your letterhead.

• **Fund-Raising Committee:** Four or more people who offer their services to do just one thing for the effort — raise money. In Greenfield, David Bete had the business contacts to make phone calls and raise "large dollar" contributions. That's what he focused on, so that I, as the paid organizer, did not have to worry about where the next check was coming from. This committee has to include the Treasurer, who keeps track of every dollar that comes in.

If you are in any kind of ballot question, initiative petition or voter referendum, you have to keep track of the name and address of every donor. However, a zoning campaign has nothing to do with electoral politics, and citizen's groups can solicit donations from residents and merchants who want to anonymously support the cause. For these people, the preferred contribution is a cashier's check made out to the coalition. Many business people do not want to be "spotted" in a campaign, but if their confidentiality can be maintained, are very willing to spend their money to stop a company that is spending its money to put everyone else out of business. Anonymous donors also have the peace of mind in knowing that their contribution to your campaign will not result in a flood of similar requests. In my first Wal-Mart campaign in Greenfield, we raised $17,000, with the lion's share of that money coming from local and regional businesses. You can't defeat Wal-Mart by holding bake sales and car washes.

The best businesses to approach for money are the real estate interests who own the "dirt" on which the local shopping malls sit. Usually the chain stores like Sears, and JC Penney are not worth approaching. They will pass you off to a comatose corporate headquarters. But the landowner who will lose his tenants is a motivated donor. One of our major supporters was the real estate company that owned the strip mall on the other side of Greenfield. The owner envisioned losing his discount department store tenant if Wal-Mart arrived.

• **Media Committee:** If you have anyone in your group that speaks well in public, or is already well-known locally to the media, he or she should act as your main media spokesperson. This committee should also take responsibility for lining up special events for the media, like press conferences, special speakers or evening forums, etc. Save all the press clippings from your campaign, and view your media effort as an on-going event that you have to recreate everyday.

A great story in Tuesday's paper is history by Wednesday. One or two people on this committee should take responsibility for generating a press release every week. Find some angle on your story, or some challenge to Wal-Mart that is newsworthy. It's always helpful to invite Wal-Mart's CEO David Glass to come to your town to hear why people don't want his superstore. Offer him a free package deal of a bed and breakfast stay and a meal at a local restaurant. Tell Glass you will give him a personal tour of the county to see what is unique and special about your community. Then release the letter to the media.

• **Research Committee:** There should be two or three people who will search the bookstore and the Internet for sprawl-related information (see "Resources" section at the conclusion of this book). The Research committee is responsible for putting together at least one basic piece of printed literature (see below) that will be used at public meetings, or other forums. This committee will try to keep current on media events elsewhere in the nation, by using resources like *www.sprawl-buster.com* to pass along stories against sprawl to local residents. Research should be a combination of "canned" stories taken from national sources, mixed in with local details about the specific project and its impact: location, size of parcel, who the developer is and other background information.

• **Letters to the Editor Committee:** An entire committee is needed for this key image-building task. I recommend that one person be assigned to be the "Letter Captain." This person's role is to do nothing but assure that letters to the editor are getting written, signed and mailed or faxed to your local newspapers.

The Letter Captain does not write the letters, but oversees the output. One or two people work at their computers generating short, one or two paragraph letters on the various themes that your group is trying to emphasize: economic impacts, lack of a traffic study, impact on the quality of life in town, etc. Letters can be variations on a theme. The Letter Captain gets these letters out to people and gathers them back up for mailing.

The reason this process has to be organized is that many people will promise you a letter, but it never happens. Even well-intentioned, motivated members of your group will not write a letter from scratch. They have busy lives and never get around to it. We help them out by composing a letter for them, delivering it to them, telling them to change the text around until they are comfortable with it. They put the letter in an envelope with a stamp — but instead of mailing it, they return it to the Letter Captain, who can coordinate the flow of letters. In this way the campaign knows how many letters have gone in, on what topics, and from whom.

We always tell people that if your letter does not appear within a week after it was submitted, you must call the editorial page editor and tell them you are a daily subscriber to their newspaper and feel very strongly about the topic you wrote about. Some newspapers print everything they receive, others print very little. But everybody reads the letters page, and in a campaign, you want to "own" that page as many days as you can by beating the opposition in volume of letters. This is how opinion in a small town is shaped, and a letters campaign rarely happens by spontaneous combustion.

2) The Legal/Expert Intervention

Wal-Mart and Home Depot go nowhere without their attorneys. This is because the process of local zoning permitting is essentially a legal process that must go by the books. If Wal-Mart is holding a press conference, or speaking at the local Chamber of Commerce luncheon, they don't need their attorney. But if they are appearing before the Planning or Zoning Board, they are going to have a local attorney present. I have even seen cases where the local attorney is also the landowner who stands to make millions off the deal.

It is important for local officials to know that a citizen's group is represented by counsel. This tells them two things: 1) you are serious and have enough money to have legal representation; and 2) if they rule against you they might find themselves sued by their own residents. This latter point is crucial, because the Zoning Board already operates in fear that Wal-Mart or Home Depot is going to drag them to court if they don't give them what they want. The big corporations figure that what they can't get by regulation, they can try to get by litigation. Most town officials quake at the thought of being dragged into District or Superior Court over a zoning decision. Even worse is being sued by your own constituents.

I recently was testifying before a Planning Board, and I began to recite the various sections of the town's zoning code that set the criteria for granting approval for a special permit for a gas station. The Planning Board chairman stopped me abruptly and said: "Mr. Norman, the members of this Board have been serving in this capacity for many years. We know what our own ordinance says. We don't need you to lecture us on the contents."

I replied: "Mr. Chairman, with all due respect, if I don't raise these criteria now as part of the formal record, I can't bring them up later if we go to appeal."

The Planning Board Chairman glanced over at his other members, and then back at me. He had no rejoinder to make — he was still sorting through what it would mean if a citizen's group were to take his Board to court.

When you go into the marketplace for a lawyer, look for the following qualifications:

• **Someone who has specialized in land use cases.** Ask for specific cases they have worked on. Don't retain someone who is good in divorce law. You need someone who has worked with zoning codes or real estate law. Don't be turned away if you find out this lawyer has represented big developers. In fact, someone with that background can be very useful to you, as long as they tell you they are interested in your case and want to see you prevail. But I have seen several lawyers sell out their group to make peace with a large developer, just so they can keep their good will in the development community.

• **Someone who does not charge an arm and a leg for a retainer.** A couple of thousand dollars for a retainer is reasonable in most rural areas, but more is not. Check at least two lawyers and compare their fees. Ask them to give you some pro bono time considering that everyone else in the campaign is offering their time for free.

• **Someone who is not necessarily from the local, good-old-boy network.** On the plus side, a local lawyer may know everyone. On the down side, he or she may be politically tied into town hall and not too anxious to rock the boat.

• **Other Experts:** While you are looking for a land use attorney, begin the process of asking around for an independent traffic engineer. You will almost always want to challenge the traffic study that is presented by the developer, and the only way to do that credibly is with your own traffic engineer. If you have a university or college near you, see if the environmental or economics department faculty has any leads on community planners or traffic experts.

You can also look for someone who can assist with an economic impact report on the proposed development. Many planning and consulting firms can prepare economic impact statements, or a market capacity analysis. Again, check with possible free or low-cost sources first, like the economics department of a local college. If you are dealing with a private consulting firm, be sure to ask for a list of clients, and discuss your perspective on the project. You want to be able to present hard evidence to a Planning or Zoning Board that the proposed project will have adverse impacts on the "general welfare" of the community through the loss of public revenues, due to loss of property value as a direct consequence of business closures in town.

Your impact statement must either be done from scratch — because the developer refused to present his own — or it can be a critique of any economic impact statement that the town asked the developer to produce. Most developers will balk at making public any of their market studies, but you should push for that to happen and then analyze with your experts what they have done. It is cheaper to respond to the developer's study, than to create your own. But an impact report is important, because the developer will base a great deal of his argument on the positive impacts this project will have on taxes, jobs, and the local economy.

As for other expert witnesses, it all depends on the issues presented by the particular configuration of the land parcel under consideration. If, for example, the land has a significant wetlands on it, you will want to hire a wetlands expert to map or delineate the wetlands, to determine just how extensive are the wetlands. You will also want to challenge the developer's plans to "recreate" the wetlands somewhere else in exchange for destroying the one on his property.

Issues like storm water runoff or siltation of streams, or groundwater and air pollution — these are all areas in which local or state universities may have some resources for you. My experience with state officials is that they are extremely reactive only, and do not like to become high-profile in any local case. They will stick to whatever regulations they have regarding wetlands, or curb-cuts, etc., but I have only rarely seen state officials step in and block a project. They are usually oriented towards mitigating any perceived problems, or giving developers wide latitude. Don't count on the state to aggressively represent your interests. A local citizen's coalition is going to have to do all the heavy lifting.

3) Gaining Visibility

Like any political campaign, visibility is critical to turning public opinion in your favor. Visibility can be achieved in a number of ways, some of which are more appropriate to your community than others: lawn signs, bumper stickers, pins/lapel stickers, display ads in the media, radio spots, local access cable, letters to the editor, special events (a walk through town to the sprawl site), use of symbols, etc. The media committee can be in charge of on-going visibility. In Greenfield, we built a four-by-six foot WAL out of lightweight particle board, gave it some footings, and displayed the WAL on Saturdays at the Town Common, at Foster's Grocery store, etc. We invited local citizens to take a sheet of paper and write their feelings about Wal-Mart on the WAL. We sent the company a letter telling them that if they wanted to know why local residents were against the project — the "writing is on the WAL." This symbol was so successful, that within eight weeks we had built three WALs to display all the letters that people — young and old — had stapled to our WAL. It provided great visibility, and gave the media something to photograph besides talking heads. We also sponsored a "Walk For Main Street, New England," in which several hundred families with children and balloons marched down Main Street, with anti-Wal-Mart signs and pro-Greenfield slogans. We assembled on the Town Common and heard from speakers, and presented a few skits about what Wal-Mart would do to our town. Area television stations carried the event, as well as local newspapers. We also ran a focused series of display ads in the newspapers with the pictures of local opinion leaders (merchants, senior citizens, homeowners), so that our ideas were presented repeatedly in paid advertisements.

4) A Source of Money

Wal-Mart, Target and Home Depot enter Town Hall with one decided advantage over local citizen's groups: money. Wal-Mart comes before the Planning or Zoning Board armed with enough paid consultants to choke any Commission: land use lawyers, traffic engineers, architects, wetlands experts, public relations firms. People in North Elba, New York were shocked when Wal-Mart revealed that it had spent $2.5 million during the application process in their small town.

Against this backdrop, citizen's coalitions often tell me they don't have enough money to even run a display ad in their local newspaper. They literally are forced to hold a bake sale to fight the world's richest retailers. For example, here's the actual fund-raising plan that was developed by the Westgate Neighbors in their campaign to keep Home Depot from encroaching on their residential neighborhood. Bear in mind that the group had already fallen into the red during a legal challenge they had made against City Officials, who had failed to properly notify the public about Home Depot hearings. But in the late summer of 1998, they put a zoning referendum on the ballot and had only two months to raise money and run a campaign at the same time. Here's the actual Westgate Neighbors plan:

Fundraising

Our fundraising plan and budget are admittedly ambitious, given the short amount of time, Westgate Neighbors' outstanding debt, and the significant spending which our opponents are likely to do.

A large proportion of our fundraising plan ($27,500) relies on house parties/coffees, small events in volunteer's homes which provide the opportunity to make a short presentation on the issue and solicit small contributions. Each volunteer house party host will be provided with a kit which includes sample invitations, instructions, and an agenda.

Proposed Fundraising Plan

1. Major Donors (10) — $5,000

2. House Parties:
   A. 5 parties @ $1000 each (10-20 people) — $5,000
   B. 30 parties @ $500 each (10-20 people) — $15,000
   C. 30 parties @ $250 each (10-20 people) — $7,500
3. Mail re-solicitation to Prior Contributors to Westgate Neighbors —
   $2,500
4. Mail re-solicitation to Major Donors — $1,000
5. Events
   A. Two senior dance parties
        (200 people each at $10 ticket) — $4,000
   B. Two smaller events--speakers, etc. — $3,000
6. Finance Committee (5 people) — $10,000
7. Institutional Support (Labor unions, businesses) — $3,000
8. In-kind contributions — $5,500
Total — $61,500

What Westgate Neighbors didn't know was that while they were planning to hold "senior dance parties" to raise petty cash, Home Depot in Atlanta was wiring hundreds of thousands of dollars at a time to their astro-turf group in Toledo. In all, Home Depot spent $444,000 on their campaign in Toledo, while the Westgate Neighbors were only able to raise $14,000. Home Depot only won the election with 55% of the vote— but financially they crushed the citizens by a 31 to 1 spending ratio. Even though the Westgate Neighbors were obscenely outspent, they got 45% of the vote, and only lost by several thousand votes. Most of what Home Depot spent its money on were multiple, full-color direct mailings to voters and telemarketing to identify voters sympathetic to the company. All of that spending was behind the scenes. Sure, they spent money on newspaper ads — but most campaign spending was invisible.

What the Westgate Neighbors did that was right was to carefully detail out a budget, and then come up with a clear fundraising plan. What was wrong was that the plan was extremely labor intensive, and lacked any major underwriters. They had a plan for raising cash, but no "Sprawl-Daddies" to come in at a top dollar level. They were counting on only 5% of their support to come from "institutional support."

You cannot beat Wal-Mart or Home Depot without cash. It's simply unrealistic to raise enough money from senior dance parties, car washes and bake sales. Can you imagine Wal-Mart having to hold a bake sale to finance their campaign expenses? If they had to live on the budget most citizens' groups work with, we'd have no Wal-Mart on our roadsides.

So what is the alternative to senior dance parties?

Major Donors.

In most of the campaigns where money is no problem, it is because local merchants were helping quietly to underwrite the campaign. You can't expect the average homeowner to come across with several thousand dollars. People in the business community play a special role in the fund-raising arena.

The best way to destroy the middle class of any small town is to break the back of the merchant class. Once they disappear, the bonds that hold the community together are gone — everything from church suppers to the little league. It was the small merchant who helped, over generations, to build up these local institutions — and the demise of the small merchant is like knocking out the nerve center of hometown America.

All the more reason for merchants to dig into their pockets for money to support citizens groups fighting sprawl.

The Special Role of the Merchant

A merchant in Decorah, Iowa was in the middle of a battle against a Wal-Mart superstore. She sent me the following e-mail:

> Same old thing: everyone comes up to you and says: "What can we do to stop it?" And when you tell them to be vocal, and write letters to the City Council and City Planning and Zoning people, they shudder at the thought, and you can tell by the look on their face that it will never be done. We have businesses donating money to the citizens group that do not want anyone to know they have given, nor their name mentioned as donating! This is small town America, and everyone knows everyone, and are not willing to go public...Did you know that (our store) is on the Wal-Mart hate board??? Their employees do not shop with us anymore! So I guess that is the joy of going public.

When we were grappling with Wal-Mart in Greenfield, we called upon merchants in town to join the effort. We did not expect them to attend weekly meetings of the We're Against the WAL Committee, but we did want them to do at least two things:

1. Put signs in their store against the zoning change;
2. Give money — till it hurts.

Some members of our business community were willing to be very visible, others were helpful with their checkbooks. One leading local merchant, grocery store owner Bud Foster, was willing to do radio spots against Wal-Mart. Bud was perhaps the best known commercial voice on the radio in Greenfield. The pitch of his voice was immediately recognizable. In the summer months, he would advertise fresh watermelon from his store. Equally recognizable were his ads pitching fresh seafood from the Boston Piers, sung like the old fish-monger he was: "FEESH, FEESH, FRESH FEESH . . ." His singing commercials for "Watta Watta Watta Water-melons!" were a trademark sound. So we had Bud do the following ad on WHAI radio:

WALLA, WALLA WALLA WALLA-MART! Does Greenfield really need a Wal-Mart? This is Bud Foster urging Greenfield voters to support your locally-owned businesses! You can spend your whole life building up a business – only to see it close down overnight! How many more X,Y and Z marts can we support in this town? There's something very FEESHY about this whole deal. Vote No, No on October 19th.

We also enlisted local camera store owner Bill Forbes to go on the radio. The Forbes logo has been on Main Street Greenfield forever. Forbes, a former town Selectman, went to the studios to produce this ad:

First they build a Wal-Mart in Hinsdale. Then they announce one in Keene. See how they operate?…This is Bill Forbes…My family has been on Main Street Greenfield for 134 years. I've never seen anything as greedy as Wal-Mart! They want a store in Orange, Deerfield, Greenfield — every 20 miles! And all profits get shipped to Arkansas. But we can stop the WAL, by voting No, No on October 19th.

The We're Against the WAL committee had a good mix of small business-people on the committee: a dry cleaner, a marketing consultant, a real estate broker, an architect, a lawyer, a food co-op manager, a hardware store owner and a department store owner. The Executive Director of our Franklin County Chamber of Commerce came out squarely against the Wal-Mart. We also had merchants who were against us, but none of them were willing to put much of an investment behind their opinions.

We also enlisted the help of merchants from other communities, like Williston, Vermont, Chestertown, Maryland and Rockland, Maine.

Here are ten reasons how and why local merchants should be actively involved in stopping superstore sprawl in their hometown:

1. Spend Your Own Money

If you believe in fair competition, and you don't want to see your community bulldozed by the highest bidder, then you should make out a cashier's check to the local citizen's group. Home Depot was willing to spend half a million on one referendum campaign in Ohio. Wal-Mart has your business targeted.

I am always amazed by those business people who will tell local reporters "it will have no impact on me," or "we emphasize service here." Privately they will tell you they are climbing the walls — or making plans to get out of the business. The Wall Street analysts are betting that your business is history. It makes little sense to just take the punches. Campaigns against Wal-Mart and Home Depot can be extremely effective and damaging to their public image, but such campaigns run on money.

2. It's Your Battle

The first thing I am usually asked in a local campaign is: "Do you own a small business?" People are surprised that anyone would try to stop Wal-Mart for other than personal economic reasons. If citizens expect small businesses to be up in arms about being smothered by Wal-Mart, don't disappoint them. I met a pharmacist in Maine who was bought out of the business and went into repairing antique clocks. He at least understood what the future held. The choice is yours: stay in business, or, as Garry Trudeau suggests, "sell corn cob pipes."

In Crescent City, California, KPOD radio station owner Bill Stamps accepted a huge advertising order from Wal-Mart the first year the retailer opened in town. But when Wal-Mart came back several years later for air-time, Stamps refused their ads. He told a local reporter that Wal-Mart had enough access to publicity without him. "I feel like the local merchants need me more," he said. Stamps decided that siding with local merchants was his battle.

3. You are An Opinion Leader

When I meet with a new community group to map out a campaign, I always ask them to think up a list of opinion leaders. Invariably some of the prominent local merchants in town appear on the list. Because business involves visibility, and creating good will in the community, business leaders are natural participants in any community organizing effort. That does not mean, however, that I want business people to chair the citizen's group, or serve as the main spokesperson. I know that a merchant can be written off as having a special interest, so the key becomes using merchants strategically and tactfully, without forcing them into one or two leadership roles.

In Cave Springs, Virginia, when residents were fighting Home Depot, a local hardware store owner became a pivotal actor in the drama, and neighbors rallied behind his store. In Santa Rosa, a group of merchants banded together to form the Redwood Merchants Association and took on Home Depot in a very direct way. Wal-Mart will aggressively be looking for opinion leaders from among the merchant class to calm the public and tell them everything will be fine. I have seen them co-opt Chambers of Commerce to turn on their small business members. If Wal-Mart appreciates the important role of merchants in the struggle to win public opinion, it should guide us to do the same.

4. Your Employees

You have some troops that can help out in a citizen's coalition. In my hometown, we had several employees of Wilson's Department Store active in our campaign, and afterwards some of them successfully ran for Town Council seats. Wilson's is the main anchor of the Greenfield downtown. A four story family-owned department store in the center of town, it's been a landmark for more than 100 years. The management of Wilson's was solidly against Wal-Mart, yet stayed out of the limelight. But they gave money and their employees were engaged. The Stop & Shop grocery chain contributed funds, and their workers, through the United Food and Commercial Workers (UFCW) union, was helpful with turnout, money and other resources.

When I held a press conference in July of 1995 in Ticonderoga, New York to announce the formation of a group called RIGHT (Responsible Intelligent Growth for Historic Ticonderoga), Wal-Mart made sure employees its were there. A local reporter described the scene:

> Heckled by employees of the mega-retailer, anti-Wal-Mart activist Albert Norman worked to deliver his message. (M)ore than a dozen employees of Wal-Mart stores in Plattsburgh and Saratoga showed up for the rally, shouting "We're No.1!" and interrupting Norman as he spoke...But none of the distractions rattled Norman as he addressed about 50 Ticonderoga area residents at the rally.

I recall driving to Cape Cod to speak at an anti-Home Depot press conference in Yarmouth, Massachusetts. As I turned into White's Way where the store was to be located, I saw people standing along opposite street corners holding signs in support of Home Depot. I pulled up to one sign-holder and asked him if he worked at the Christmas Tree Shops, which was selling the land to Home Depot. "Naw," the man said. "We're from the Depot!"

Wal-Mart and Home Depot are prepared to call their troops out to attend hearings and defend their company. Small merchants should do the same.

5. Being High Profile

Many business people avoid any controversy. They somehow believe that by remaining neutral on all issues, they will stay out of harm's way and not alienate any of their customers. Then there are other businesses who understand that risk-taking is part of being in business, and that being in the news can create important name recognition and visibility for their business.

In a confrontation with a superstore, where there is documented proof that your business is economically at risk, if you remain low-profile you take the greatest risk of all: having no profile. Companies like Wal-Mart are investing a fortune in image-making, because they know at this point that even their shadow cast over a community is enough to stir up a storm of protest. They expect negative publicity at the local level, and they respond to it by trying to turn the discussion around to the issues they feel most comfortable presenting: EDLP (everyday low prices). If Wal-Mart is prepared to be quoted on the front page of your local newspaper, you should be prepared to do the same.

In Eureka, California, merchants initially tried to avoid visibility in the Friends of Humboldt County campaign against Wal-Mart. But pro-Wal-Mart people made it look like the friends were trying to orchestrate a "secret" campaign, and the Friends quickly released the names of its Board members. Merchants should be proud to defend their business, and leave the stealth to Wal-Mart.

6. Fund-Raising Ability

In the first campaign that I waged against Wal-Mart, our citizen's group was headed up by David Bete, who owned an industrial company in town that manufactured fog nozzles. He was clearly not financially threatened by Wal-Mart. David purchased a lot of raw materials for his business from local vendors — everything from paper products to cleaning services. He offered to perform one major task for our group: raise money. He knew where the money was, and he had the connections to make it happen. David headed up the budget committee. The We're Against the WAL committee raised small donations from homeowners — but most of our money came from businesses — and the people who knew this community the best were other businessmen. Merchants play a critical role in not only tapping their own business for financial support, but helping a citizen's group find other dollars as well. Having David Bete focusing on money meant that I could run a campaign without having to knock on doors for cash, which was a tremendous relief, and a good delegation of labor.

7. Protecting Competition

I hear small business people saying all the time that they can't take up arms against Wal-Mart because "I don't want to look like I'm against competition or the free market."

When you think about it, Wal-Mart is the beginning of the end of competition in your local trade area. Initially, shoppers will welcome the "competition" from big stores, until they start to see the smaller stores folding, and the plywood going up on the windows. If the idea of Evander Holyfield coming to fight a kid from your local high school sounds like competition to you, then you'll love the fight between Wal-Mart and the local pharmacist — if you have any left in your town. By slowing down the spread of Home Depot, or Target, you are helping to preserve a level of competition among relative equals in town. If Aubuchon's and Tru-Serv are scrapping it out on Main Street, neither company has the wherewithal to put the other guy under. But when Home Depot comes to town, it's like Evander Holyfield stepping into high school gymnasium. Wal-Mart isn't looking for a piece of the pie, they want the whole pie. That's what one-stop shopping is all about. To prevent one or two stores from dominating the marketplace, small merchants should do what they can to keep Main Street viable, and to keep some semblance of competition alive.

8. Marketplace of Ideas

If local businesses don't tell their story, Wal-Mart will have free reign to tell theirs. I have found that local residents are quick to criticize Main Street merchants — but they also know very little about what it's like to try and build up a business and keep it going. Wal-Mart is not going to tell that story. It's up to you. Instead of putting on this false front of bravado that says "My own business is not going to suffer" — which most smaller retailers do — it would be more useful in galvanizing people to publish a list of the businesses that would likely be hurt by the Wal-Mart, and to point out that superstores sell mostly what is sold already elsewhere in town. Don't assume that people know who the competition is. Be honest about what you think the impact will be in town, and appreciate the fact that if you are going to get your message out you've got to spend some money on media and direct mail to local residents.

9. Saving Your Business

It's not the burden of citizens in your town to understand the full financial impact your business has on your community. But you can help calculate that figure. Wal-Mart is very quick to tell people the volume of goods and services it buys in your state, what its tax bills come to, and so on. Your financial statistics should not be a trade secret either. Use the list of local businesses that are threatened by superstores to generate data on how much these establishments pay in property taxes, or sales taxes. How many people do they employ? What is your annual payroll? What local vendors do you use to keep you in business? Add all these items up, and then present them in the form of a letter to the editor. It's important to let people know what really is the real "cost" of losing a business like yours. Look over your list of five major suppliers, and get them involved in this battle as well. Because if you cannot save your business, you may be placing their business in jeopardy as well.

10. Leveling the Field

All of the actions on the list above are ones that your competition is willing to take to get rid of your business. This is what the competitive struggle is all about. It's not about finding niches, or trying to hide, or down-playing the impact. It's about using the same tactics as the competition. It's about making the rules work for you as well as them. I certainly don't blame Home Depot for trying to get Zoning Boards to rezone residential land. Conversely, I don't blame you for standing up at the same Zoning Board meeting and listing out the reasons why rezoning is a bad land use precedent.

If we examine the resources that our opponents are bringing to the table, and try to match those resources as best we can, then we are doing what it takes to level the playing field. This is, after all, what companies like Wal-Mart have done to us. They have studied our tactics at the grass roots level, and imitated what they found successful against them. That's why they create astro-roots groups. That's why they do telemarketing to quantify their base of support. That's why they have hired more public relations companies to organize the community.

The hardest thing to watch is the small business that goes down without firing a shot. In December of 1998, the *Philadelphia Inquirer* ran a story about the demise of the Ridley Park 5 & 10:

> After more than 25 years in the heart of the borough, the 5 & 10 on Hinckley Avenue will close tomorrow when James "Bud" Geddis retires

after 15 years as proprietor. The closing is a disappointment for many who will miss Geddis, and his old fashioned wares. But more significant, many say, the closing is symbolic of the continuing decline of small business districts in the face of competition from malls and giant retailers. "I think a small businessman can't compete with the large stores," said Geddis…"These big chains carry everything. They sell it cheaper than I can buy it for." Geddis, who said last week that his favorite part of the retail business was "meeting people and making friends", started sweeping floors at the Woolworth store at 52nd. and Market Streets in West Philadelphia in 1943. By the time he left 40 years later, he was manager… There are no immediate plans to fill Geddis' store, which sits across from the former Carole's Casuals, which has been vacant for more than a year.

Other Campaign Ingredients

In addition to the structure of the Coalition, there are other decisions that must be made in a successful campaign:

• **Office Space/Phone line:** Storefront visibility is useful, but not essential. But at a minimum you must have a way for people to reach you, offer services, exchange information. This can be done with a Coalition Hotline, which is nothing more than a local phone line hooked up to an answering machine. The other side will do the same thing, which is all the more reason why the Coalition must respond in kind.

• **Paid Coordinator:** If your finances allow, you should try to hire someone for roughly 24 hours a week (three days) to oversee the activities of the group. The Coordinator understands that everyone else in the group is a volunteer with many other priorities in their lives, and so someone in the group has to ensure that the press conference happens on time, that the fund-raising committee event is going off smoothly, that the traffic engineer has received his copy of the study, etc. This is the role of the Coordinator. A well-organized person can assume this role without working full-time to make things happen. The coordinator keeps track of all the volunteers, by committee, and can staff the office space, if you have one.

• **Opposition Literature:** Every group has to distill its message down to a short "literature piece" that explains to the public why you are opposed to this project, what it means to the community. In Greenfield, we produced a "Retail News" tabloid insert into our local newspaper that was very effective. This was printed on newsprint, and had the feeling of hard news. It contained stories about Wal-Mart as an employer, letters from other towns where Wal-Mart had done damage, and myth-busting articles about their "Buy American" campaign and employee relations. We printed up 6,000 of these newspapers and used them as one of the main literature pieces in the campaign.

• **Campaign Theme:** People become confused by too many messages, or changing themes. It's helpful to have the whole Coalition think through at the outset what are the main message you are trying to deliver, and to boil that message down to a sound-bite. In Greenfield, at the bottom of all our newspaper display ads, we ran the slogan: "We're not gaining a store, we're losing our community." We felt that a large factor in our campaign was the fear of losing our small town, rural identity, our special sense of place. In other areas that may not resonate, but something else will be dominant: a traffic stranglehold; crime; loss of the downtown; pollution of a river, etc. Ask yourself: What do I fear most about this project? What makes me the most upset about what is happening? Then convert that thought into a media blurb, and stick with it throughout the campaign, unless the reaction you get from the public is not supportive.

• **Developing A Timeline:** It helps to know how and when the municipal decision-making process will unfold. If you approach the town planning department, they should be able to tell you what kind of permits this project will require, who grants that permit, when the Planning Board will meet on it, and when the Zoning Board will meet. From such conversations, develop a flow chart or timeline that shows your members who will make decisions, and in what order those decisions are expected to be made. This will help you determine when you need to act, when certain players, like expert witnesses, need to be ready, etc.

If the planners are not forthcoming, go directly to your town manager, town clerk, or Mayor for this information, even if you think they are "in the tank" with Wal-Mart. They still have a public responsibility to explain how the hearing process works. You need to understand if you are up against a special permit process, or perhaps a conditional use permit or only a site plan review. Your land use attorney can help explain this process, but make town hall work for you as well.

• **Key Documents:** Obtain a copy of two documents: the zoning ordinance and the town's master plan/comprehensive plan. In some communities, it may be helpful also to get a hold of the county's comprehensive plan and zoning ordinance to put a regional perspective on the proposal. After all, these large-scale projects are regional in nature, and should not be the province of any one town. As a practical matter, your town may not want to hear from surrounding communities, but since these contiguous towns will be strongly impacted economically, they should make their feelings known whether they are invited to speak out or not. Such comments from neighboring towns are all part of building up the pressure inside your town for officials to do the right thing. The Zoning Ordinance and the Comprehensive Plan are public documents, and must be made available to you. Some towns will charge you a copying fee for these documents. Ask also for a copy of any site plans or studies that the developer has submitted to date.

• **Petitions/Referendums:** While you are in town hall, ask for a copy of the town charter or bylaws. Research your rights to bring a referendum to overturn a zoning decision. This procedure will not be found in the zoning ordinance, but more likely in the town's general code or ordinance. In my hometown, the right to mount a citizen's referendum was the key strategy we employed to overturn a favorable vote for Wal-Mart. If we had not had a referendum ordinance, Wal-Mart would be in Greenfield today. The specific process of how many signatures are required, and over what time period, will all be spelled out in the ordinance. You should determine if this option exists, and use it as your plan of last resort.

Companies like Wal-Mart and Target are now turning to the ballot themselves to initiate referendums. These companies use this tactic because they know that running successful voter campaigns involve two things: voter turnout and money. If you have enough money, you can turn out your vote. Citizens are actually at a disadvantage in such match-ups, because the Home Depots and Wal-Marts can spend a fortune in voter turnout efforts, like direct mail and telemarketing.

• **Writing/Calling the Permit Boards:** In addition to writing letters to the editor, all the members of your Coalition should receive a list of public officials who sit on the permitting boards, and a personal letter should be written to each of them. When the final shot is fired, it all comes down to how many people on the Town Council, or how many members of Planning and Zoning will vote on your side. I have seen some of these officials testify that they keep a pencil and pad by their phone to record how many constituent calls they received. They will announce at a public hearing that their mail or phone calls have been running four to one against the project. You have to make sure that everyone on the Board — even those you suspect are not with you — receive a substantial amount of mail and phone calls. But you must train your members in how to make such calls.

A phone call or letter must be short, concisely state what the objections are to the project, what a positive alternative might be, and your personal concern with the plan. Letters and phone calls must NOT be threatening, long-winded, or attack local people. Have your local letters committee or research committee develop a short "telephone script" for people to use when calling members of the Board. It's important to remember that Planning or Zoning Board members are supposed to act like impartial judges during the hearing process, so don't demand that they take a position on your side, and don't expect them to tell reporters how they feel about a project. Board members may say something subtle about their attitude on the project, or reveal how they are leaning — but restrict your comments to why you want the project defeated, and ask Board members if there is any information you can help them get.

If you come across a Board member who is publicly making statements in support of Wal-Mart before the case has been presented fully, you can make the claim later in court that they were predisposed to the project and prejudiced their fellow Board members.

• **Telemarketing:** In a ballot campaign, there is no way around the need to do telemarketing outreach to your voters. We spent $4,000 in Greenfield on a local firm that specialized in mass phone calling. The goal of this effort was to create a list of voters who were leaning in our favor, so we could later turn them out at the polls. Here is essentially the phone script we used for our calls:

"Hi, this is _____ calling. We're taking an opinion poll on behalf of the 'We're Against the WAL' committee. I'd like to ask you one question about the proposed Wal-Mart project. OK? Here's the question: Which of the following statement describes how you personally feel TODAY about Wal-Mart building three stores on the edge of town?

- I'm leaning AGAINST Wal-Mart
- I'm leaning FOR Wal-Mart
- I'm UNDECIDED."

We coded voters who indicated they were against or undecided. This gave us a master list of voters to work from later in the campaign, and it also showed us where our support was strong in town, and where we were weak. On election day, we used our coded list to do "poll-watching", which allowed us to call people we determined had not come to vote by 5:00 P.M. We spent the last three hours of the campaign calling several hundred voters who our poll-watchers told us had not yet come out for us. It's called GOTV: get out the vote!

Even if you are not in a ballot campaign, some voter polling like this is extremely useful if you can raise the money to pay for it. You can commission a basic poll of town residents to find out if they are leaning for or against your position on the Target or Home Depot project. Such a poll can be published if you like the results you get, or at a minimum used to tell you in what parts of town you need to do more work. A poll can also be useful to identify key themes which resonate with voters – and which do not.

More Campaign Principles:

- **Incorporating:** Some groups believe that they must incorporate to protect members from liability lawsuits. In my experience over the past six years, I have seen very little justification for setting up non-profit community groups that are going to dissolve after the major battle is over. Retaining an on-going identity, and using a sprawl-battle to build a larger constituency and momentum on growth issues is fine, but if it distracts from the immediate objective of stopping sprawl-mart, then this kind of internal organizational work is counter-productive. Beat Wal-Mart or Home Depot first, and then worry about incorporating.

- **One Target At A Time:** In many places where I have worked with local citizen's groups, the members have become fixated on the need to replace unresponsive local officials. "That Mayor's got to go!" "Can you believe that

County Supervisor? Just wait until he comes up for election." In fact, in places like Mansfield, New Jersey, Old Saybrook and Plainville, CT and others, anti-sprawl activists ran for public office and won. When they saw how lame some elected officials were, they decided to run for office. But during a sprawl campaign, it is dangerous and divisive to get distracted by a wayward public official. Stay focused on the main target: Wal-Mart, Home Depot, whatever the logo is. The Mayor is not the target. The County Supervisor is not the target. You can address those shortcomings later. The task at hand is to educate your fellow citizens about the dark side of Wal-Mart. Too many targets dilutes the message, and splinters the group.

• **Heart as Well as Head:** A campaign cannot appeal only to the head. Yes, you must have a list of strong "talking points" about sprawl that measure the damage in statistics about jobs lost, falling property values, sales captured, etc. Numbers are essential in building credibility for your message. But behind the numbers is a deeper argument that you must find in your community. Most people respond to the argument about the unique sense of place. "There are thousands of Rite Aids, but only one Henniker on earth." Pride of Place, Commitment to Community — whatever you want to call it — is vital to the success of your campaign. You can't talk about this too much. After all, Wal-Mart does not live in your hometown. They live in Arkansas. Home Depot lives in Georgia. Rite Aid lives in Pennsylvania. Target lives in Minnesota. Local control, home rule, and control over the future of the place your call home — these are the themes of the heart you must play.

• **It's a Campaign:** By definition, a campaign is an on-going series of events with a start and a finish. Too many people believe that a battle against sprawl happens on one evening, and then you read about it in the next day's newspaper. In a campaign, every day is a new day, and all the victories of yesterday don't mean much if you lose today. You have to keep your message before the public, day after day. It's important that the core group forming the campaign's nerve center understand this concept of the continuous campaign. Otherwise, their energies will wax and wane, and they will drop energy levels just at the time they need to be rising.

• **Delay is Good. Take Your Time:** In a campaign, the more time you have to get out your message, the better. For this reason, delay is good — no matter-what the source. If a Planning Board wants more time to review a project — let it happen. Developers generally rely on quick decisions, short time frames, to keep community groups from building up momentum. You, on the other hand, want as many delays as possible, during which time land deals can fall apart, adverse media publicity can grow, and turnout at public hearings can increase. The downside of this is that you have to keep the troops motivated by coming up with fresh angles from which to tell your story, new ideas for getting on the front page of the newspaper, and innovative ways to turn the public against sprawling projects.

Using these simple organizing tactics, I have personally helped stop at least thirty Wal-Mart or Home Depot projects. These experiences have convinced me that it is far easier to preempt a Wal-Mart than to react to one. In other words, it is better to head them off at the pass than to hold a showdown on Main Street.

9

Creating A No-Sprawl Zone

"Local zoning authority is a critical element of community self-determination that allows local people to mediate the pace and pattern of residential change and manage the economic and social dislocations attendant on local development."
— **Jonathan Moore Peterson, "Urban Lawyer," Spring 1995**

If you don't define growth, it will define you.

Everyone knows of a stretch of road near them — usually within a short drive away — that is just one neon sign after another. It's the kind of unsightly sprawl that people drive by and comment: "Nice place to shop — but I sure wouldn't want to live there."

The issue of sprawl is ultimately an issue of local control. Control over how your community looks. Control over what you pass on your way home from work, and how long you sit in traffic eating other people's car exhaust. Control over the supply and mix of retail business, and the type and availability of decent-paying jobs. Control over what happens to your consumer dollars.

When Gladys Keller, a senior citizen from Westville, New Jersey first called me about stopping a Wal-Mart in a neighboring town, she told me: "I can't find anyone who is willing to fight this. They all tell me: Gladys, there's nothing you can do. You can't beat them." What the Sprawl-Buster's record shows, is that you can beat them — you just have to know where they are vulnerable.

There is no single word in the Developer's Lexicon that is so hated as the six letter word "zoning." Zoning is a powerful tool for local control, and yet most communities are totally unprepared to use their zoning bylaws to stop undesirable growth. Most of our hometowns have what I call "Alice's Restaurant zoning": you can get anything you want at Alice's Restaurant. Developers have created designer zoning in such communities. The zoning map ends up looking like the counties of Yugoslavia. Many zoning codes were written in the 1960s when retailers like Wal-Mart and K-Mart were just getting started. It's time to bring zoning into the new Millennium.

The average citizen in Sprawlville, U.S.A. has never read a zoning bylaw. He or she couldn't name anyone who sits on the Zoning Board of Appeals or the Planning Commission. Yet the Zoning Board, and the Planning Board, the Master Land Use Plan, and the Zoning Bylaws, are the best tools the Sprawl-Buster has for stopping the invasion of superstores in hometowns across America.

Everyone fighting sprawl should have a basic grasp of some of the zoning concepts used to regulate growth. I remember Rite Aid's attorney telling a Planning Board in Henniker, New Hampshire: "This land is zoned commercial and retail use is permitted 'as of right,' so there is nothing you can do to stop us." If the Planning Board had believed that, there would be a Rite Aid in Henniker today. But Rite Aid lost the argument and their store. It all came down to fine points of zoning.

If Tip O'Neill had been asked about zoning decisions, he would have said: "All sprawlitics is local." Local cities and towns have an enormous amount of discretion in shaping the future of their communities. They hold one of the most powerful tools for stopping sprawl: zoning. Developers and their lawyers don't want town officials to understand just how much discretion local police powers give a community, but it's your job to help empower local decision-makers.

Any citizen's group that wants to stop a Wal-Mart, Kmart or Home Depot needs to understand the basics of zoning. Your lawyer will help you craft an argument before a Zoning Board that responds to the specifics of your community's situation.

As Attorney Jonathan Moore Peterson has written in the "Urban Lawyer":

Zoning is certainly the preferable mode of dealing with the predation of box retailers. Zoning has the greatest potential for excluding dangerous firms from a market protective of local interests . . . Zoning has the distinct advantage of being useful before significant economic damage can occur upon America's historic Main Street area.

The New Jersey Office of State Planning advises local planners that some communities may want to attract big box retailers, but "others may not have adequate infrastructure capacity to accommodate it." Either way, says the OSP:

> Big box retail uses are regulated by local land use controls — the municipal master plan and land development ordinances . . . municipalities in New Jersey and elsewhere can to a remarkable extent influence site layout, building location and the overall configuration of retail development through the planning and zoning tools at their development.

Here is a crash course in "Sprawl-Zoning 101":

Introduction: The "Property Rights" Argument

Local zoning ordinances or bylaws have the force of police power, and allow a community to dictate the number, location, and size of land uses — like superstores. Power over land use decisions has been delegated to localities with minimal constraints on its use by the state or federal government. As the New Jersey Court has said: "localities . . . could use their powers for the exclusive benefit of local residents" as long as the zoning ordinances are "reasonably calculated to advance the community as a social, economic and political unit." In New York state, for example, Section 261 of the Town Law gives towns the authority by ordinance to regulate and restrict the height, number of stories, and size of buildings, the percentage of the lot that may be occupied by a development, and the location and use of buildings. Unfortunately, many Planning and Zoning Boards do not seem to remember that they have these powers, and when you tell them they have the right to limit the size of buildings, they look incredulous.

Developers will complain that their property rights are being violated, or that tough zoning rules stifle competition. "It's my property, and I'll do with it as I please," say the developers. "You have no right to tell me how to use my property." In response, the citizen's group says: "You have no right to use your property for a purpose that would destroy the value of property of other residents."

In 1922, the United States Supreme Court ruled that a government regulation that severely restricts property use can be so onerous that it has the same effect as a "taking" of property. But over the past twenty years, various Supreme Court decisions have clarified that a "taking" is involved if a regulation renders an owner's property completely worthless. A regulation that reduces the value of land, such as rezoning land from commercial to residential, is not in itself unconstitutional. The regulation must be so burdensome as to remove all practical use of the property, so that it has no reasonable value left.

A landowner whose property is zoned office park, cannot simply demand that his land be rezoned for retail commercial because it will have more value, or claim that leaving the land office park leaves him with worthless land. I saw a developer try to make this case in New Jersey to pave the way for a Wal-Mart, but without success. Most land use restrictions – such as limiting the size or location of superstores leave the property owner with many other options for his land. The developer may complain loudly about his property rights, but he is unlikely to prevail in court.

The courts have also ruled that "the power to zone and rezone necessarily has foreseeable anti-competitive effects." As long as a city or town in a reasonable way is pursuing a clearly stated objective to serve the public welfare of its residents, or enhance property values, or sustain the vitality of a community's commercial center, its zoning restrictions on big box retailers will be legally supported in the courts.

If a community tries to implement its zoning bylaws in an arbitrary or capricious manner, then it could have problems. In a Virginia case (*National Memorial Park v. BZA of Fairfax County*, 348 S.E. 2d at 250) the Supreme Court said that zoning boards "must exercise their discretion when making decisions on proposed special uses. Judicial interference is permissible only if the Board's action is arbitrary and capricious, constituting a clear abuse of discretion."

In *Ames v. Town of Painter*, the Virginia Supreme Court wrote that "A board of zoning appeals, acting under a delegated power to grant special use permits, acts in a legislative capacity . . . its action is presumed to be reasonable . . . the litigant attacking the legislative act has the burden of producing probative evidence of unreasonableness . . . The zoning board must only produce evidence sufficient to make the question of reasonableness 'fairly debatable' for the legislative act to be sustained." In other words, the burden of proving that a zoning board's decision was capricious lies with the developer, who must show that the town's unreasonableness isn't even debatable.

Listed below are several key legal concepts and landmark cases in zoning law can be cited by local citizen's groups when working with Town Councils, or Planning and Zoning Boards:

• Promoting the General Welfare

Just about every zoning ordinance in America begins with a general purpose statement that says the zoning ordinance is meant to promote the health, safety and general welfare of the community. In Plymouth, Massachusetts, for example, home of the rock where the Pilgrims first got us started, Section 100 of the Zoning Bylaw states:

> In pursuance of authority conferred by the general laws of Massachusetts, chapter 40A, sections 1-17 inclusive, and all acts in amendment thereof; and for the purposes including but not limited to promoting the health, safety, convenience and welfare of the inhabitants of the Town of Plymouth; and more particularly to promote the most appropriate use of land throughout the town in accordance with a comprehensive plan; to preserve and increase its amenities; to secure safety from flooding and other dangers; to lessen congestion in the streets; to prevent the overcrowding of land; to conserve the value of land and buildings; to facilitate the adequate provision of transportation, water, sewerage, schools, parks, and other public requirements; and for other appropriate purposes; the town of Plymouth does hereby enact the following regulations to be known as the Zoning Bylaw of the town of Plymouth.

In this typical zoning statement of purpose are at least four legal openings for sprawl-busters to promote at the local level:

• Sprawl development will have a negative impact on the local economy, and such adverse consequences reach into the general welfare of the community by causing declining property values and loss of public revenues.

• Rezoning farmland or industrially zoned property is not the highest or best use of land for the community.

• A sprawl-mart is not harmonious with the town's comprehensive plan, which calls for avoidance of strip development and enhancement of the central commercial district.

• A big box development will harm the value of land and buildings, which the zoning bylaw seeks to protect.

All of these arguments can be made, depending on what your local comprehensive planning and zoning ordinances say. But don't expect local zoning boards to rise to their feet applauding. Most boards take a very narrow interpretation of their powers to shape major developments. There are two major reasons for this "know-nothing" attitude:

1) Many zoning officials really know nothing about their broad powers. As Attorney Jonathan Peterson of the American Bar Association has written: "Few communities are sufficiently foresighted to realize and accept the potential for economic, social and cultural harm that box retailers bring."

2) They are afraid that if they turn down the developer they will be perceived as "anti-growth" or "anti-business" — and, most importantly — they may be sued by the developer. Most zoning boards are extremely risk averse, and don't want to be remembered for having caused the town to run up legal bills.

When Home Depot spokesman Amy Friend told a newspaper reporter that Al Norman was "definitely anti-growth," my response was: "Home Depot is definitely anti-community." Home Depot, which promotes out of scale development that clashes with the rest of the built environment, is showing contempt for local community values. If being pro-growth means being in favor of uncontrolled, out of scale development, then I am anti-growth.

There are court cases in which an application for a special use permit for a shopping center or retail commercial use was denied on the ground that the grant of such a permit would devastate or otherwise adversely affect existing commercial business or business districts in the surrounding community, and thereby undermine the public welfare.

In a 1957 case in Virginia *Board of County Supervisors of Fairfax County v. Davis,* 200 Va 316, 106 SE 2d 152, 157 (1958)], the Virginia Supreme Court said that it was proper to consider the economic effects of a shopping center project, in so far as such effects reach into the general welfare: "The only point at which it is proper in zoning to consider economic effects is the point at which the economic effects reach into the general welfare."

Public welfare is an argument most boards try to ignore. But in the *Village of Belle Terre v. Boraas* case [416 U.S. 1 (1974)], the United States Supreme Court wrote that "the concept of public welfare is broad and inclusive . . . the values it represents are spiritual as well as physical, aesthetic as well as monetary." As long as a zoning ordinance does not deny an applicant of a fundamental right protected by the Constitution, the courts will not subject the ordinance to strict scrutiny and will generally defer to a municipality's discretion.

Maintenance of Property Values

In a 1985 case in Iowa [*E&G Enterprises v City of Mount Vernon*, 373 NW 2d 693 (Iowa App. 1985)], a furniture store was unable to locate near a highway because such retail uses were limited to the city's downtown. The Court of Appeals ruled that Mount Vernon's "effort to preserve its downtown business area is a valid exercise of the police power, and the preservation of that area promotes the public welfare, including the maintenance of property values." Many local zoning ordinances have a purpose clause that says the ordinance is designed to "protect the value of land and buildings." Sprawl-busters should use such language to demonstrate that Wal-Mart will not protect property values, but harm them. If necessary, some groups have hired a land appraiser to measure the loss of value in nearby residential properties that lie along roadways leading up to the megastore.

Economic Need

Many city councils will allow developers to enter into the record statements about the positive impacts that big box retail will have on jobs, property taxes, sales taxes, etc. I have even seen developers argue that their project will give the community enough revenue to build a new senior center or library. In one case in Warrenton, Virginia, Wal-Mart actually tied their land use permit to the deeding of abutting property for a future school. The Superintendent of the Warrenton schools came to the zoning hearing to argue on behalf of Wal-Mart as a vehicle for constructing a much-needed elementary school.

On the other hand, the same officials will turn off the microphones when citizens start talking about the negative economic consequences if a Home Depot or a Wal-Mart is built. Citizen's groups should not structure their argument as an attempt to save one or two, or even half a dozen specific businesses. Instead, the argument should be based on the eventual impact on public revenues caused by the loss of productive commercial properties.

Sprawl busters can also assert that the community already has sufficient retail establishments, and that continued development of large scale projects will push the limit beyond what the community can absorb, leading to negative economic impacts on public revenues. If there is no need, or adequate population base for an additional large regional shopping center, then the grant of that application would therefore likely lead to the destruction of other nearby commercial businesses, leaving unattractive vacant buildings, lower quality businesses, and the financial ruin of local business people and their employees. Approval of the shopping center would not promote the public welfare. Rather, by denying the application, the general welfare would be protected by preventing the deleterious effects of destructive competition among a surfeit of retail commercial businesses.

In a 1960 case in Barrington, Rhode Island [*Laudati v. Zoning Board of town of Barrington*, 91 RI 116, 161 A.2d 198, 201, 202 (1960)], the ZBA denied a special exception for a shopping center, arguing that the proposed use would not serve the public convenience and welfare since adequate shopping facilities of a similar nature were located only 1,200 feet distant from the land in question.

In a 1977 California case (*Ensign Bickford v. City Council of Livermore*), the City Council denied an application to rezone land to create a shopping center based partially on the fact that "the population base to support a neighborhood commercial area . . . is not adequate at this time, nor is it anticipated that the neighborhood population will become large enough in the immediate future to justify rezoning at this time." The California courts ruled: "The City Council determined that the area needed and would support one shopping center...the city is attempting to regulate where within the city business will be developed. In furtherance of this legitimate end, it is necessary to permit business development in one area before allowing commercial development in another . . . the Council was regulating the commercial growth of the City as it related to the needs of the residential areas for that commercial development."

When the North Elba Planning Board ruled against Wal-Mart in January of 1996, the Board addressed the issue of need:

> The Planning Board recognizes that it may not approve or disapprove the application based on the basis of effects on competing merchants . . . The Planning Board may consider the potential impact economic matters may have on the character of the community . . . To the extent that the project would result in long term chronic vacancies, the ambiance of the community would be adversely impacted, resulting in loss of a portion of the tourist trade. Such loss would have economic impacts on the remaining merchants, resulting in a downward spiral in which increasing numbers of businesses could close their doors, further reducing the community's desirability as a tourist destination.

In Napa, California, the city's Planning Director asked the City Attorney to write him a memo regarding to what degree Napa could consider the "economic" impacts of a Home Depot. Here is what City Attorney Tom Brown concluded in 1997:

> While the City clearly may not deny the application solely based on a desire to either regulate competition or provide advantages to local businesses, the City nevertheless has broad discretion to deny the Home Depot application based upon "economic" considerations, namely, considerations of whether there is a sufficient market to be served by the proposed new Home Depot business, and whether the additional intensity of the use proposed by Home Depot would create an over-saturation of that use within either the area, or the City as a whole.

Napa's attorney told the city that they could deny the Home Depot request to build, in part at least, upon a finding that "the applicant has failed to demonstrate the need for the new or increased intensity of use." Quoting the *Ensign Bickford* case noted above, Brown continued:

The law in California is that irrespective of whether its decision might have indirect impacts on economic competition, cities properly may, by ordinance or adjudicatory action, deny or restrict certain uses based on a determination that there is an inadequate market or need for the proposed new or increased use . . . (W)hile the City Council may not deny the Home Depot application solely upon a finding that the application would provide additional competition for local businesses, or to exclude an out-of-town business for the sole benefit of local businesses, the City has broad discretion to deny or otherwise limit the application based upon the "economic" considerations that the City already is adequately served by uses similar or identical to the proposed Home Depot use, or that the intensity of the use proposed by Home Depot would create a condition of "over-saturation" unwarranted by local market needs.

In the 1971 California case of *Van Sicklen v. Browne* [15 Cal. App. 3d 122, 92 Cal. Rptr. 786 (1971)], the city of Milpitas denied an application for a gas station where there was already an over-supply of gas stations in the nearby area. The Planning Commission said that approval of another gas station "would create a further proliferation of this type of land use in a neighborhood already adequately served by service stations . . . (T)here is no demonstrated need for an additional service station in this neighborhood at this time."

The Courts ruled that "the Planning Commission is vested with considerable discretion in determining whether the proposed use subserves the Master Plan's objectives." Denying the application was a "legitimate exercise of the discretionary power vested in the Planning Commission."

The California Appeals Court in this case wrote: "The traditional purpose of the commercial use permit is to permit a municipality to exercise some measure of control over the extent of certain uses, such as service stations, which, although desirable in limited numbers, could have a detrimental effect on the community in large numbers."

The developer complained that the city was using zoning to regulate competition, but the court responded:

(A)lthough cities may not use zoning powers to regulate economic competition, it is also recognized that land use and planning decisions can not be made in any community without some impact on the economy of the community . . . Today economic and aesthetic considerations together constitute the nearly inseparable warp and woof of the fabric upon which the modern city must design its future. . . . (W)e perceive that planning and zoning ordinances traditionally seek to maintain property values, protect tax revenues, provide neighborhood social and economic stability, attract business and industry and encourage conditions which make a community a pleasant place to live and work. Whether these be classified as planning considerations or economic considerations, we hold that so long as the primary purpose of the zoning ordinance is not to regulate economic competition, but to subserve a valid objective pursuant to a city's police powers, such ordinance is not invalid even though it might have an indirect impact on economic competition.

In a 1969 case in New Jersey, the town of Tenafly had an ordinance designed to restrict retail sales to the town's central business district. When a developer wanted to build a supermarket outside of this retail area, the courts said: "(I)t is true that a municipality may not, by zoning or otherwise, exclude a particular use only because it will compete with an existing business or businesses . . . but if the exclusion of competition happens to be an incident or effect of otherwise valid zoning, it does not invalidate it."

The Comprehensive Plan

A town's comprehensive plan can make the general welfare argument easier, by adding more definition of what serves the public welfare. When a comprehensive plan is specifically mentioned in a town's zoning ordinance, it becomes part of the zoning rules for the town, with the full force of law. For example, in the case of *Visconi & Jacobs Company v. City of Lawrence* [927 F2d 1111 10th Cir. (1991)], the city's planning commission set up a comprehensive downtown plan with the policy to "eliminate or substantially reduce competition for downtown business interest and support the central business district (downtown) as the only retail center in the city."

A developer alleged that the Lawrence, Kansas Downtown Improvement Committee had engaged in a conspiracy to prevent the developer from building a suburban mall, and that this was a violation of antitrust law. The courts found that the goal of "sustaining the vitality of the city's center" was a valid public purpose.

When the Planning Board in New Paltz, New York was preparing its decision against a Wal-Mart development, it cited its Comprehensive Plan as one reason to say no:"The Comprehensive Plan's mission statement clearly states that the Town of New Paltz places high value on its small town feeling and wishes to retain the character of the Town while enabling responsible growth."

In a 1997 decision in Westlake, Ohio blocking a Kmart from being built, the Court of Appeals in Cuyahoga County ruled that Westlake's Guide Plan (Comprehensive Plan) had the force of law because it was specifically referenced in the town's zoning ordinance. Kmart had argued that the Guide Plan was just a guide, but the town insisted that Kmart could not use the land for a supercenter, based on its Guide Plan. The courts ruled in favor of Westlake.

When the Planning Commission in St. Petersburg, Florida ruled in November of 1998 against a rezoning for a Wal-Mart, one of the reasons cited was the Comprehensive Plan:

> The requested commercial general land use is not consistent with … the City's Comprehensive Plan which states that the City has an adequate supply of commercial land use to meet existing and future needs, and that future expansion of commercial uses shall be restricted to infilling of existing commercial areas and activity centers except where a need can be clearly identified.

Aesthetics and Harmonious Development

Development in your hometown should be harmonious with the character of the rest of the community. Local zoning boards do not think of themselves as art critics, and the very word "aesthetics" scares them. But local groups should insist that all retail projects be aesthetically in keeping with what the community wants. What the community wants should be found in its state statutes, comprehensive plan and zoning ordinance. Some big box retail projects have been denied, in part, based on aesthetic considerations.

When the town of Henniker, New Hampshire said "Rite Aid, Wrong Town," one of the considerations the Planning Board listed was the aesthetic impact on the community and the "incompatible appearance" of the building in the middle of a residential neighborhood. One Planning Board member said, "The plan is too intensive for the site. Just because something is commercial doesn't mean any commercial venture is appropriate to any commercial lot."

Rite Aid took the town to court, but the Superior Court in Merrimack County ruled that, "A planning board may permissibly consider issues of safety, traffic circulation, lot coverage, and even purely aesthetic issues pursuant to the enabling act in granting or denying site plan review applications."

The Court pointed out that New Hampshire site plan review regulations permit planning boards to adopt regulations that "provide for the harmonious and aesthetically pleasing development of the municipality and its environs."

A New Hampshire newspaper editorialized after the Henniker ruling that the courts had helped determine "how far towns can go in determining and then protecting the look and feel of their own communities."

In October of 1996, the Nantucket, Massachusetts Planning Board turned down a proposal for a large supermarket saying that the structure was "a large, monolithic structure not in keeping with the character of commercial development in Nantucket."

In the North Elba, New York Wal-Mart case, the Planning Board said a large scale project was inconsistent with the land use code purpose "to promote aesthetic values" and "to preserve the character and quality of life enjoyed in the town at present." A portion of the proposed Wal-Mart was in a Scenic Preservation Overlay District, which was created "to provide regulatory power to the Planning Board to protect the view of Whiteface Mountain from this area, and the surrounding view, and the area's other scenic qualities." A similar issue of "viewshed" was part of the reason Wal-Mart was rejected in Ithaca, New York.

Perhaps the most comprehensive treatment of the issue of aesthetics and zoning is found in Vermont's landmark land use regulation, Act 250, which was passed in 1970. The law has ten criteria on which to judge developments. Criteria 8 deals with aesthetics, and states:

> Before granting a permit, the board or district commission shall find that the subdivison or development will not have an undue adverse effect on the scenic or natural beauty of the area, aesthetics, historic sites or rare or irreplaceable natural areas.

Developers challenged the legal and constitutional basis of this criterion in Court, but the Environmental Board and the Vermont Supreme Court have ruled that the aesthetic criterion is legal. When the state Environmental Board is analyzing an application for its aesthetic impacts, the Board first inquires whether there is an adverse aesthetic effect. Then, the Board has to determine whether any adverse impact is "undue." The most critical factor is whether or not the project "fits its surrounding context." Aesthetic resources protected by Criterion 8 do not just mean a pristine area of scenic or natural beauty. The Board has considered the aesthetics of "settled areas and farmlands" also. The term "aesthetics" has been broadly applied in Vermont to include natural beauty, visual harmony, and "peace and quiet" as aesthetic values. According to the Vermont Act 250 Handbook, the typical "Vermont scene" is a feature that the Environmental Board has protected under the state law:

> This scene usually consists of an open valley dotted with farms and traversed by stone walls. The hillsides are a patchwork of field and forest. From approaching roads, the heart of a nearby village is often marked by a white church spire projecting from its center. The Board has characterized this "typical Vermont scene" as open, rural areas punctuated by village centers — what it calls the Vermont settlement pattern.

Or, to paraphrase Vermon't Robert Frost: " Something there is that doesn't love a WAL."

Reinventing Local Zoning to Keep Out Sprawl

We have the choice to lead growth or follow it. In all likelihood, your town's zoning ordinance and Master Plan were written before anyone conceived that stores as large as 220,000 square feet would come before your Planning Board. The superstore movement is really only about ten years old. Your current code is inadequate or silent on the issue of big box retailers. It's time to dust off the ordinance and Master Plan, and bring them into the twenty-first century.

Instead of trying to defend our communities against Sprawl-Mart applications on a case-by-case basis, we can be pro-active to stop the megastores cold. Here are a dozen pro-active strategies that can stop sprawl in your hometown, and examples of where each of these strategies has been employed:

1. Neighborhood Commercial Zones: We can rewrite our zoning bylaws to create "neighborhood commercial" zones with smaller trade areas. We can require that commercial establishments demonstrate that their size and scope of business is designed predominantly to serve a neighborhood, or town-only customer base. Large retail establishments clearly could not satisfy this requirement. In Palm Beach, Florida, the community has created "town-serving zones," with the intention to:

> (P)reserve and enhance an area of unique quality and character oriented to pedestrian comparison shopping and providing a wide range of retail and service establishments, to be developed whether as a unit or as individual parcels, serving the short-term and long-term needs of towns persons. Further, it shall be the intent of this district to enhance the town-serving character of this area through use of limitations on maximum gross leasable area (GLA), thereby reducing the problems of parking and traffic congestion determined to result from establishments of a region-serving scale.

The Palm Beach code requires that applicants for a special exception use which exceeds district space limits must satisfy the Town Council that not less than 50% of the anticipated customers will be "town persons," which is defined as full time or seasonal residents or visitors living in accommodations and working in Palm Beach. The applicant has to demonstrate that the principal portion of anticipated customers will not be attracted from off-island locations. This ordinance was justified as a way to deal with the public problems of traffic and parking, and to limit displacement of businesses by larger, regional establishments. The "C-TS" zone in Palm Beach permits "a maximum of 2,000 square feet of gross leasable area."

2. Central Business Districts/ Growth Boundaries: We can focus future commercial growth in core downtown areas. If your local zoning ordinance and comprehensive plan indicate that this is a growth goal of your community, a developer has to comply with such an "infill" plan, because the courts will uphold such plans as a legitimate land use objective. In Rochester, New Hampshire, the city's 1993 Master Plan had the intent of "encouraging commercial and retail development of the downtown over expansion of old, or development of new, retail shopping centers." The Master Plan's objectives included 1) the revitalization of downtown areas to attract more business ventures and local and tourist shopping; 2) the improvement of the small business environment and 3) the promotion of growth and expansion of the retail sector. When a Wal-Mart proposal was dropped in Rochester's lap, a local citizen's group went to court and argued that building a new Wal-Mart two miles away from the nearest retail business area would directly contradict the intent of the goals and objectives of the 1993 Master Plan.

This same principle of designating a core business area can also be applied as a "growth boundary" in any community zoning code, which delineates an area of town where retail growth is permitted, and areas outside of the boundary do not permit such development to occur. Oregon has perhaps the best known "urban growth boundary" law, which was passed more than 25 years ago. The Oregon Land Use Planning Act provides for "an orderly and efficient transition from rural to urban land use." Local governments have the power to estimate how much land they need for economic development, for example, and then draw a bright line around that land to prevent additional development outside the growth boundaries. The goal of Oregon's law was to prevent sprawl development from encroaching on open spaces, and to encourage new "infill" development in urban areas, where the water, sewer and utility infrastructure was already in place.

3. Caps on Building Size: Your town can place strict caps on the overall size of retail buildings, and limit the square footage of first floors, forcing developers to build up — not out. In March of 1996, the City of Hailey, Idaho enacted a 36,000 square foot cap on the size of retail stores. In Skaneateles, New York, the town concluded that "it is appropriate and in the best interest of the town to reduce the size of "shopping centers" currently permitted in the town . . . and critical to the existing town comprehensive plan and the future welfare of the entire community to maintain the Village as the center of the township and to prevent the 'suburban sprawl' which has so decimated other townships." The town enacted the "1994 Shopping Center Development Criteria Amendment," which said:

> The site on which a shopping center is to be located shall be no smaller than five acres and no larger than 15 acres, excluding off-site landscaping. The size of a shopping center shall be no less than 15,000 square feet of gross leasable area, and no larger than 45,000 square feet of GLA.

In Westford, Massachusetts, where activists repulsed a Wal-Mart proposal in 1993, the town went on to close the door further, by enacting an amendment to their bylaws "intended to prevent construction of a very large retail development . . . and to provide a long and more thorough review period for retail buildings between 30,000 and 60,000 square feet." The Westford amendment stated clearly: "Buildings larger than 60,000 square feet gross floor area shall be prohibited."

In April 1999, the city of Clermont, Florida passed an ordinance limiting the size of retail buildings to 100,000 square feet. Wal-Mart was reported to be unhappy with the Clermont vote. "I don't think that they will let this stand because of the precedent it would set," warned Wal-Mart's lawyer.

4. Architectural Review Guidelines: Communities have the power to ban flat-roof, windowless boxes of dead architecture. This should be done by creating a section of the ordinance called "Architectural Review Guidelines." The city of Eureka, California, for example, produced in 1996 a sixty-three page

"Core Area Design Guidelines Manual" covering a fifty-block area of historic waterfront and downtown area, so that "any new buildings be compatible with the older more traditional buildings located in the Core Area." The community's goal was to "maintain and enhance the 'Victorian Seaport' flavor" of the area. The Eureka fully-illustrated manual covers such topics as "rhythm of facade widths," "perceived scale of structures," "pedestrian-oriented activity," etc. The manual warns the town to avoid "long, blank, unarticulated street wall facades." Unfortunately, when Wal-Mart brought plans to Eureka for a 130,000 square foot superstore, even though the company called their store a "downtown" Wal-Mart, it was located in a section of the waterfront that was outside the "core area" of the Design Guidelines Manual.

5. Economic Impact Analysis: Your town can reject projects which do not pass an independent public cost-benefit economic analysis — but you must add a section to your zoning ordinance that requires such an impact study to be conducted. This study should be underwritten by the applicant (Wal-Mart, Home Depot, etc.), but should be performed by an independent consultant chosen by the town, not the applicant. The best language on economic impact is found in a Vermont state law enacted twenty-five years ago, known as Act 250, the land use regulation law.

Under Act 250, a project of regional impact must be measured by a series of criteria, one of which is the extent to which a project will place an unreasonable burden on the ability of the local governments to provide municipal or governmental services. A mall developer, for example, must gather evidence of how the mall will impact the tax base in not just the host town, but in surrounding communities as well. A mall in Williston would cause neighboring Burlington to lose a substantial portion of its downtown retail businesses. Burlington would lose tax revenues as property values declined, and the mall would create an unreasonable burden on the ability of Burlington to provide municipal services. Under such circumstances, the mall could be rejected.

One former chairman of the state-wide environmental board that oversees the implementation of Act 250 listed ten steps that would be necessary for assessing the impact of a regional retail project on neighboring towns. These ten steps should be incorporated into every town zoning ordinance requiring an economic impact review by an independent contractor::

    1. Define the market area.
    2. Show the distribution of shopper's good sales in the market area.
    3. Determine future market growth.
    4. Project sales distribution without the applicant's project.
    5. Determine the applicant project's characteristics.
    6. Project sales at the project.
    7. Measure market changes caused by the project.
    8. Measure the loss of sales on commercial property values.
    9. Project the loss of municipal tax revenues.
    10. Quantify the impact of lowered tax revenues on municipal services.

Act 250 also requires an applicant to measure the cost of "scattered development" whenever a project is not "physically contiguous" to an existing settlement. A note in the law says, "Strip development along highways and scattered residential development not related to community centers can cause increased cost of government, congestion of highways, the loss of prime agricultural lands, overtaxing of town roads and services, and economic or social decline in the traditional community center."

When a developer tried to build a shopping center off Route 100 in Waterbury, VT, the Environmental Board ruled, "The Board concludes that the proposed project will not be in an existing settlement and will not respect the historic settlement pattern. Instead, the project has most of the characteristics of strip development and will likely lead to similar highway-oriented development."

6. Create Major Development Review Criteria: Developers will not present any data harmful to their application unless they are required to do so. All communities should have some form of comprehensive Major Development Review Criteria (MDRs). When my hometown of Greenfield, Massachusetts was confronted with a Wal-Mart development, we already had in place a set of MDRs dating back to 1991. Here is the stated purpose of the Major Development Review process in my hometown:

The purpose of an impact statement is to provide the Special Permit Granting Authority with sufficient information to conduct a detailed review of uses which have the potential for significant impact on the Town. The impact review process is intended to promote and protect the natural resources and aesthetic qualities of the Town, and to mitigate any adverse impact to Town services, traffic patterns, abutting properties, the economy of the Town, the character of the Town, or the public health, safety and welfare of Town residents.

Any town can decide what the threshold should be for determining who needs to go through an MDR process. When Greenfield created its MDR process, the threshold was any project that created more than 500 car trips per day. A building size threshold, such as 40,000 square feet, could be added as another threshold measure. Applicants who bring a project to town that exceed these standards must comply with the MDR process.

In Greenfield, an applicant has to produce, at its expense, an impact statement that covers four areas:

1. A detailed description of the proposed project and its design features, including existing conditions on the site, and in the vicinity of the project.

2. Identification and assessment of the impacts of the proposed project, including positive, negative, direct and indirect impacts.

3. An evaluation of how the project will meet the design standards required in these Rules and Regulations.

4. Proposed measures to mitigate adverse impacts and/or maximize positive impacts, including design modifications and provision of infrastructure or public service improvements sufficient to support the project. Any adverse impacts which cannot be mitigated shall be identified. Mitigation measures to be implemented by the applicant shall be identified.

The Impact assessment itself requires several standard features:

• A traffic impact study
• Impact on municipal utilities and services (water, sewage, storm drains, solid waste, emergency services, schools)
• Environmental impact (air quality, surface water, wetlands, groundwater, plant and wildlife, temperature, wind, noise levels)

But what is unusual in the Greenfield MDRs is the inclusion of the following two criteria:

- **Community Impacts:**

    1) Describe the impact on surrounding neighborhoods

    2) Describe the scale of the project, relationship to scenic views.

    3) Evaluate the relationship of the design to surrounding areas and prevailing architectural style

    4) Identify the impact on historic properties

    5) Estimate the number and types of jobs created and impact on existing employers

    6) Estimate spin-off development impacts, changing land use patterns, development pressure on surrounding neighborhoods, impact to the downtown business district

    7) Identify potential impacts to neighboring communities

- **Fiscal Impacts**

    1) Evaluate the projected costs and benefits to the community, including:

    - projected costs arising from increased demand for and required improvement to public services and infrastructure
    - projected tax revenues generated by the project
    - projected impact of the project on surrounding land values and any potential loss or increase in tax revenues to the Town
    - short-term and long-term projection of increased Town revenues and costs resulting from the proposed project

    2) Evaluate the market and financial feasibility of the project. Include any market studies for the project and any plans for phased development

Each of these areas of review have standards for the Zoning Board to employ when evaluating the response from a developer. Under "Community Standards," the project must "be compatible with the character and scale of neighboring properties." Under the Fiscal Impact Standards, a project "shall not have a significant adverse impact on the Town in terms of balancing as near as possible, the cost of public services and public revenues provided through taxes and other income." The project must also be designed "to minimize any negative impacts to adjoining property values."

When Wal-Mart came to Greenfield, they had to pay for a $35,000 impact study that showed, under a "high-sales impact" model, that their project would trigger the closure of 232,000 square feet of retail space — or more square footage than the three stores they proposed to build on the edge of town. The MDR process helped unveil the real impact of Wal-Mart on the local community.

7. Create a Commercial Acreage/Population Ratio: In St. Petersburg, Florida, when Wal-Mart proposed to build a 220,230 square foot supercenter, city planning staff recommended against the proposal in a November 1998 report. One of the criteria they used to reject the plan was an objective in their Comprehensive Plan that read, "The City's Future Land Use Plan and Map shall provide for identified future land use needs, and that additional commercial acreage is not required to serve the future needs of St. Petersburg. An oversupply exists based on the standard of one acre of commercial land for every 150 persons in the community."

The City conducted a report in 1996 for its Comprehensive Plan that showed St. Petersburg had one acre of commercial land for every 143 residents, lower than the standard of 150 persons per acre. The report also found that the City's existing supply of commercial land would satisfy resident's demands until the year 2010. The Planning Staff therefore denied Wal-Mart's request by arguing that adding more commercial land

> ... is not consistent with the objectives of the City's
> Comprehensive Plan ... the addition of 30 new acres of general commercial land use will exacerbate existing problems related to the over supply of commercial land. Job creation and tax base enhancement resulting from commercial development of the subject site must be balanced against compatibility issues, traffic impacts, and the need for additional commercial acreage within the City and especially at this time.

The existence of a commercial acre-to-population ratio allowed planners to point out that "conditions of community build out and slow population growth are evident," and that the Wal-Mart project "could result in increased vacancies" of business properties. The project in St. Petersburg was rejected.

8. Limit Locations for Large Scale Retail: Another way to restrict the location of big stores is to tie them to specific locations, which are limited in availability. In the city of North Olmstead, Ohio, for example, the zoning code permits superstores only when 60% of the property is within half a mile of an interstate highway interchange. What would make more sense is to write a town zoning ordinance that requires 60% of a superstore property to be located within half a mile of the existing downtown central commercial district. If such a restriction meant that only smaller commercial lots were available, then companies like Wal-Mart would either have to downsize their stores, or consider a footprint that stacked stores on more than one level, to be able to accommodate smaller lots. Wal-Mart has only occupied one store in the entire nation that has two stories.

9. Require Mandatory Referendum Zoning Ordinances: Some communities in Ohio have changed their City Charter to require that any rezoning of land for large-lot retail be approved first by a city-wide popular vote — plus a majority of votes in the ward or precinct where the project is located. North Olmsted, Ohio, which prevented a Home Depot from locating in an office park zone, approved the following charter amendment in May of 1999:

> Every Initiative or Referendum measure submitted to the voters, which involves the rezoning of any parcel or parcels of land in the city (must) be approved by a majority of the voters residing in the ward or wards of the City in which any part of the parcel or parcels is located.

An ordinance like this means that a developer could win a city-wide vote, but lose the project in the ward where it is located. This forces developers to woo local residents, and win them over with real concessions, not just minor cosmetic changes. In a number of towns surrounding Cleveland, for instance, the "majority ward" zoning amendments have been adopted. In Fairview Park, any change to a zoning text or map must be taken to a city-wide vote, and must pass in each ward where property would be rezoned. The same is true for Highland Heights, North Ridgeville, Macedonia, Twinsburg, Seven Hills, Solon and Strongsville. According to the Cuyahoga County Planning Commission, as of 1994 there were thirty-four communities with mandatory referendum zoning ordinance. The recent North Olmsted vote was backed by the mayor and passed with 87% of the vote.

10. Batched Zoning: Washington State's Growth Management Act, which was passed in 1990, requires local communities to engage in growth planning for a twenty year period. Once a local land use plan is adopted, any amendments to the zoning ordinance must be batched, and handled all at the same time — once a year. This forces communities to look at the cumulative impact of zoning requests, rather than a piecemeal "spot zoning" approach. If Kmart proposes a superstore in December, and Wal-Mart submits a superstore in March, the two projects would have to be considered side by side, and the impacts of both developments added together. This simple scheduling change in zoning requests improves the planning process by forcing upon it the discipline of coordination.

11. Enact a Moratorium: If your goal is to simply buy yourself more time, a moratorium on commercial development is a useful tool — but it only buys a limited respite from the pressures of growth. But a six-month moratorium can give a town enough time to develop an ordinance that will help guide growth in the future. However, a community must be careful to develop language for an ordinance that will not be challenged by developers or landowners. According to a Legal Memorandum for the New York Secretary of State:

> Moratoria have been upheld in New York where they are of reason-able and limited duration, where legitimate efforts are being pursued to enact or amend land use regulations, and where all procedural require-ments have been complied with . . . A municipality should consider allowing uses of property which will not frustrate the purpose of the moratorium and should consider providing a relief mechanism to ensure that some reasonable use may be made of property subject to a morato-rium. Today, the use of moratoria is very, very common, and the short-

est ones are least likely to be challenged.

The town of Pulteney, New York passed a moratorium on development for a period of three months citing the town's "unprecedented growth and development." The town decided that its lake shore and lake view land was the town's most valuable resource, and this land "may be in jeopardy if comprehensive land use regulations are not enacted at this time." The town empowered its Planning Board "to investigate and prepare comprehensive land use regulations for the Town of Pulteney as a means to develop the Town on an economical and environmentally sound basis." The Town Board found that:

> (S)ignificant development in Town prior to the completion of the planning process will substantially reduce the effectiveness of any land use regulations subsequently enacted and interfere with the ability of the Town Board to afford adequate facilities for the distribution of public services, comfort, convenience, public health, safety and the general well-being of the citizens of the Town of Pulteney.

The Town passed a moratorium that stated that for a period of three months "no applications for building permits or subdivision approval shall be accepted or considered by officials by officials, boards or commissions of the Town of Pulteney."

12. Tax-Base Sharing: Many developers have mastered the art of playing one community off of another by moving their developments like checkers across the landscape. Town warfare over property or sales tax revenue pits one community against another. This 'if we don't take them, another town will" mentality has helped build hundreds of malls across America.

The simplest solution to this revenue warfare is "tax-base sharing," and the most prominent example is the 1971 Fiscal Disparities Act in Minnesota. Officially known as the Charles Weaver Revenue Distribution Act, named after the state lawmaker who authored the bill, the Fiscal Disparities Act was developed to reduce differences in tax-base among communities in the Minneapolis-St. Paul metro area. The law allows cities and towns in a seven county area to share part of any commercial or industrial tax-base growth anywhere in the region – so that one town cannot gain by stealing another town's mall.

According to the *Minnesota Journal*, communities that are covered by the law contribute 40% of their commercial and industrial tax-base growth, above a 1971 base year, into a regional pool. Each community gets back a portion of that pool based on its share of population and tax base. Towns that have a low per capita tax base take more from the pool than they contribute, and those with relatively wealthy tax bases per capital put in more than they take out of the pool. For taxes payable in 1999, for example, the amount of tax base shared is based on commercial and industrial property values and property tax rates from the 1998 tax year. Taxes generated by the property tax pool are collected through an area-wide tax paid on the shared portion of each commercial and industrial property. These funds are then distributed to cities, counties, school districts and special districts based on the amount of shared tax base each unit was assigned.

There are 60 communities with populations over 9,000 listed in the twin Cities Tax-Base Sharing program. In addition, the seven county "Iron Range" region of Minnesota passed their own tax-base sharing program in 1996, covering Lake and Cook counties, much of St. Louis and Itasca counties and Aitkin, Crow Wing and Koochicing counties. The law is now in its second year of operation and provides for sharing 40% of the commercial/industrial tax-base growth since 1995 throughout the Iron Range area.

Tax-base sharing is an example of regional land use planning that eliminates the incentives for communities to rob Peter to pay Paul. Developers can no longer leverage support in one town by using their neighbors as bait. This also can prevent the proliferation of superstores, because tax-base sharing requires a regional approach to the proceeds from such development.

10

Buster's
Megastore Diet

*"They blame Home Depot for putting them out of
business. They can't blame Home Depot. It's not our fault.
It's really the consumer who did it."*
— **Bernie Marcus, Home Depot, December 15, 1997**

It is truly inspirational what some people will say about Wal-Mart, their red-white-and blue store. It's a form of retail patriotism:

• The woman in Clermont, Florida who went to a zoning hearing on a 187,539 square foot Wal-Mart superstore in November of 1998 and told officials: "Before Thanksgiving, I couldn't get whipping cream in three stores. If I had a Wal-Mart here, I would have had it."

• The man in Norman, Oklahoma who told City Councilors that "homeowners want to live where they can get full services." Full-service living in Norman, Oklahoma means the Wal-Mart three miles away on the east side of town is not close enough for the west side of Norman. Wal-Mart wanted to open up both stores on the same day, but citizen opposition has snagged their west side plans.

• The man in my own hometown who wrote a letter to the editor castigating me for blaming Wal-Mart for the loss of 22,000 jobs at the failed Caldor discount store:

Individual families are looking out for themselves. A person would be foolish not to take advantage of the best deal offered to them. Why would I, Mr. Norman, purchase a hedge trimmer from a local hardware store for $42.99, when I can drive a short distance to Hinsdale, New Hampshire, and buy the same product at Wal-Mart for $29.99? I'm sure you would have done the same . . . Just remember, Mr. Norman, when you go out this spring to purchase a lawn mower, a bag of fertilizer or a garden hose, the company you purchase it from. I'm sure you will look for the best deal.

In fact, if you factor in the gas and wear and tear on this man's car driving forty-four miles round trip from Greenfield to Hinsdale, New Hampshire — not to mention the hour and fifteen minutes of down time in the car — I'd rather walk to Carr Hardware in downtown Greenfield and look for a garden hose.

Hedge trimmers. Cheap underwear. Whipping cream. Mickey Mouse lawn furniture — the items will vary, but the message is the same: The Most Important Thing In America Is Getting The Best Deal! It doesn't matter how many people get laid off along the way, or what the real economic cost is to your town. Most of the people that I hear testifying for Wal-Mart or Home Depot have a sense of community that is no bigger than the dimensions of their own shopping cart. They want their whipping cream — and they want it now! An e-mail I received recently from a Wal-Mart supporter says it all:

> If you don't like Wal-Mart don't shop there. I envision an American culture where I can pull up in a drive through store and buy a pack of smokes, a bottle of booze, and a hand gun, and use them all before I get home!

There's a bumper sticker that is attributed to Wal-Mart that epitomizes this demand for "full-service" living:

"Outta My Way, I'm Going to Wal-Mart!"

At any point in time, there may be as many as several hundred citizen's coalitions across America fighting to keep sprawl-marts from coming to their town. Wal-Mart has become the main target for sprawl-busters — yet the problem is not Wal-Mart or Home Depot at all. It's us.

We, the consumers, are the real problem. Just ask David Glass, the CEO of Wal-Mart. He has said: "At the end of the day, the only vote that counts is the consumer's." His mentor, Sam Walton, said that small businesses were not like whooping cranes— they had no right to be protected. Walton actually bragged in his autobiography that he put out of business the old Ben Franklin store in Newport, Arkansas that he had once managed:

> As it happened, we did extraordinarily well with our Newport Wal-Mart, and it wasn't too long before that old Ben Franklin store I had run on Front Street had to close it doors. You can't say we ran that guy, the landlord's son, out of business. His customers were the ones who shut him down. They voted with their feet.

Bernie Marcus, Chairman of Home Depot, said in a 1997 interview with the *Home Center News* that blaming Home Depot for destroying small town America is just not fair:

> When you look at a graveyard full of . . . those folks (competitors) out there, the consumer wasn't very impressed with what they had. And they blame the Home Depot for putting them out of business. They can't blame the Home Depot. It's not our fault. It's really the consumer who did it. They just didn't want to shop there anymore.

Newspaper reporters often ask me if I shop at Wal-Mart, fully expecting me to sheepishly admit that I do. The truth is, I bought a bag of popcorn in 1993 at the Wal-Mart in Hinsdale, New Hampshire while I was on a fact-finding visit to check the store out. That's the full disclosure of my shopping at Wal-Mart. My entire family of five spent $0 at Wal-Mart this year. The bumper sticker on my car reads: "I don't shop at Sprawl-Mart." Target. Costco. BJs. Home Depot. Rite Aid. The logo really doesn't matter to me — the impact of these "sprawl-marts" are all basically the same. This "Wal-Mart: Love it or Leave it" attitude is the 1990s update of the "America: Love it or Leave it" movement of the 1960s. I agree with the sentiment completely. I DON'T shop at Wal-Mart or Home Depot. When a BJs Wholesale store opened up on the western edge of my hometown, I was quoted in the paper as saying "I wouldn't be caught dead in that store."

The personal solution to megastore sprawl is to go on what I call "the megastore diet." There are two things that we Americans do to excess: eat and shop. It's possible to combat both indulgences at once by going on a megastore diet.

We are what we shop. As the ad from BJ's Wholesale Club says: "You are what you buy." When we shop, we are doing much more than just making a purchase. We're making an investment. We have the choice to invest in a business that respects our community, or one that is bent on milking it dry. If we use our income to invest in companies that are wasting our hometown, then we've made a bad investment. Wal-Mart's appeal to you is as a customer. My appeal to you is as a citizen. My shopping cart can hold as much as yours, but I am increasingly fussy about who I allow to fill my shopping cart. I never thought there was a politics of shopping. Now I realize that everything I buy has a political value attached.

The decision to shop at a superstore, like Wal-Mart or Home Depot, may seem like a personal decision — but it actually can affect an entire community. Because of the "one size fits all" mentality of the big box retailers, citizens groups are actively fighting to protect the uniqueness of their towns. Overstuffed retail giants dominate the economic and social life of small towns, turning them into homogenized, faceless sprawlvilles.

The megastores have demonstrated over the last few years that they are increasingly unwilling to modify their behavior to meet local standards of acceptability. Local communities have become simply pins on a map to the developers and superstore owners.

We, as consumers, control the future growth of these companies. The bottom line for megastores is sales revenue. All of us as shoppers have the right and the ability to make a statement about what we value in our community by choosing where we take our business. Will we continue to invest in companies that disinvest in our communities? Will we fatten the companies that pursue a scorched earth policy against our own neighborhoods? Is our quality of life worth more than a cheap pair of underwear?

We, as consumers, are the real problem. For two reasons: 1) we have left our Zoning Bylaws and Comprehensive Plans wide open for developers and megastores to exploit, and 2) we have become a nation of binge shoppers, consuming Barbie Dolls and coffee filters as if there were no tomorrow.

We are in a unique position to go on a Megastore Diet. It involves no special preparation, no patches or medications, and we don't even have to deprive ourselves of any "stuff" that we want. Simply follow these diet guidelines:

• If you find yourself in a megastore parking lot, throw the car into reverse, and do a Sprawl-Busters U-turn out of the lot.

• Calculate roughly how much you spent at superstores this past month, and make the commitment to cut your intake by 25% this month, and 25% each month following until you have weaned yourself gradually from Home Depot or Wal-Mart.

• Exercise daily your right to shop at stores that do not waste land, locate on the edge of town, and cause severe economic dislocation.

• Send an e-mail to Wal-Mart (*letters@wal-mart.com*) once a month telling company officials how much you have saved by not shopping at their store.

• Push the "mute" button when any Wal-Mart, Target or Home Depot ads come on TV. This will help lower the craving to impulse shop.

• Encourage your family and friends to go on the Megastore Diet, too.

• Create a megastore support group in your community to help consumers who are fighting the addiction to superstore sprawl.

Tom Naminsky, an auto mechanic from South River, New Jersey, told the *Wall Street Journal* in January of 1999 that he shops at a local hardware store instead of Home Depot. "Why make big companies richer," Naminsky asks, "when there's someone around the corner trying to make a living?" Naminsky is a typical poster boy for the Megastore Diet.

In July 1997, Angela Francis, who is the wife of a Wal-Mart manager, explained the Megastore Diet succinctly:

"If a community doesn't want a store, all they have to do is not shop there!"

11

You Don't Need
A Shotgun

*"If I was a city father, and Wal-Mart wanted to move in,
I tell you what I'd do. I'd sit out there on the city limits
with a shotgun."*

— **Merchant in Livingston, Texas quoted in the** *Arkansas Gazette*,
March 15, 1988

You don't need a shotgun to stop a superstore.

There are other, more civilized ways to take down a Wal-Mart. As citizen's groups across the country have learned, it just takes a group of committed local citizens with energy and financing to trip up Goliath. When you take on a big box retailer, you are also taking on a developer and a landowner. All of these parties have deep pockets, and all are willing to try to use intimidation to get what is not possible through regulation.

But things are not as they appear at Wal-Mart. Behind that yellow, round-faced "Mr. Smiley" is the Great American Dust Machine. What we see at companies like Wal-Mart and Home Depot is only that small fragment of what the companies want to reveal.

We don't see the "hate board" where employees list businesses they're working to destroy.

We don't see the Asian children in Saipan "hotboxes" making Wal-Mart label clothing.

We don't hear about the 5,000 shoppers who are seriously injured each year shopping at Wal-Mart, or the customers who are crippled by Home Depot fork-lifts.

We don't read about the major fires that have taken place at Home Depot, inside these vast repositories of hazardous materials.

We don't know the landowners who lost their shirt when Wal-Mart abruptly pulled out of its lease.

All we know is that the megamerchants spend hundreds of millions dollars of shopper's money to depict a friendly giant, a good neighbor, where "good things happen."

But behind the relaxed, folksy image advertising, is a predator that has left its mark on Hometown America.

Things are never as they appear at Wal-Mart. A perfect example of this is the "People Greeter." Wal-Mart has prominently featured its "Greeters" as part of its corporate culture, and as a "classic example of associate empowerment." The Greeter story is a profile of what Wal-Mart calls a "dual purpose" — the superficial meaning of a word or policy, versus the corporate attitude that hides below the surface.

Wal-Mart employees are given this explanation in their Associate's handbook of the purpose for store "Greeters":

> The important position of People Greeter would not have existed in all stores if Sam Walton did not truly believe that the best ideas for our Company come from associates at all levels of the Company. The success of our Company depends on you and your ideas. You have the power to take your ideas as far as they can go!
>
> The Greeter idea actually came from a "store coach" in Crowley, Louisiana. Sam Walton and Tom Coughlin visited the Crowley store in 1980, and returned to the Home Office "with what (Walton) thought was one of the greatest ideas he ever heard. Sam took the idea from the store Coach and built a position that has become a trademark symbolizing customer service for Wal-Mart." The Greeter is Wal-Mart's peculiar form of "aggressive hospitality" — similar to Mr. Sam's "10 Foot Rule", whereby employees are instructed to "make customers feel welcome, smile, look them in the eye, and greet everyone who comes within 10 feet of you.
>
> But it wasn't just "customer service" or "associate empowerment" that

caught Sam Walton's eye. Compare another version of the Greeter story as it is told by Wal-Mart's Chief Operating Officer, Tom "We Make Dust" Coughlin:

> The first thing we saw as we opened the door was this older gentleman standing there. The man didn't know me, and he didn't see Sam, but he said: "Hi! How are ya? Glad you're here. If there's anything I can tell you about our store, just let me know." Neither Sam nor I had ever seen such a thing so we started talking to him. Well, once he got over the fact that he was talking to the chairman, he explained that he had a dual purpose: to make people feel good about coming in, and to make sure people weren't walking back out the entrance with merchandise they hadn't paid for. The store, it turned out, had had trouble with shoplifting, and its manager . . . didn't want to intimidate the honest customers by posting a guard at the door, but he wanted to leave a clear message that if you came in and stole, someone was there who would see it . . . The greeter sent a warm, friendly message to the good customer, and a warning to the thief.

Calling a "guard" a "greeter";
Calling 28 hours a week "full-time";
Calling workers with no job security "associates";
Calling an "anti-union" company "non-union";
Calling Chinese imports a "Buy American" program;
Calling a tax break for the company "life insurance" for workers.
These are all examples of the dual purpose behind companies like Wal-Mart. You can shrug it off and say, "That's just business. It's part illusion, mostly deception." But this is why more and more Americans see Wal-Mart as a bad neighbor.

Companies like Home Depot simply say it's war. Business is combat. That's what Home Depot teaches its managers. The company hired a training outfit called Afterburner Seminars to teach its managers how to prepare and carry out a business mission like fighter pilots. In 1996, Afterburner Seminars taught 1,800 Home Depot Managers the rigors of retail combat. The managers were divided into squadrons of twelve. A war game was simulated in which a country called "Lowesnia" was on the attack. To motivate its managers, Home Depot tells them that a coalition of competitors — Lowe's, Menards, and others — have banded together to destroy Home Depot's dominance over the home improvement business.

Fortunately, it is still possible to turn these companies away from your local community. "We did the impossible," Kathleen Warfield from Gilbert, Arizona wrote to me:

> The local newspapers announced today that Wal-Mart is pulling out of their site on Lindsay and Warner Roads in Gilbert. Life is good. I'm not yet sure what happened, but apparently Wal-Mart has dropped its proposal. I like to think it was because of our grass roots efforts (and noise) but we don't know for sure. Whatever the reason, they won't be in my face at least ...It was a lonely fight at times, because the town government seems so ready to buy what Wal-Mart is selling. Seems they don't really understand what really happens when Wal-Mart comes to town. For now, this obscene monster seems to be out of my neighborhood. But I remain "on guard" in case they try to inflict themselves somewhere else.

She thought it was impossible. But it wasn't. She slam-dunked Wal-Mart.

12

Confessions of a Sprawl-Buster

"You made me realize I like what you like."
— e-mail from Wal-Mart employee, April 1999

I'm not a crusader.

In fact, when my friends first approached me to help them stop Wal-Mart, I was a little irritated that they were distracting me from my other work. When the anti-Wal-Mart effort first got underway in my town, I sat it out. For months there had been an organizing effort to prevent our Town Council from rezoning the land for Wal-Mart. It was only after the Council voted to rezone that I was approached.

So I was late to joint the cause, and I can relate to those people whose initial response to a Wal-Mart or a Home Depot is one of indifference — because I was there, too. I had to be convinced that it made sense to fight these stores. I took the job of heading the Greenfield campaign with the assurance that the whole campaign would end twelve weeks after I signed on. Six years later, I am still fighting the battle.

Why the change?

Maybe its because I'd rather support the Little Guy than the Big Guy.

Maybe its because I like doing business with people I know.

Maybe its because I think Americans deserve more than one store.

Maybe its because I think communities should not all look the same.

Maybe its because I don't think anyone deserves Wal-Mart as a nightlight.

Maybe its because Wal-Mart makes a union job look like heaven.

Maybe its because I'm not ready to surrender my country to "Walmartians."

Maybe its because I think land is a finite resource.

Maybe its because I like buildings that have windows somewhere.

Maybe its because I think Wal-Mart knows the price of everything and the value of nothing.

Maybe its because my brother-in-law lost his job twice when Home Depot put smaller companies out of business.

Maybe its because I like a fair fight.

I receive a significant amount of mail from Wal-Mart employees. Some of them are off the deep end, or just profane. But recently one young Wal-Mart "associate" wrote me in defense of his company. His notes helped remind me of why I have become passionate on the subject of Wal-Mart. Here is his correspondence, and my reply:

April 14, 1999

I work for Wal-Mart and they care a lot about customers and employees. Times are changing, so go with the flow. If you don't like Wal-Mart don't shop there but don't make it so other people got to shop at the other higher priced stores.

Sincerely,

Eric

Wal-Mart Associate

April 14, 1999

Eric —

All I would ask you to do is read through my website "newsflash" page and see what is actually being said about Wal-Mart. I don't invent any of this stuff, it's all from local newspapers. I have nothing against anyone who happens to work at Wal-Mart, but I think the company is doing very destructive things to small towns. I also think that the quality of life in small towns is worth more than a cheap pair of underwear.

But thanks for your civil note. I get some Wal-Mart employees who just write me swear words and snarling. I guess it makes them feel better.

I also encourage people not to shop at Wal-Mart, and I don't shop at

Wal-Mart. But you're in luck, because millions of people are drawn by the promise of cheap goods.

Yours,

Al Norman

April 16, 1999

I can see where you're coming from. Where I live used to be a nice small town with a few stores. Now it is filled with chain stores and more crime. There really isn't nowhere to shop other than Wal-Mart but K-mart etc. They do put business out and really don't pay that great and only give 10% off, that's not much. They built the Wal-Mart where I'm at where ponds used to be so the birds lost most of their homes. I agree a town with a lot of small stores where it is a little higher but you get to know the people and not just sale ads, that would be nice. I know I would like it. I basically got to work there for a while so I can look for a good job and pay bills and such. You made me realize I like what you like.

Eric

Wal-Mart associate

This was not the response I had expected. I felt badly that my letter had arrogantly referred to the millions of Wal-Mart shoppers who would keep him in a job. Yet Eric responded by saying YOU MADE ME REALIZE I LIKE WHAT YOU LIKE! Here was a high school kid, making $5.50 an hour (as he later told me) trying to make ends meet with a part-time job until he graduated, and he was concerned that the "birds lost most of their homes."

There, beneath the thin veneer of Wal-Mart slogans, handbooks and rules, was the beating heart of an environmentalist and an anti-Wal-Mart activist! All the corporate training, and all the corporate "culture" could not rob Eric of his common sense: he liked small towns and he knew Wal-Mart was destroying them. For me, Eric's straightforward response was an affirmation that a little bit of education can go a long way.

I am also consoled that after six years of fighting sprawl, I am still a puzzle to Wal-Mart. The folks in Bentonville don't have a clue about how to respond to me. Almost every time a reporter has asked Wal-Mart about my criticisms of their company, they have attacked the messenger, even more than the message. Here's a recent example from the *Exeter News* in New Hamphire:

Wal-Mart: Crusader looking to profit at retailer's expense
STRATHAM – A Wal-Mart spokesman says an anti-Wal-Mart crusader who spoke recently to a Stratham group is out to make a profit from public speaking and that he makes unsubstantiated allegations about the national retail giant.

Keith Morris of Wal-Mart's corporate offices in Bentonville, Ark., said that Al Norman of Sprawl-Busters is out to get Wal-Mart and is making money from it …He's getting $2,500 to $5,000 (to speak to the Planning Board and citizen's groups) said Morris. "It's an anti-Wal-Mart strategy that he finds very profitable."

Jon Hanna, head of the Citizens for Stratham, said his group paid the Massachusetts consultant $400 to speak.

Morris also said Norman makes untrue claims against Wal-Mart. "A lot of the information that gets out by this individual…is meant to discredit Wal-Mart…and has no basis in fact," said Morris. "The information he puts out has all the makings of a Stephen King novel. It's not based on factual conclusions."

I can only assume from these now familiar attacks by Wal-Mart that they can only ascribe one motivation to most human behavior: greed. Perhaps that is because it is part of the Wal-Mart "corporate culture" to think in these terms. On an hour per hour basis, I could make more money by being a bagger at Wal-Mart than from busting sprawl. But behind Wal-Mart's words is the message that my voice matters to them. Sprawl-Busters has more than caught their eye. If sprawl-busters are so insignificant, why set the PR attack dogs on us? This huge behemoth, with over 900,000 employees and the largest retail bottom line in the world, sends out public relations hacks to compare my work to a Stephen King novel.

If one voice can elicit this corporate time and attention, then there is truly hope for all of us in battling these international conglomerates. Wal-Mart claims to have small town roots, but they have long ago forgotten what it means to live in a small town, and how people in a neighborhood relate to each other. Their girth has grown so large they can no longer see their feet. Sam Walton said in his autobiography that being big "has ruined many a fine company — including some giant retailers — who started out strong and got bloated or out of touch or were slow to react to the needs of their customers." Wal-Mart has been slow to react to the sense of outrage at the bulldozing of small towns and neighborhoods.

It is almost four decades since Wal-Mart was founded in Rogers, Arkansas. The company's icon is dead, and so is the company that said it would rather "walk away" from a community than "going in and creating a fuss." The "fuss" is now all around them, from Ketchikan, Alaska to Clermont, Florida. Wal-Mart and Home Depot have created a coast-to-coast fuss.

Sam Walton wrote that the secret to Wal-Mart's success was that "they went into small towns when nobody else would." The same can be said for the sprawl-busters movement today in America: We went after Wal-Mart and Home Depot when nobody else would. "Certain folks figured they could create a niche for themselves," Walton wrote, "a platform from which to express their views about small town America, by zeroing in on us." Walton had it totally backwards. It was WAL-MART that zeroed in on us. Years after Mr. Sam took aim at our hometowns, we are only now learning how to slam-dunk him back.

If I had the Walton family money, I would print this book and make it available to every American for free. Forget "everyday low prices." I would pass it out at Planning Board and Zoning Board meetings – gratis. This may demonstrate that fundamentally I don't have the mentality to be a mega-merchant.

Wal-Mart has said "Al Norman is a legend in his own mind."

I say back: "Wal-Mart is a legend in our mind."

Sam Walton understood where the real power of Wal-Mart comes from. When I went to Bentonville in 1998 with over 2,000 union activists, I walked across the little town square just like Sam must have done thousands of times. I looked up at Town Hall and saw these words chiseled above the entryway as I addressed the crowd:

"Sovereignty rests with the will of the people."

It was the will of the people that stopped Wal-Mart in my hometown. Nearly six years after Wal-Mart tried to flatten Greenfield, there are renewed rumors that the company might still be interested in locating here. When it comes to corporations like Home Depot and Wal-Mart, I have learned that you have to sleep with one eye open.

If you thought that my Wal-Mart story in Greenfield ended with our victory in 1993, you're wrong. The sad truth is that my hometown still has not taken the steps necessary to zone out big box retailers. We could very well face another rezoning battle, and another nail-biting outcome.

Two decades ago, small town poet Archibald MacLeish said the "spreading ruin of our countryside" was not inevitable. The key, he said, depends on "what the people think they are."

The future of our communities cannot be measured in shopping carts. Our personal environment cannot be purchased at a drive through window.

In his autobiography, Walton left us the first real clue as to how to stop sprawl in our hometowns:

"Our customers are supporting us. If they stopped, our earnings would simply disappear, and we'd be out looking for new jobs."

The goal of this book, and that of sprawl-busters everywhere, is to help Wal-Mart look for a new job.

We have the power to slam-dunk Wal-Mart.

FAQs

Ten Frequently Asked Questions

Q: Are there any differences in fighting a Wal-Mart versus a Home Depot, Target or a Rite Aid? Is one worse than the other?

A: There are no differences. Only the logo changes.

Q: How long does a sprawl battle take?

A: I have seen some towns drive out Wal-Mart in a matter of weeks, as in Walpole, New Hampshire or Brookfield, Wisconsin. In other cases, like Plainville, Connecticut or Lake Placid, New York, it took three or four years. In Chestertown, Maryland and in Keene, New Hampshire, the Wal-Mart debate has been going on at least six years. It is hard to determine at the beginning how long a fight will unfold — so it's best to make no promises about when the fight will be over. The longer the struggle, the better for the citizen's group, because the more time you have to educate people, the more anti-Wal-Mart they become. The advantage of a ballot question is that you know exactly when the campaign ends: election day.

Q: How many people does it take to have a successful citizen's group?

A: Your core group, who will make the key decisions of the campaign, should not be larger than around twelve people. You may end up involving more than a hundred volunteers to do everything from phone polling to pounding in lawn signs, but the Steering Committee should be no larger than a dozen or so people. A larger groups tends to be hard to keep focused.

Q: Is it a good idea to challenge a pro-Wal-Mart vote on the ballot?

A: Community groups should be conscious of the fact that Wal-Mart, Home Depot, Target and Rite Aid will spend a small fortune to win a ballot question. In Fort Collins, Colorado, Wal-Mart outspent the opposition by 24 to 1. In Toledo, Ohio, Home Depot spent $434,000 on one ballot question. The larger the population base, the harder it is for citizens to financially compete. That's why it is important to announce at the outset of any campaign your challenge to the Wal-Marts or Home Depots to leave their corporate money in their pocket, and let local citizens finance local ballot questions.

Q: How much money does it take to run a campaign against Wal-Mart?

A: It depends. To start off, I recommend that your group try to raise $20,000 as a goal, assuming that most of that will be spent on legal and technical expert fees. You should expect to retain a lawyer to work on your zoning case before local officials. That could cost several thousand dollars at the outset. Having a traffic engineer review the developer's traffic study could cost another $1,000 or more. Having someone review a developer's economic impact statement could cost several thousand dollars. If city officials rule in Wal-Mart's favor, and you take the case to court on appeal, you could spend anywhere from $10,000 to $60,000 or more in legal fees and technical experts.

Q: What about the cost of going with a ballot question?

A: If your city or town permits a voter initiative or referendum process, you can expect to need at least $30,000 to run a decent campaign in a community of 20,000 people or less. If the community is larger, the budget can increase considerably. Generally expenses are under $100,000. We spent less than $20,000 in our Greenfield, Massachusetts campaign against Wal-Mart in 1993.

Q: Do you recommend that a citizen's group become incorporated?

A: No. I don't think its necessary, unless your group plans to remain active after the sprawl battle is over. Some groups, like the Citizens for Responsible Development in Decorah, Iowa want to go on to address other issues like rewriting the comprehensive plan, or redrafting the zoning ordinance. But for most groups, it is distracting and time-consuming to incorporate as a non-profit group.

Q: Should I be concerned that Wal-Mart will come after my personal assets?

A: No. It is very unusual for a large corporation or a developer to go after an individual in a group. These so-called SLAPP suits (strategic lawsuit against public participation) are uncommon, and very rarely get anywhere in court. "Although suits against such individuals rarely prevail in court, their true goals of retaliation and intimidation are frequently accomplished," writes Attorney Dwight Merriam. Defamation, including libel and slander, are the most common claims that a developer will bring, accounting for roughly half of the suits.

There are also business-related suits involving contract interference or restraint of trade.

In the hundreds of battles I have seen, only one or two involved SLAPP suits by developers. I don't believe a company like Wal-Mart wants the negative press of going after an individual. Even if a citizen's remarks in a zoning debate are knowingly false, if the citizen is furthering some interest of social importance, like protecting his town from the negative impacts of sprawl, it will be very hard for a developer to get a court to find a citizen liable for his remarks. Citizens using their First Amendment right to petition government are largely protected from any civil action brought against them by a developer. A developer could file a SLAPP suit hoping that the suit will distract the opposition during the public hearing process, but it is unlikely he expects to prevail in court.

Q: Who should lead the citizen's campaign?

A: Anyone except a local merchant or a union member. I only say this because the average citizen will fall for the Wal-Mart argument that a merchant or a union member represents a "special interest" — as if Wal-Mart itself is not a "special interest." It always amuses me that Wal-Mart will call a union "an outside special interest," when Wal-Mart is from Arkansas. The best people to use up front in a campaign are well-known opinion leaders in town: a civic leader, a former City Councilor, a retiree, a "housewife." Someone who wears no affiliation on his or her sleeve. When I first fought Wal-Mart, they didn't know how to deal with me, because I was not a local merchant. To this day all they can figure out is that I'm trying to make money off their misery. The financial motivation must be the easiest thing for Wal-Mart to understand.

Q: Some businesses say they can survive a Wal-Mart. What do you tell them?

A: A public official recently theorized that after a Wal-Mart comes to town "in the long run, small stores revitalize themselves." It's a curious theory. The best response to the idea that small business can "survive and thrive" in the shadow of a superstore came from Donald Aronson, president of the Englewood, New Jersey Chamber of Commerce, and a former Mayor. When Home Depot suggested that merchants should "keep their eyes on their business" and develop niches or join buying cooperatives, Aronson replied: "Adapt means I can now eat half-rations because you're taking away half my food." Small businesses do not have to settle for half a loaf. If the "niche" you find becomes too successful, companies like Wal-Mart will start carrying your niche, and try to force you to move on. It makes more sense to proactively keep Wal-Mart out of town, than to spend years trying to continually adjust to their presence.

Appendix I

Sprawl-Busters Strategy Check List

Things Don't Just Happen

This list is an "audit" of your capacity to get organized at the local level to fight a large megastore. These items are to be reviewed by your core group of members, to assign people to work on matters that need to be done, e.g. fund-raising, media, etc. Every community is different, but go through each of these items to plan for your campaign:

1. Creating a Core Group: Two Options
   A. Look for what already exists in the community: a citizen's group, church group, civic group, taxpayer's group, environmental group, etc.
   B. Create your own group: from friends, a neighborhood, customers, etc. The key is that membership must be as broadly-based as possible and inclusive.

2. Basic Organization of your Group
   A. Selecting a name: factors to consider. "Westfield First": positive, we come first, developers come second.
   B. Size of group: Core group of twelve, build to active membership of fifty to sixty. Core group should consist of a mix of people: property owners, local business people, opinion-leaders in your town.
   C. Delegate labor: Prevent burn-out. For the tasks below, assign them to different people.

3. Issues Research
   A. Review town zoning bylaws and the comprehensive land use plan (Master Plan). Ask Planning or Zoning Board staff to explain the decision making process on zoning/land use issues.
   B. Get a complete copy of the applicant's proposal as submitted.
   C. Review your town's general municipal ordinance with your lawyer.
   D. Research who makes initial, and final, zoning-related decisions.
   E. Is there a citizen's referendum process in your town bylaws?

4. Time-lining the Campaign

Map out the expected timeline for your entire campaign. Understand who
makes the decision at each point, and rough timetable.

Decision　　　　　*Made By*　　　　　*Date*

Make sure you understand the timeline for your appeal rights.

5. Develop a Campaign Budget

Project what your major expenses will be: land use attorney, special studies
(traffic, wetlands, etc.), media ads, etc.

6. Resources to run a Campaign

A. Legal assistance — you will need to retain an attorney who has
experience with zoning and land use issues. Look for someone who has
worked with public interest groups before, or with developers.
Sometimes preferable not to hire an attorney from your town. Ask for a
couple of relevant references.

B. Paid coalition coordinator — you should budget enough funds to cover
a person coordinating your efforts (phoning, ensuring that fund-raising
is being done, etc.) Plan on a person assisting one day per week at
minimum.

C. Media spokesperson — assign one volunteer to be the main
spokesperson for your group with the media. Should be someone with
public relations background or good speaking ability and sense of
humor. This person should also be responsible for collecting all press
articles about sprawl in one place.

D. Local phone line — set up a new line, or use an existing one. This line
allows people to easily find you and offer their help. Many people will
not want to be visible, but will call to ask how they can assist.

E. Fund-raising committee — two or three people who will accept the
responsibility for soliciting funds to meet the coalition's budget. Should
be people with business roots in the community.

F. Treasurer — one person who will keep the books for the organization,
listing all income and expenses. Pick a person with fiscal background.

7. Getting Started

A. Press conference at the site – sound basic themes of neighborhood
character, saturation of land uses, traffic, congestion, promoting the
general welfare of the community.

B. Gaining visibility – Letters to the editor, bumper stickers, lawn signs. Media ads: display ads in print media, radio spots using local people. Local access cable: use of videos produced already, use of symbolism or a key sound bite. Special events/ speakers.

8. Public Hearings Strategies

A. Public officials behave differently when they know they're being watched. Have speakers assigned in advance. Leave little to chance.

B. Divide speakers to focus on certain topic areas.

C. Speakers should have short, concise statements: 2-3 minutes maximum.

D. Mix neighborhood people with merchants, opinion leaders, etc.

E. Speak to the heart as well as the head.

F. Present any rebutting studies about traffic, runoff, etc.

G. Have your attorney present to show you're serious about potential litigation.

9. General Campaign Principles

A. The Sprawl-Mart is the ONLY target. Do NOT attack or focus negative energy on any local person, newspaper, or other group. Always direct your remarks towards the Sprawl-Mart impact.

B. Use humor whenever possible. Be factual, but point out the absurdities of the proposal.

C. Be prepared to have pro-sprawl groups attending all your events. Never be negative towards your fellow citizens.

D. Use whatever facts you have against the project, but appeal to emotional issues as well: pride in community, uniqueness of this place, loss of small town life, loss of property values, etc.

E. Ask for equal time: if a pro-sprawl story appears in the newspapers, ask for equal time to present your point of view.

F. Think like a reporter: is there a local symbol, or sound bite?

G. Challenge statements from developers and Sprawl-Mart that their plan is good for the town. Ask them to prove it.

H. Grow your visibility. A campaign is an on-going event. It doesn't end with one hearing, or one newspaper article. Build momentum.

I. Assume zero knowledge: when you make a public presentation of any kind, assume your audience has no background about the subject of sprawl – because they don't.

Appendix II

Economic Field Reports: Dust to Dust

At Wal-Mart we make dust. The file on the Wal-Mart Dust Machine is growing, as evidence comes in from around the nation. Here are fifteen examples of economic impact reports from around the country, ready for you to copy and mail to your local officials.

Iowa State University, March 1989

An economics professor at Iowa State University released a study of the economic impact of a big box retailer on typical small towns in Iowa. "Some people misinterpret the sales changes after a Wal-Mart store comes into a town," the report concludes. "They observe an increase in general merchandise sales and in total sales and believe that all is well. But, upon further study, it is clear that the Wal-Mart gains are at the expense of other merchants." Stores selling apparel, building materials, grocery stores, specialty stores — all lost money to the big box retailer. Wal-Mart sales in the typical town increased by $10 million, yet overall sales increased by only $1.7 million. In other words, even though town sales increased, the large retailer's gains were at the expense of an $8.3 million loss to existing merchants. "My basic principle is this," explains Professor Ken Stone. "When Wal-Mart comes into a small town, they're going to take a big hunk out of the retail pie, and the size of the retail pie is virtually fixed. Somebody loses."

Amherst, Massachusetts, September 14, 1989

Two economic researchers release a report on the Fiscal Impact of Mall Development, a study of 9 malls in New England. Among the conclusions: 1) Malls create traffic problems and tend to increase far beyond the estimates provided by mall developers; 2) Malls create strip development. These strips cause increased traffic, use additional sewer and water capacity, and are typically a blighting influence; 3) Malls continue to grow after they are built:

if there is land designated as open space beyond that required by the community, one can expect further expansion some time in the future; 4) Malls disrupt downtowns, sometimes for as long as five to ten years. If the downtowns survive, they have a smaller retail base, are less active commercial centers, and cease to serve as the heart of the community; 5) Vacancies in downtowns will range from 10 to 20%. After the mall comes, higher quality stores in the central business district tend to be replaced by lower quality stores. The sale price per square foot in the downtown will drop, and taxes collected from downtown properties will decline.

DuPage County, Illinois, January 1992

A study by the DuPage County, Illinois Department of Planning concludes that property and retail sales tax revenues generated by new, regional commercial development, including superstores, will not cover the County's costs associated with extending highways and physical infrastructure, expanding service coverage (such as police, fire and ambulance services), providing financing, and offering development incentives.

Dedham, Massachusetts, April 8, 1992

The Homart Development Company abruptly withdrew its plans for a $140 million, 850,000 square foot shopping mall in Dedham, with 125 speciality stores and 3 large, unnamed anchor stores. Five days before Town Meeting was set to vote on rezoning 108 acres from residential to commercial, the developer bailed out. "I don't think it would have passed," the director of development told the press. The Dedham project was the second Homart project to fold in 1992. A mall in Hudson, Massachusetts was also abandoned. The developer offered the town $500,000 to build a new senior center. Concerned citizens against the mall showed charts indicating a dramatic increase in property crimes (larceny and auto theft) and car accidents the mall would bring. The local police chief said the mall would burden his small department. "The mall might be an upscale mall," Chief Dennis Teehan said, "but I can assure you that the thieves will not be." According to local citizen opponents, the mall would increase area traffic seven to eight times. The group also showed the impact of an existing mall on town services: The Dedham police budget increased nearly 100% within five years after the mall opened, and the fire budget increased by 50%. In years six through ten after the mall opened, police costs went up another 29%, and fire protection up 51%. The conclusion: "Even accounting for reasonable inflation over this ten year period, a 129% increase in the police budget, and a 101% in the fire budget is a simple indication of the effect a mall had on Dedham taxpayer's wallets."

Greenfield, Massachusetts, April 2, 1993

A $35,000 independent study underwritten by Wal-Mart indicates that under a "high-impact" scenario by the fifth year after opening, Wal-Mart would control 80% of the total annual retail sales in the town, and existing stores would have lost 64% of their sales. Instead of generating 270 new jobs, as promised, the retailer would create only 29 jobs. Greenfield would lose 232,000 square feet of existing retail business to the Wal-Mart mall. Roughly 49% of Wal-Mart's sales would come from existing businesses, for a total transfer of $37 million a year. The developer's projected property tax revenues are estimated to be only one-third of that promised.

Washington, D.C., January 18, 1994

The Congressional Research Service releases a report on the effect of the discount retail industry on small towns. The report concludes that for any community to evaluate the significance of any job gains created by large retailers, "they must be balanced against any loss of jobs due to reduced business at competing retailers." Retail jobs, the report notes, "provide a significantly lower wage than jobs in many industries, and are often only part-time positions, seasonal opportunities, or subject to extensive turnover...In short, it is easy to overestimate the true benefit to wouldbe workers and the local economy."

St. Albans, Vermont, December 23, 1994

The State of Vermont Environmental Board ruled that a proposed large-scale retail proposal "is likely to cause a job loss in the Franklin County region, and a negative impact on the downtown city of St. Albans." The Board found that "the credible evidence is that the proposed project will have an adverse impact on the tax base of the affected municipalities, due to competition with existing retail business." On an overall basis, the public cost of the proposed project was projected to outweigh the public benefits. For every one dollar in public benefit, there was $2.87 in public cost. The state study found that the retail project would cause local towns to lose state aid to education, create increased direct costs to the Town of St. Albans, reduce property tax revenues due to changes in the Grand Lists of four towns, result in regional job loss and loss of public funds which had been invested in downtown revitalization or preservation of historic buildings. Total public benefits: $109,400. Total public costs: $314,500.

East Aurora, New York, February 10, 1995

An overflow crowd of more than 500 people turned out in this town just outside of Buffalo, New York to oppose the conversion of industrial land to house a 228,000 square foot commercial project. The town had no other large parcels to offer existing industries that wanted to expand or to attract new industries. An independent economic analysis paid for by local citizens said that the Town's own impact report understated the negative impacts of the project. The independent study showed that 38%, nearly $30 million, of the sales at the new mall would come from businesses already located in East Aurora. The study also found that a total of $236,200 in property tax revenues would be lost annually due to the new project. The mall "will simply transfer sales tax revenues from one location in Erie County to another . . . Nearly no net gain at all is most likely." Finally, the impact report projected that overall retail employment in the region would fall "due to the higher sales per employee experienced in newer stores, especially megastores, as compared to downtown stores and older shopping center stores." A total of 329 jobs would be lost, the consultants said. By contrast, industrial use of the property "would not have an adverse effect on existing commercial properties containing retail uses."

Windsor, California, October 1995

A proposed 350,000 square foot mall in Windsor, including a Wal-Mart anchor store and a Home Depot was the subject of several impact statements. One study conducted for the town said that "in spite of increasing population, and an increasing number of retail outlets opening in Sonoma County, retail sales have been essentially a zero-sum game, with overall sales declining slightly. This means that any gains in sales by one outlet have come at the expense of other outlets, rather than through increased overall spending in the County...

(O)verall sales in the general merchandise category, which includes big box discount stores such as Wal-Mart, Kmart and Target, have not increased since the beginning of 1990." The study showed that Wal-Mart and Home Depot sales combined, around $92 million annually, would be greater than Windsor's total current retail sales...(The) resulting negative effects for these existing stores include reduced profitability and possible store closures...Even under a best case scenario, some existing retailers are likely to either close or see a decline in profitability."

North Elba, New York, January 1996

The Town of North Elba's Planning Board disapproved 3-1 the conditional use application for an 80,000 square foot Wal-Mart. "The Planning Board may consider the potential impact economic matters may have on the character of the community...Total jobs at Wal-Mart are estimated at 134, with 112 displaced over the short term in existing businesses...(P)otentially impacted square footage exceeds the size of the proposed Wal-Mart store...(T)o the extent that chronic vacancies affect existing downtown areas by causing fewer people to shop there, downtown merchants may be additionally impacted...having a significant adverse impact on the overall ambiance and appeal of downtown Lake Placid and Saranac Lake to tourists."

The Planning Board said this would result "in a net downward spiral in which increasing numbers of businesses could close their doors, further reducing the communities' desirability as a tourist destination...(A) substantially smaller store would have lesser impacts, since these impacts are scale-related... (T)he proposed project would not be consistent with the Town Plan to preserve the character and quality of life enjoyed in the town at present."

New Paltz, New York, March 1996

Four economic impact statements were prepared in New Paltz when Wal-Mart tried to build there. The New Paltz Planning Board released its finding that the trade area spending potential was $141 to $148 million, and that the proposed project would capture as much as $45 million, and cause a $29 million erosion of existing retail space, or a 21% loss of retail sales to existing businesses during the first year of the new store's operations.

"In the long term," the Planning Board wrote, "it is foreseeable that a decline in the viability of the three major existing plazas would produce secondary ripple effects on other local businesses and small plazas...(T)here will most likely be a net loss of jobs and income in the community because of the new plaza."

The Board found that the plaza would result "in substantial job losses, closed businesses, requests for property tax abatements, increased vacancies in the downtown and other retail centers, and would result in far less dollars in the local economy as a big box retailer consolidates its gains and expands...(T)he impact of underused, vacant or boarded up shopping centers could very well start a chain-reaction in a continuing contraction of investment leading to disinvestment and blight."

Iowa, May 1996

Economists Tom Muller and Beth Humstone published an economic impact report entitled "What Happened When Wal-Mart Came to Town?" Commissioned by the National Trust for Historic Preservation, the Muller/Humstone report examines three communities and seven counties in Iowa.

According to the report, Wal-Mart diverted sales from existing business in the counties studied, ranging from 77% of their sales, to 100% of sales. "There were clearly identified losses in downtown stores after Wal-Mart opened. General merchandise stores were most affected. Other types of stores that closed included: automotive stores, hardware stores, drug stores, apparel stores, and sporting good stores. Some restaurant closings also were noted."

Five years after Wal-Mart came to these Iowa towns, new stores opened in the downtowns of all three communities studied, but there was still a net decline in the number of stores downtown. There was no evidence to support the claim that Wal-Mart had boosted downtown shopping.

In the nine counties studied, about 84% of all sales at the Wal-Mart stores came from existing businesses. None of the nine cases studied was experiencing a high enough level of population and income growth to absorb the Wal-Mart store without losses to other businesses. "Wal-Mart believes, and its founder has stated, that the company has 'created thousands of jobs' in rural America. Such impressive gains would be a major boon to these small area economies. Our data, however, do not support this positive assessment. Although there is an initial increase in general merchandise employment in the year Wal-Mart opens, this gain is at least partially offset over time as employment in this category declines." Muller and Humstone found that the local tax base added about $2 million with each Wal-Mart, but the decline in retail stores following the opening had a depressing effect on property values in downtowns, and on shopping strips, offsetting gains from the Wal-Mart property.

Easton, Maryland, October 1996

The Urban Studies and Planning Program at the University of Maryland released a study of Wal-Mart's impact on the community of Easton, Maryland. Wal-Mart had opened in that town in November of 1991. The University study, which examined the impact on Talbot County, concluded that "numbers of establishments and employees have declined since the store chain's arrival in 1991."

In competing businesses, there was a net decline of 25 establishments (13%), a loss that researchers called "significant". From 1990 to 1993, overall employment in retail trade in the county fell by 5%, or 176 jobs. "However, looking more closely, seven of the thirteen industries that might compete with Wal-Mart experienced declines in employment totaling 435 jobs. This is a decline of 19%." The report says "it is likely that these job losses will continue as small merchants lose their ability to survive the competition." Based on these findings, the study concludes that "it would be very possible that total job loss could be significantly higher."

Concord, New Hampshire, November 1998

Richard Gsottsneider is the president of a consulting firm that does retail economic impact studies. It was Gsottsneider's firm, RKG Associates in Durham, New Hampshire, that conducted the economic impact study in Greenfield, Massachusetts, underwritten by Wal-Mart.

In an editorial published in *Planning* magazine, Gsottsneider warns that "municipalities pursue economic development with an almost religious fervor. What they don't consider is the overall real estate impact their economic development initiatives will have on the local tax base." He cautions that the danger "is that a community will neglect its existing tax-producing development – including older shopping centers and industrial areas – while public attention is focused on new development. Even if the new projects are extremely successful, however, they seldom contribute more than one or two percent to the tax base. Meanwhile, the existing tax base declines." This is exactly what happened in Concord, the state capital of New Hampshire.

Between 1986 and 1998, this city of 39,000 people added more than 2.8 million square feet of new commercial and industrial development. But during the same period, total assessed valuation dropped by 19%, from $1.9 billion in 1990 to $1.5 billion today. Gsottsneider explains the reason for this decline: "We found that the much-touted new retail development was a mixed blessing. While retail property values were relatively high in the major development corridors, they were stagnant in older areas, in part because of the new competition. In addition, commercial and industrial encroachment into some residential neighborhoods had a negative impact on residential property values. Because residential property represented 57% of the municipal tax base, the overall impact on assessed values was sizable."

Gsottsneider believes that Concord was so focused on economic development, "it was inadvertently undercutting the private sector and harming property values." The lesson from Concord? "A shopping center may be a boon for the community at large, but it may also have an adverse impact on other shopping areas. As a result, the community may gain tax base in one location, only to see values decline in another."

Kilmarnock, Virginia, January 1999

A new economic impact study from Kilmarnock, Virginia and the Northern Neck peninsula quantifies the likely impact of a proposed Wal-Mart superstore in this trade area. Written by economist Tom Muller, the report concludes that a 109,000 square foot Wal-Mart would have average sales of $330 per square foot, or total sales of $36 million. However, total retail sales in Lancaster County only totals $110 million. That means Wal-Mart sales would equal about one third of all taxable sales in the trade area.

The study suggests that Wal-Mart would draw roughly 25% ($8.5 million) of its sales from "leakage" — sales leaving the trade area for other stores. But the other $27.5 million would come from existing merchants. Of this total, $13 million would come from other grocery stores, and $14.5 million would come from general merchandise stores. The study notes that Wal-Mart's supercenter would "likely lead to the closure of at least one, but more likely two of the weakest Kilmarnock supermarkets."

"Were this to happen," Muller says, "the local shopper would have less choice than at present." Even with a larger trade area, "the market could not absorb an enlarged Wal-Mart. The result: closed stores that are an eyesore and reduced value as commercial property. The significance of this shift in retail activity is obvious. Wal-Mart pays property taxes, but the gain, in the absence of rapid market expansion, is offset — and could be more than offset — by reductions in other locations."

Appendix III

Hometowns, Not Home Depot
A Consumer's View of Home Depot

For community groups fighting Home Depot, the following profile of the world's largest building supply company should be shared with your local officials and with the media.

Not in Our Hometown: The Orange Wars

All across America, the headlines in daily newspapers describe a battle between citizens' groups and a company that one magazine describes as "America's most admired retailer." If Home Depot is so admirable, why are so many community groups and homeowners fighting hammer and tong to keep them out? Here is another side of Home Depot that you won't find in their Annual Report. Thousands of local residents are engaged in the Orange Wars — an effort to save their home towns from Home Depot.

Corporate Background

Home Depot, the company with the orange box logo and the cartoon carpenter with his cap pulled down over his eyes, is proud to tell you that they are the world's largest home improvement center retailer. As of May, 1999, Home Depot had 750 stores across 44 states, 43 Canadian Home Depots, 1 in Puerto Rico, 2 in Chile, and 9 Expo Design Centers. The company plans to add nearly 800 more stores "in the Americas" by the end of 2002. That's a new ribbon-cutting almost every other day somewhere in the hemisphere for the next three years. Over the 3 month period from May to July of 1999, Home Depot plans to open 35 new stores. Home Depot sales have risen from $19.5 billion in 1996, to $24 billion in 1997, and $30.2 billion in 1998. There are now more than 181,500 people working for Home Depot, up from 67,300 in 1994. By 1997, Home Depot controlled 66 million square feet of selling space.

According to its report to the Securities and Exchange Commission in December 1998, Home Depot conducted 1.8 million transactions per day at its stores, with an average sale of $45.62 per transaction. The typical Home Depot store rang up $847,000 in sales per week, or $44 million a year in business. Sales per square foot averaged $412.

Home Depot was founded by Bernie Marcus and Arthur Blank, who tell their employees that they were fired from Handy Dan, a California company. Bernie was the President of Handy Dan, Arthur was vice president for finance. They didn't like how Handy Dan operated, so they started a new company called Home Depot, which opened its first stores in Atlanta in 1979. Home Depot notes that Handy Dan is a "former home center retailer" that is now out of business largely because of Home Depot.

Home Depot is targeted primarily towards DIYs: do-it-yourselfers. The new concept was to create a store that made you feel like you were in a wholesale warehouse, which Home Depot describes as a "no frills environment with a simple merchandise presentation that reduces overhead costs and allows us to pass those savings on to the customer in the form of lower merchandise prices." The typical Home Depot has eleven departments (lumber, building materials, flooring, paint, hardware, plumbing, electrical, lighting, garden, kitchen and bath, millwork, and decor). The average store is 105,000 square feet.

Home Depot has a three part merchandising philosophy: 1) good customer service, 2) low day-in, day-out (DIDO) pricing, and 3) a large assortment of stuff. "If a competitor does offer a sales price lower than our DIDO price," Home Depot says, "we meet and BEAT that price."

In addition to the DIY (do-it-yourself) market, Home Depot has two other kinds of customers: BIY (buy-it-yourself) customers who don't have the time or expertise to install materials, and PBC (professional business customers) who need truckloads of materials delivered to their site.

The Home Depot Culture: Orange-Blooded

Home Depot describes its own corporate culture as "definitely a feeling — it is commitment, belief and faith." Employees at Home Depot have been described as "orange-blooded," and it is clearly important to the company to make its workers true believers in the culture.

Home Depot's corporate culture appears modeled on Wal-Mart. In fact,

Home Depot has been described as "Wal-Mart with a hammer." Here are some examples of how the corporate culture in Atlanta and Bentonville are similar:
- Their founders are given revered, messianic status: Sam, Bernie, Arthur.
- Customer Service Hype: Sam Walton's ten foot rule (if you come within ten feet of a customer, greet them) is expressed at Home Depot as: "we never walk by a customer without speaking."
- Everyday low prices (ELP) versus day-in day-out pricing (DIDO).
- Calling employees "associates."
- Wal-Mart says the customer is the boss. Home Depot says "only a Store Manager may ever say 'no' to a customer."
- Both companies are pursing a saturation strategy – locating stores as close as seven miles apart. Both companies have an ambitious projection of new store openings.
- Both companies depend on a low mark-up/high volume discount image.

War-Like Environment: Death to the Competition
Two examples of Home Depot culture will help explain the attitude that exists inside corporate headquarters:

The Tombstone Affair: At the Colma, California store (#624), associates wore t-shirts with the motto "Colma Buries the Competition With Day-In Day-Out Low Prices and Great Service." The logo bore a picture of Homer, the Home Depot cartoon carpenter, leaning on a grave-digger's shovel, next to four tombstones, with R.I.P. on each marker. Home Depot's main competition each had a tombstone, included Pay N Pak, which had been put out of business. One manager from a competitor store says he saw such tombstone t-shirts elsewhere. "I have seen these MARKERS in front of stores in Colma and Fremont...the idea that Home Depot wants to coexist with other area stores is almost insulting to us who compete with them." Since Home Depot opened in the Pittsburgh (Pennsylvania) area, the local True Value store, in business since the 1930s, has disappeared; two local nurseries, a flooring store, and a landscape supply yard are also gone or sold.

Afterburners: Business is Combat. That's what Home Depot teaches its managers. Home Depot uses a training company called Afterburner seminars to teach its managers how to prepare and carry out a business mission like fighter pilots. In 1996, Afterburner Seminars taught 1,800 of Home Depot's managers. First, they conjure up a scenario that threatens Home Depot. The managers then divide into squadrons of twelve. The enemy is "Lowesnia", after Home Depot's competitor Lowe's. Home Depot said it chose Afterburner to train its management team because the retailer wanted to instill a sense of teamwork and reinforce competitive spirit. To do this, managers are told that a coalition of competitors — Lowe's, Builder's Square and Menards — have banded together to destroy Home Depot's dominance over the home improvement business.

Home Depot As Competitor: Saturation

The signs are obvious. The home improvement industry's retail food chain is being eaten from the bottom up. The mom and pop stores withered, and now the regional chains are dying. Companies like Rickels, Handy Andy, and Grossman's are history. In 1993, after one year in the Chicago market, Home Base closed all its stores and transferred its leases to Home Depot. "The smaller regional players are getting squeezed," said an analyst with Brown Brothers Harriman. "They are banding together or getting out entirely, or shrinking back to a base where they think they can continue to exist."

"Local merchants have no choice but to give way," a market analyst with Hancock Institutional Equity Services told the *Christian Science Monitor.* "Regional chains and small independents are likely to feel increasing pressure to merge with rivals, or quit," said the *Wall Street Journal* in January 1997. It has been Home Depot's mission to "bury" its competition. James Inglis, former Executive Vice President for Home Depot noted that "Orchard Supply (in California) proved to be one of the few regional chains Home Depot failed to take a real bite out of."

Grossman's is a perfect illustration of what has happened in the home improvement market. Its service area is littered with orange-and-white striped empty stores. Grossman's at its peak in 1983 once controlled 345 stores, but went into Chapter 11 in January 1997.

There is no question that Home Depot dominates the home improvement market. As *Countryside Retailing* magazine put it: "Having almost saturated the major metro markets, the company is seeking new avenues of growth. President Arthur Blank announced in May of 1994 that Home Depot is developing a store prototype 'which we think will be more appropriate for rural America.' He could not say how large the stores might be."

As an analyst for Citicorp Securities told the *Wall Street Journal* in January of 1997: "Home Depot and Lowe's are going to make it very difficult for anybody else to get in."

Napa: A Case In Point

In most towns it enters, Home Depot has not been challenged to show how its need for $41 million in sales will impact other area businesses. But a significant amount of register sales at Home Depot are "captured" from other competitors. In Napa, California, for example, the developer of a Home Depot claims that the area is under-retailed, yet acknowledges: "There's only so many retail dollars around."

In fact, according to the city's 1996 General Plan, Napa's market capacity for building supply goods was $38 million in 1993. This means that the addition of a store with sales of $41 million would more than double the entire sales capacity of the community. The same studies show that Napa has very little "leakage" of shoppers going outside of the area to purchase building supplies. "For building materials, the recapture is low, since these store categories currently display a limited leakage of sales to other areas." In other words, for Home Depot to succeed, it will have to largely cannibalize sales from other merchants. Because Home Depot already has stores in Vallejo, Fairfield, Rohnert Park, San Raphael, and El Cerrito, it will "import" little or no new business into Napa. As much as 70% of the expected building supply sales at the proposed Marketplace would be shifted from other businesses, creating a form of economic displacement — rather than economic development. Simply stated, what Home Depot brings to Napa, is already there. Although residents and merchants banded together to fight Home Depot in Napa, a store was eventually built.

Market Share: The CASH study

There is very little published data that examines the market dominance of Home Depot. One survey, however, provides useful data in a market with roughly a quarter of a million adults. For the past seven years, the *San Diego Union-Tribune* has been conducting its "CASH" study of market share in the building supply industry. CASH stands for "Continuing Analysis of Shopping Habits in San Diego." Based on interviews with 3,600 households annually, the

CASH study shows Home Depot gaining significant market share of commonly purchased products.

• In the 1996 study, for example, 50% of the consumers surveyed said they had purchased exterior paint in the last twelve months from Home Depot. This is an increase from 26% of the market in 1990. The nearest competitor had a market share of 12.6%. Home Depot had nearly four times the market share of its nearest competitor.

• For interior paint, Home Depot increased its market share from 27% in 1990 to 48% in 1996. Its nearest competitor had only 13% of the market.

• For hardware and building materials, Home Depot moved from 60% market share in 1990 to 75% in 1996. Its nearest competitor was Home Base, at 8%!

• For hand or power tools, Home Depot rose from 28% market share in 1990, to 45% market share in 1996. Its closest competitor was Sears, at 24%.

• For plant, lawn or garden care products, Home Depot increased from 26% share in 1990, to 51% share in 1996. Its closest competitor had less than 10% of the market.

Studies like this indicate that most communities should expect to see significant competitor losses when a Home Depot comes to town. For this reason, it is imperative that communities conduct a market capacity study to understand their market potential, before they take action on a Home Depot proposal. Communities are increasingly asking the applicant to underwrite the cost of an independent analysis of market capacity and Home Depot economic impact on property taxes and sales revenue generated at other businesses.

No other home improvement company is positioned to add 100 new stores to its base. As seen in locations like Napa, California, Reno, Nevada and Nashua, New Hampshire (see stories below), Home Depot is positioning stores only a few miles apart, hoping to reach the enviable position of competing with itself for market share. In this regard, Home Depot does not represent healthy competition. It represents a dangerous drive towards monopoly.

Home Depot As Employer: The X-Files

Home Depot places great emphasis on its workforce. "Our people set us apart from our competitors," they brag. Sounding like an episode from the X-files, Bernie Marcus explains, "The Home Depot culture is passed on generation to generation of orange-blooded associates."

Yet people who come to work for Home Depot have no job security, and are, in fact, employees at will. Here is an excerpt from the Home Depot Associate's Guide: "As an associate of Home Depot, your employment is guaranteed for no set definite term, and you have the right to terminate your employment at any time, at your convenience, with or without cause or reason. Understand that Home Depot also has this right."

In other words, the company can let you go any time, without any justification or cause. The company's termination policy also includes a "reduction in force" policy, in which an associate is involuntarily discharged because the company is down-sizing. "Home Depot plans and schedules to keep RIF terminations to a minimum," the handbook explains.

Home Depot employees can also be subjected to "substance abuse" drug tests, and this extends to prescription drugs. Any employee who tests positive for a prescription drug, but does not have a written prescription, will be terminated.

Home Depot employees must also agree to submit to "a search of personal belongings while on company property." Each employee is issued a locker for storage of personal and company-issued equipment. Personal locks are prohibited. "Home Depot reserves the right to search associate lockers."

Female employees at Home Depot are allowed to wear skirts, but they cannot be shorter than three inches above the knee. Clothing which reveals midriffs, cleavage, or shoulders is not allowed. No spandex, or exercise clothes are allowed. No t-shirts are allowed.

For male employees, hair must be neat, clean, and "conservatively styled." Beards, mustaches and sideburns must be kept "neatly trimmed."

Cashiers: Trapped

Here is how an inter-office Home Depot memo describes their cashier's position: "In our culture of customer service, the cashier is ALWAYS in the spotlight. A cashier is trapped in their assigned three by five foot area and can't even go to the bathroom without permission. They are put into this incredibly stressful situation and told that they are to remain upbeat, positive and superefficient for eight hours a day. They are the gatekeeper. They are the last person the customer has contact with, so they've got to be the best performer in the store to leave the customer with a positive impression."

The Glass Basement

Home Depot assures its employees of its commitment to an Equal Employment Policy. "The company will not, under any circumstances, discriminate against an associate with regard to race, age, sex, color, national origin, religion, or disability," says the employee manual. But here's what has happened in practice:

• Several hundred thousand women employees and applicants claim that Home Depot has trapped them inside a glass basement of employment discrimination. The Depot was actually facing at least three such lawsuits.

• In March 1997, the United States Supreme Court refused to stop a huge class-action lawsuit encompassing current and former employees and job applicants in the Home Depot Western Division, covering 150 stores.

• In the same month, the federal Equal Employment Opportunity Commission moved to intervene in a 1995 lawsuit covering 310 Home Depot stores east of the Mississippi. A third lawsuit was pending in New Jersey. This was the largest sex discrimination case the EEOC has ever taken on. The Home Depot response? Home Depot said it was "puzzled and outraged" that the federal government has intervened in a class-action sex discrimination lawsuit against the nation's largest building supply retailer.

As of 1998, ^5% of the employees at Home Depot were men, 35% were women. Only 18% of Home Depot's officers and managers are women. There were 5 male managers for every 1 female manager. Discrimination against Home Depot was alleged in hiring, job placement, training, promotions and compensation. An attorney with the EEOC said: "While Home Depot has a glass ceiling, it traps its female employees in what amounts to a glass basement, with glass walls." According to the EEOC, "in too many instances, women at Home Depot were hired only for jobs such as cashier's positions — but not others."

The company told reporters: "We are very proud of our record of hiring and promoting women to every level in the Company." In a memo to employees entitled "What We Are Committed To," Home Depot's management said: "The Home Depot is not going to bend to the pressure of those who seek to capitalize on our success — and your success — so that they can pursue their own self-interested agendas . . . (W)e are fully confident that the truth will ultimately be realized by all — that there is no better place for women and men to work than The Home Depot."

In September of 1997, Home Depot announced that a federal District Court Judge in New Orleans had approved a settlement agreement in the gender discrimination lawsuit and other class action lawsuits. The agreement cost Home Depot $104 million, of which $65 million went to the women plaintiffs in the lawsuits, $22 million went to the lawyers, and $17 million to pay for internal improvements to Home Depot's human resource programs. "We are committed to putting these lawsuits behind us," said Bernie Marcus, "and focusing everyone's attention on what we do best — serving our customers, providing outstanding returns to our stockholders, and growing our business." Home Depot said the $104 million settlement had left Home Depot's "unique culture" intact.

Recycling Employees

Home Depot made headlines in 1995 for firing a janitor in its San Jose, California store because he spent 10 minutes of his workday separating recyclable garbage. Home Depot was besieged with 120 calls from supporters of janitor Bard Reynolds. Four members of the San Jose City Council introduced a proposal to require large companies like Home Depot to recycle garbage, and the city's recycling department offered the company a free environmental audit to set up a better program.

Overtime Pay: Employees Are Abused

Zaira Guerrero was recruited by Home Depot out of college. She began as an associate manager in Home Depot in Miami. In theory, she was in training. In practice, she worked 70-hour weeks for a fixed annual salary of $24,000. "I was in training a year and a half. I had the manager title," she said. "Overall, I was doing regular employee work — helping customers on the floor, stocking shelves, even being a cashier when they needed one." It wasn't until Guerrero left Home Depot in 1994 that she questioned whether the company owed her overtime pay. After she filed a complaint, the United States Department of Labor investigated Home Depot's associate manager program nationwide. It took more than two years to reach a settlement, which entitled Guerrero to

$4,205.55 — a fraction of what she figured her overtime pay would have been worth. By then, the two year statute of limitations had run out, so Guerrero no longer had the option to sue Home Depot. The company says it worked closely with federal officials to answer their concerns. Home Depot now says that it makes sure that associate managers don't work more than 40 hours a week. "Employees don't know their rights, and they are being abused," says Guerrero.

Home Depot as Philanthropist: 29 cents per week

Every Home Depot store has a budget for making contributions to local community organizations, says the company. Its workers "volunteer their time to make our communities better places to live."

"We do more than just hand out checks to charities," says Home Depot, "we help make advances in community service, environmental concerns," etc. The fact is, Home Depot says it contributed $8.6 million to charity in 1996, a year in which total sales exceeded $19.5 billion. In 1999, Home Depot's philanthropic budget was $15 million based on sales of $30.2 billion. By comparison, if a family with $35,000 annual income gave at the same rate as Home Depot, it would equal a donation in the church plate of 29 cents per week. Not much to write home about.

Furthermore, half of many gifts come from the workers, not from the company. Under the "matching gift" program, the worker's gift is matched 50 cents on the dollar by Home Depot. The "Team Depot" program is a group of employees in a store that offers its time to work on a community project. Workers are reminded that Home Depot does not pay for time spent helping the community: "Participation in Team Depot takes place during your personal time."

Home Depot does not allow "non-associate groups," like the Girl Scouts, church groups, Boy Scouts, the military, etc. to raise funds on Home Depot sidewalks or parking lots.

And finally, sometimes charity begins at home — Home Depot, that is. In 1997, Home Depot gave a charity called Christmas in April, $265,000 in merchandise credit. Christmas in April then spent $878,000 at Home Depot, giving the company a more than three to one payback for its "charity."

Home Depot As Environmental Citizen

Groups like Greenpeace and the Rain Forest Action Network have been hammering away at Home Depot for years on the subject of "old growth" lumber. Environmental groups charge the Home Depot has become the world's largest retailer of products made from old growth lumber. In November of 1998, when Home Depot was assailed on its old growth lumber policy, the company responded in typical megacorporate fashion: it's not our fault. "We don't cut down any trees," said Home Depot spokeswoman Suzanna Apple. "We don't manufacture any products . . . We sell 50,000 products. It's difficult for us to know, difficult for anyone to know, the content of products in our store."

The company said criticism of its policies to sell old growth products was, therefore, "misdirected." When 40 demonstrators protested outside of its Rohnert Park, California store in August of 1998, Home Depot again took an evasive position on the issue. A Home Depot spokesman told reporters "different groups define 'old growth wood' differently . . . the term need defining." At Home Depot, environmentalism comes with a dictionary.

Taking Care of Customers: Poor Citizenship

Home Depot says that "taking care of customers is our #1 priority." Home Depot took care of Soon Kim — but not the way she expected.

According to a personal injury lawsuit filed in April, 1997 in King County, Washington. Superior Court, Kim, a 51 year old woman, suffered a traumatic head injury shortly before Christmas in 1995 at a Tacoma Home Depot.

Kim went to the Home Depot that day in search of supplies for her kitchen remodeling. She asked a Home Depot employee to retrieve a cabinet door located high above the sales floor. Climbing the shelving units to reach the item, the employee slipped and lost his footing just as he was pulling the door off the shelf. He dropped the heavy door on Kim's head, and then landed on top of her as he too plunged to the sales floor ten feet below. Kim was knocked unconscious. Home Depot's assistant manager was called to the scene, where he took a photograph of Kim. Kim's lawyer says Home Depot did not offer to to assist Kim out of the store, and did not call an ambulance. Kim left 15 minutes after the accident. On the way home, she could not remember how to get to her residence. Once home, she complained of a headache and felt dizzy. She has no recollection of the doctor's visit she made that afternoon.

Her lawsuit seeks damages from Home Depot to pay for her medical expenses, which have reached $25,000 and are climbing, plus pain, suffering and loss, as well as lost earnings. Kim's seventeen-year-old son says his mother has been unable to work since the accident and can no longer drive a car. "She simply can't remember how to get home," he said. Kim's lawyer says that despite Home Depot being clearly negligent for these injuries, the company has refused to help with any of her medical bills. "The corporation is aware of Kim's financial situation, and figures they can reduce their financial exposure by forcing Kim into a premature settlement. This is a prime example of poor corporate citizenship on the part of Home Depot." Home Depot's "adjustment policy" is reportedly not to pay medical bills of injured customers until the victim agrees to settle the entire case.

The Home Depot store in Tacoma reportedly has a history of safety violations. In 1996, the Washington State Department of Labor and Industries fined the store after an inspection revealed "serious" violations related to faulty electrical equipment. That same inspection revealed the store had no plan in place to report unsafe conditions — such as the practice of climbing store shelving.

In the past few years, there have been thousands of injuries at retail warehouses, some fatal. Home Depot says that "no one is more important than our customers." Washington State Inspector Mark McHarg says: "I don't particularly like walking up and down the aisles in most stores because of my experience with it."

Taking Care of Customers: "You Got That Right"

According to a media story in the December 18, 1995 issue of the *Fairfield County (Connecticut) Business Journal*, in November 1995, a lawsuit was filed in Stamford, Connecticut Superior Court, claiming that two Home Depot employees at a Danbury store refused to accept a customer's return of a $155 thermostat. The lawsuit claims that the Home Depot employees called a Jamaican-born customer a "nigger" and threatened to beat him. According to the suit, the customer did not have a receipt for the thermostat and was not offered a refund or a store credit. The plaintiff claims he saw a white woman exchange merchandise for cash without a receipt. The customer claims he told a Home Depot employee: "I bet if a white person were returning this thermostat, you wouldn't give them such a hard time." To which, the Home Depot employee is alleged to have responded: "You got that right."

After some arguing took place, another Home Depot employee came over, and the customer stated "he had no intention of leaving the store until this matter was taken care of." The customer claims that the second Home Depot employee said: "If you don't shut up, I'm going to kick your black ass and have you arrested."

The customer says he was "crying, humiliated and extremely upset." As he was leaving the store, he told the Home Depot employees: "You'll hear from my lawyer," to which the second employee allegedly replied: "Whatever, nigger."

The lawyer representing the customer says he can't sue Home Depot on civil rights grounds, because a private company can discriminate as much as they want to. Instead, the claim was filed as an unfair trade practice, because Home Depot did not follow their own return policy, which permits returns of merchandise without a receipt in exchange for a store credit. Customers must have an ID for record-keeping purposes, and can't make more than three claims in any twelve-month period.

Fire Danger at Home Depot: Clouds of Hazardous Smoke

Communities considering a Home Depot application need to seriously examine their fire-fighting capacity. In May 1995, a fire broke out at the Home Depot in Quincy, Massachusetts. *The Patriot Ledger* described the fire this way:

> Burning stacks of fertilizer, pool chemicals and plastic lawn furniture at Home Depot created billowing clouds of toxic smoke that sent dozens of firefighters to local hospitals last night...The fire created a toxic mix of hydrogen chloride and other gases...Every firefighter who went into the building was washed down at a decontamination station in the parking lot...two school buses and 15 ambulances were called to take firefighters and police officers to hospitals.

The smoke was considered hazardous enough to call the 26 members of the regional hazardous materials team. The firefighters were fighting chemicals that could have caused burns on exposed skin. The crush of customers in the parking lot hindered the arrival of fire engines and ambulances.

According to reports, because of the way Home Depot stacks its merchandise, much of the material continued to burn because water could not reach it. "You had about a minute to get out of the store – it happened that fast," said the Quincy Wiring Inspector, who said it was a matter of seconds before the heavy, thick smoke spread through the store. "I would say that anybody that lingered more than a minute wouldn't have got out," said the Inspector.

City Council President Mike Cheney said he was worried about the smoke danger. "It's scary, because you know there are a lot of chemicals in there. There was a blanket of smoke rolling through the neighborhood."

"People were panicking," said a Home Depot cashier. "What would you expect? The building was on fire."

There was a second major fire at a Home Depot in Tempe, Arizona on March 19, 1998. According to the Tempe Fire Department, the fire began in a rack that contained lawn furniture seat cushions. The cause was determined to be incendiary, and was started by someone using a point and click type of lighter to ignite the seat cushions. Firefighters arriving on the scene reported that "smoke had filled the building from floor to ceiling, and that visibility was zero." The official report by the National Fire Protection Association concludes that the fire "overwhelmed the inadequately designed sprinkler system, destroying 96 linear feet of racks and product, and causing $6 million in damage."

The NFPA added: "The level of protection being provided in bulk retail stores is a matter of concern for many local fire and building officials . . . considering the potential number of customers that can be in one of these stores and the speed with which this particular fire grew, there is a concern over potential risks. There is also a strong concern for firefighters that must attack fires in these buildings. Due to the nature of the business, there are very wide and varied commodities being sold in these buildings. Some of these products, such as pesticides, herbicides, oxidizers, flammable and combustible liquids, and aerosols, can present significant hazards to fire fighters. The additional risk of product that is stored on pallets on the upper shelves dropping during interior fire-fighting operations creates another serious hazard that must be addressed during fire attack."

Hometowns, or Home Depot?

Home Depot likes to say: "Good Things Happen When Home Depot Comes to Town." Many communities around the nation have fought bitterly to prevent Home Depot's brand of "good things" from happening to their town. Here is a "hometown tour" of more than two dozen communities that have had close encounters with the orange-blooded company:

• **Santa Rosa, California: Journey's End for Home Depot.** On a warm afternoon in early June 1995, Lola Strom, a senior citizen who lives in the Journey's End Mobile Park in Santa Rosa, opened her mail to find a letter from a company called Crossroads R/W. It says on their letterhead that they are "Governmental Acquisition & Relocation Specialists." The letter informed Lola that the owners of her mobile park were planning to change the zoning of her park and close it down. "They have found a buyer," the letter continued, "the Home Depot company, who plans to build a new retail store on the property after the park closes and after all the residents are properly relocated into new housing situations." Lola learned that Home Depot would prepare a Relocation Plan for all the elders in the park. They would receive information, counseling, moving assistance and other benefits which "will ease the burden and costs of moving."

"We fully understand the effects of relocating from a place that has been 'home' for many years," the company assured Lola. "Please do not feel compelled to move out," the letter added, "until the new store and the Relocation Plan are approved" by the Santa Rosa City Council. Lola was told she would be given six months notice of the park's closing. The 200 elderly residents would have to move so that Home Depot could lease the land to build a 154,000 square foot store on the north end of Mendocino Avenue. "It'll break our hearts when we have to leave here," one elderly resident told the media.

But Lola and her neighbors never had to move. They began gathering petitions asking city officials to reject Home Depot. The City Manager came out against converting thirteen acres of residential land into retail. After all, Santa Rosa's General Plan for land use called for "preserving existing mobile homes, and preventing conversion of mobile home parks to other uses." Home Depot was undeterred. "We're confident that the opposition will recede," the Home Depot lawyer said, calling conversion of the park "inevitable." Home Depot had recently converted thirty-nine mobile homes in Seattle, Washington into a new store – so why not here too? "They have a great tiger by the tail," warned the mobile park residents. The elders began appearing weekly at City Council meetings, and plans were underway for a five-hour picketing session at a nearby Home Depot.

The picketing never happened, because Home Depot decided to "relocate" their proposal instead of relocating the elders. "They said it was generating more heat than they wanted to endure," said Mayor Jim Pedgrift. For Home Depot, it was the Journey's End. But it was a Journey that never should have begun. Home Depot unsuccessfully tried to add one more "home" to their chain, by closing the homes of the elderly. Since withdrawing from Journey's End, Home Depot has explored at least two other sites in Santa Rosa. Each time, the elders have followed their moves, urging public officials to keep them out of Santa Rosa city limits. Eventually, Home Depot abandoned plans to locate in Santa Rosa, and moved their plans to Windsor, California instead.

• **Yarmouth, Massachusetts: Home Depot Scrapped.** It was an early Christmas gift from Home Depot to the town of Yarmouth, when company officials announced in March of 1997 that they were pulling out of this Cape Cod community. The building supply chain told reporters that they could not agree on an extension of the purchase and sales agreement with the Christmas Tree Shops, owner of the industrial warehouse they wanted to rent. "We have put a lot of time and effort into it," admitted Home Depot's public relations manager, "but we just couldn't come to an agreement." Members of the Yarmouth Citizens for Responsible Development suspect other motives for the sudden withdrawal. "Maybe Home Depot came to the realization that is not economically feasible to open that store on Cape Cod," said one resident. "The real reason I suspect," wrote group leader Harriet Ronander, "is that Home Depot couldn't meet the conditions laid down by the Cape Cod Commission and the Regional Policy Plan." Because of regional land use planning on Cape Cod, the Commission was expecting Home Depot to produce a detailed economic impact report, and that report would be critiqued by an independent economic analyst. Home Depot never supplied the necessary reports, and may have anticipated a lengthy legal battle if they pursued the project. The company lost the vote in a special town meeting in Yarmouth in August of 1995, 549 against to 342 for. A second vote was held in April of 1996: 24% of voters supported Home Depot, 20% voted against, and 56% didn't vote at all. Home Depot bussed in its employees from other stores onto the Cape to hold signs on streetcorners promoting a Home Depot vote. The votes, however, were non-binding, and Home Depot ending up withdrawing from the project. Home Depot then picked another site in the neighborhood of Cedarville in Plymouth, Massachusetts, near a rotary just off the Cape, where the Cape Cod Commission could not reach them. Home Depot was rejected in Cedarville in 1998, and began exploring yet another location in Plymouth.

• **Nassau, New York: No Corporate Responsibility.** Lieutenant Rick Capece of the Nassau, New York police told *Newsday* that Home Depot managers at the East Meadow store "were sort of playing deaf, dumb and blind" when confronted with neighbor's complaints about idling trucks in the parking lot. "They're saying it's trucks delivering to them — so they're not responsible for them," Capece said.

• **Encinitas, California: Home Run?** Home Depot hired a series of political consultants to help them win an election in Encinitas. The consultants later wrote about the campaign in a magazine, explaining how they overcame "highly motivated environmental-leaning voters." The consultants wrote,"Behind this solid victory was a careful strategy by Home Depot's consulting team."

Home Depot paid for four consulting groups; a media relations firm; a field operations consultant; a consultant to shape strategy and message; and a polling/voter targeting firm. Home Depot urged town officials to quickly hold an election, because "support for Home Depot could only diminish over time… as opponents raised fears…a (quick) election deprived the opposition of sufficient time to mobilize effectively." Home Depot paid for a phone bank to make calls to voters, a computer-generated mailing, and an advertising campaign. Consultants conducted an absentee voter campaign that they credited with giving them the margin of victory, which was 63% for Home Depot to 37% against.

Like a politician running for office, Home Depot spent its money liberally on voter turnout, instead of hammers and nails. The consultants proudly called this vast expenditure of corporate money to win an election a "Home Run for Home Depot."

- **Lansing, Michigan: Abysmal Record.** In May of 1998, Michigan Attorney General Frank Kelley announced that his office had filed a lawsuit against Home Depot over violations of his state's Consumer Protection Act and item pricing statutes. Kelley said that Home Depot had "knowingly and persistently" violated state unit pricing laws. Kelley said: "Home Depot's compliance record with Michigan consumer law is abysmal. The management of this company has consistently failed to live up to past agreements . . . Item pricing is one of the most popular laws with consumers. I hope shoppers will keep this case in mind when making decisions on where to shop in the future."

- **Nashua, New Hampshire: Flip Flop.** Residents of Riverview Garden sued Home Depot for proposing to put up a 130,000 square foot store only 70 feet from their apartments. The Nashua Planning Board in November 1996 approved a request to amend previous zoning approvals for the mall where Home Depot wanted to locate. The Nashua Zoning Board overturned that decision in January 1997, but a week later backed down and voted to support Home Depot. The Zoning Board denied the project initially based on noise, traffic and pedestrian safety. The residents in the abutting apartments said that Home Depot would ruin the character of their neighborhood. The owner of the housing complex took the decision to court. Nashua, by the way, already has a Home Depot located several miles away on the other side of town.

- **Reno, Nevada: More Saturation.** Home Depot petitioned the City Council in May of 1996 to change its Master Plan and Zoning Ordinances, grant variances, and issue special use permits to build a second Home Depot in Reno, six minutes from the first store. The City's Planning Commission rejected the proposal unanimously because it didn't meet any of the ten findings needed for a special use permit, was in violation of hillside development ordinances, and ignored buffer requirements between residential and commercial properties. But the City Council voted four to three to approve it. The Home Depot is literally just feet from neighboring houses.

- **Clarendon, Virginia: Too Big.** Homeowners in this community told a County Planning Commission that a Home Depot would only bring "noise, traffic, air pollution, and decreased property values." Abutters said the 103,000 square foot store was too big for the site. Residents successfully defended against Home Depot's request to have the land rezoned for retail. County planning officials warned Home Depot to either reduce the size of their project, or "stack" a second story onto a smaller store base. The project received a "resoundingly negative response."

• **Mansfield, New Jersey: Letter-Writing Campaign.** Residents near this historic district of Beattystown spent more than four years fighting a mall that was to be anchored by Wal-Mart at one end, and Home Depot at the other. As the project grew more unpopular and more heated, Home Depot eventually withdrew from the project. The developer's lawyer blamed a citizen's letter-writing campaign as the reason why Home Depot dropped out of the proposal. The project ultimately received approval, without a Home Depot.

• **Greensboro, North Carolina: Citizens Spooked.** In 1994, nearly 800 petition signers fought to rezone eighteen acres of hillside land for a Home Depot. After the Guilford County Commissioners approved the rezoning, residents took the decision to court. The lawsuit fizzled, after homeowners ran scared. They were "spooked," according to one newspaper account, when Home Depot and the developer sought damages from them that could have totaled thousands of dollars. City and county planners opposed the rezoning because of traffic and pollution. Home Depot made important concessions to the angered community: they gave the store a red brick facade and agreed not to use the loudspeakers in the garden center.

• **North Olmsted, Ohio: Zero-To-Bad for Home Depot.** The welcome mat was not out for Home Depot, which wanted to locate across the street from a Wal-Mart in North Olmsted. Home Depot and three other retailers wanted twenty-four acres rezoned from office park to retail. According to the *Sun Herald* newspaper, the developer "is sure to be stalled by a ring of fire from area residents." Ward Four councilman Dean McKay predicted: "I'd give it a zero-to-bad chance of getting through. The fact is, we already have too much retail in North Olmsted. There's a lot of vacant stores."

McKay said he doesn't have a problem with retail development. "It's when they start infringing on a residential area that there's a problem." The developer mailed a fact sheet to area residents warning that "to maintain its position as a leading regional retail center . . . North Olmsted must continue to attract new retailers that are the cornerstone of today's market." But according to the newspaper, "it is doubtful that many North Olmsted residents would mourn if shoppers chose to go elsewhere."

A real estate developer offered local homeowners an "above market price" to entice them to sell out. Last spring, Former Mayor Ed Boyle gave the project 0% chance of happening. "Not if they painted it red, white and blue and presented it on the Fourth of July," Boyle said. The Park West Homeowners Association organized to stop the project, but the developer conducted a survey designed to show that consumers want a Home Depot. But what one Ohio newspaper called "the Home Depot invasion" finally drew up short in North Olmsted. The City Council in February 1997 voted unanimously to deny a zoning change, which effectively blocked Home Depot's efforts on that parcel. The developer persisted in going to the ballot to try and get his land rezoned from office to commercial. In November of 1998, the voters of North Olmsted resoundingly defeated the rezoning plan. Home Depot then moved its planned store to a nearby existing mall, where it encountered virtually no opposition.

• **Cary, North Carolina: Wrong Color.** In 1993, city planners in Cary objected to the orange color of Home Depot's proposed store, saying that only the main sign could have that color. Home Depot resisted that demand, but finally gave in when the Town Council sided with their planning staff.

• **West Roxbury, Massachusetts: Misinformation Suit.** In this Boston neighborhood, Home Depot sued an opposition group's lawyer for libel. In a letter to the editor of a local newspaper, lawyer James Rosencranz claimed the company spread "misinformation" in its two year battle for zoning permits. A judge dismissed the Home Depot suit a month after the store opened.

• **Costa Mesa, California: Dog on a Hydrant.** Home Depot is developing a store location just three miles from its existing store in Santa Ana. When asked why Home Depot would build another store so close to an existing store, Scott Bell, president of ICI, the development company working on the project, simply said: "It could be they want to protect their turf."

• **St. Charles, Illinois: Corporate Welfare?** Home Depot, a company with annual sales of nearly $20 billion, asked the city of St. Charles for $8.5 million in tax incremental financing to help spur a development in the Cave Springs area. The new TIF district proposed by Home Depot would receive tax subsidies over the next ten years. TIF has been a "controversial form of public assistance," said the *St. Louis Business Journal*, "since taxing jurisdictions, especially school districts, don't reap the tax benefits of new development." Home Depot originally asked for $8.5 million, but the city negotiated the amount of tax subsidies down to $3.9 million.

• **East Liberty, Pennsylvania: More Corporate Welfare.** It was announced in July of 1998 that Home Depot was building a new store in East Liberty, Pennsylvania that would cost $10 million. But 43% of that cost was being picked up by the state of Pennsylvania. Home Depot paid the state's Urban Development Authority $1 million for land, and another $5.2 million to build the store. The rest of the financing, $3.8 million, came from the Authority, city bond money, the Pennsylvania Department of Commerce, and a tax-increment financing proposal. The competing building supply stores in East Liberty must have wondered why the world's largest building supply retailer was given government assistance in putting local companies out of business.

• **New York, New York: No Thanks, Mr. Mayor.** The City Council of New York in December 1996 voted thumbs down on a proposal by Mayor Rudolph Giuliani that would have opened the door for megastores like Home Depot to open outlets in industrial areas of the city. Manhattan City Councilwoman Ruth Messenger led the effort to block the rezoning plan. When Home Depot was expanding in Queens, New York, citizens claimed that Home Depot's two top executives had tried to buy political favor. In 1992, Chairman Bernie Marcus and President Arthur Blank each gave $6,500 (the maximum allowed) to Giuliani's campaign. Most recently, residents in East Harlem are fighting a proposed Home Depot store in their neighborhood.

• **San Francisco, California: A Terrible Idea Whose Time Has Come.** Cable cars aren't the only things that go up and down in San Francisco. So have the fortunes of Atlanta-based chain Home Depot. In 1996, Mayor Willie Brown called Home Depot's proposal to lease space in San Francisco's Pier 80 "a terrible idea...We must discourage the encroachment of large chains and outlets which tend to stifle job growth and export dollars out of the community." Seven months later, Home Depot hired the Mayor's former campaign manager, Jack Davis, to nail the deal shut. Davis was paid $30,000 by Home Depot to meet with the Mayor and "discuss plans and exchange information" regarding a Home Depot for the Port. These discussions led to a 45-minute tour by Mayor Brown to a nearby Home Depot. Hizzoner emerged from Home Depot with a change of heart. "He had a very positive experience," Davis said. "I'm definitely Home Depot shopping," the Mayor told reporters. The residents of the Mission Park neighborhood successfully kept Home Depot from locating a store in their community.

• **Riverside, California: Papa, Why Do We Have Too Move?** Jacob Hernandez and his Madison Street home stood in Home Depot's way of building a 131,000 square foot store. His seven-year-old son scrawled a sketch of the family home, with the words [sic]: "Papa, Why Do We Have Too Move?" Hernandez enlarged the paper to a sign and put it on his front lawn. Hernandez refused to sell his home to Home Depot. He inherited the home from his father, and wants to pass the house on to Jacob, Jr. "At least I've tried," Hernandez told reporters. "That's what I can tell my son. At least I didn't roll over."

Residents of Riverside were angered when their own Redevelopment Agency offered to loan Home Depot $730,000. Home Depot would actually loan the Agency the money, and the Agency would pay Home Depot back with interest out of tax incremental financing. "Why does a multi-billion corporation need help from Riverside's Redevelopment Agency?" asked the citizens' group.

• **North Greenbush, New York: Need a Fire Station?** Citizens in this small (population 15,000) community that overlooks Albany vowed to fight off a developer who has already put up a Wal-Mart/Grand Union mall in their community, and now wants to add another shopping mall anchored by Home Depot. The mall is slated for the intersection of Routes 4 and 43, in the Defreestville neighborhood of town, in a Professional Business District in a predominately residential area with 1,300 residents. To build the mall, the developer, John Nigro, needed the five member Town Council to change the zoning.

Residents feared he would try to overlay a Planned Development District which might allow a large mall. But the town was in the final stages of adopting a new zoning plan, including a more progressive PDD district that requires the built environment to be compatible in scale and character with the residential character of the town, limits stores to community businesses, and restricts retail use to buildings no larger than 40,000 square feet gross floor area. The developer offered to build a new fire station, much to the pleasure of the Defreestville Fire Department. But the Defreestville Area Neighborhoods Association fired back: "Our Association will not be "blackmailed" by any developer seeking to develop our community in a manner that is inconsistent with its current residential/neighborhood business character and the proposed Master Plan for the area." The North Greenbush Democratic Committee came out "firmly opposed" to the Home Depot project. The developer said publicly that he had no agreement yet with Home Depot, and declined to give any details of his negotiations with the company. But the residents of Defreestville had a letter directly from Home Depot. Mark Bander, the Real Estate Manager for the Atlanta-based chain, wrote to neighbors and told them "the existing Route 4 corridor has the best roadways to service the development with the least concerns to the community."

The developer said the Home Depot site was the ideal place for such a development. However, the thirty-five acres that Home Depot wanted was zoned "professional business district," and was bordered by single family homes to the north and east. The North Greenbush Master Plan committee presented a new zoning map that keeps the property zoned office park. In addition, local officials offered the developer at least three other sites, including one just across Route 43. The developer rejected all offers. "It's smaller, and the elevations and esthetics would not be as pleasing as the one across the street," the developer explained.

"Permitting commercial activity on this site would seriously undermine the town's ability to contain commercial development to only this site," the Master Plan Committee warned the Town Board. "The act of allowing commercial development on (this site) would set a precedent that would lead to a step-by-step dismantling of the professional business district zone." The neighbors stated their position very clearly: "Runaway commercial development in our neighborhood would be a disaster."

The developer summed up his case by saying: "Home Depot and the others know where they want to be." The citizens of North Greenbush also knew where they didn't want Home Depot to be. The Master Plan committee handed Home Depot a rejection, voting to keep the land zoned professional business. But Home Depot found another location in North Greenbush, and managed to build a store at the second location, without opposition from community neighbors.

• **Manalapan, New Jersey: An Outright Ban.** Public opposition to a Home Depot in 1991 became so intense that officials in this New Jersey town decided to rewrite their zoning bylaws to exclude building supply stores. Home Depot then sued the town, and the litigation lasted four years until it reached the New Jersey Supreme Court, where Home Depot lost. The Court affirmed that the Manalapan ordinance had been properly adopted and was valid, "even if in response to public opposition," and was not inconsistent with the town's Master Plan. Home Depot's lawsuit forced taxpayers in Manalapan to pay for the town's legal defense for four years. But today there is no Home Depot in Manalapan.

• **New Hartford, Connecticut: Home Depot Yo-Yo.** Residents of this small community sent a letter to Bernie Marcus, CEO of Home Depot, urging his company to drop plans to build a store on Route 202 just feet away from the more populated Torrington town line. "This land is in the Farmington River watershed," the group wrote. "There are wetlands on the land, it is isolated from other commercial uses, and surrounded by residences . . . there is no water or sewer service, no storm drainage, and no professional fire department." The residents told Bernie, "We are adamantly and unequivocally opposed to construction of the type that Home Depot represents . . . we will do everything we can to prevent such construction."

The company said that it had "nothing pending" in the town, but the town's Zoning Officer said "a major retailer" had requested an application to build on the site. Local residents went to Town Hall and photocopied a check paid by a Manhattan engineering firm for site maps. On the memo line of the check it said"Home Depot." The check was dated December 26, 1996 — nearly three months earlier. One neighbor told a local reporter: "I'll be close enough to see the glow of its lights, and hear some yo-yo calling for 24 two-by-fours on the intercom from my yard." Home Depot eventually located a store in New Hartford, despite resident opposition.

• **Rutland, Vermont: Another Letter to Bernie.** A group of citizens and small businesses, Rutland Region First, has formed to oppose efforts of Home Depot to locate a store in the town of Rutland, Vermont, which circles the city of Rutland. The citizen's group has sent a letter of opposition to Home Depot's CEO, Bernie Marcus. The first Home Depot in Vermont was located in Williston, when a last minute switch was pulled between a Sam's Club and the Home Depot. Sam's "assigned" its lease to Home Depot after the project had already battled through its approval. The city of Rutland is the community that allowed a Wal-Mart to come to town – but only if it located in downtown Rutland in a 78,000 square foot vacated Kmart. Home Depot is trying to build a store in the town of Rutland. It will not only face an organized opposition group of taxpayers and business owners, but the regional land use board, known as Act 250, as well. In the spring of 1999, Home Depot began to surface again in Rutland with a proposal to locate in a dead mall outside of the city. The Governor of Vermont has urged Home Depot to locate downtown.

• **Napa, California: No Special Deals for Home Depot.** A group called Napans for Responsible Government challenged a developer's efforts to add a 118,000 square foot Home Depot to the South Napa Marketplace, which was anchored by a Target. The master plan for the Marketplace called for a limit of 80,000 square feet for the available space. The developer underplayed the sales that Home Depot would take from other area businesses. "What is Home Depot going to do to the home improvement business in the area?" the developer asked. "Personally, I believe they won't do all that much." However, a 1994 study done for the city of Napa showed that the building supplies market was around $40 million. A Home Depot in nearby Rohnert Park was bringing in $46 million in sales. This means that Home Depot alone required more revenue than the entire sales pie of roughly 50 other stores in the city. The same study showed that Napa lost very little in sales leakage for building supplies to other communities, because the city already had a good cross-section of hardware and building supply stores. Residents asked town officials to keep the limit at 80,000 square feet and not give the Atlanta-based retailer any special deals, but with municipal help, Home Depot opened in the mall in Napa in 1998.

• **Port Chester, New York: Murder the Local Merchants.** A Home Depot proposed for the village of Port Chester, New York spawned two lawsuits: one from the neighboring city of Rye, and one from the Rye Citizens Committee. According to the *Westchester County Business Journal*, both suits accuse Port Chester of trying to push the Home Depot project through with no regard for any negative impact that might occur in surrounding communities. The lawsuits seek to nullify Port Chester's zoning change resolution that would clear the way for a 101,000 square foot Home Depot. The project site is currently a mixed-used zone with small retailers and more than 400 houses. Home Depot would be the largest retail project in Rye, Port Chester and Greenwich.

Home Depot first tried to get into Port Chester in June of 1992. The lawsuit says that the Port Chester Planning Commission held a meeting to consider the Home Depot plan, but it was not on the regular agenda. The citizen's lawsuit contends that during the process the Port Chester officials hindered access to public documents, and "retained purported independent consultants paid by Home Depot without disclosing to the public the facts of said retailer."

The suit also charges that Port Chester limited comments from the public, and did not limit the presentation from Home Depot. The Rye Citizen's Committee says that the village was predisposed to approve the project, which will "murder the local merchants and devastate local neighborhoods." According to the Metropolitan Chapter of the American Planning Association, a 150,000 square foot store will directly increase congestion costs by $5 million per year. The report also said that a store of that size would increase the number of traffic accidents and add to noise and air pollution. "These impacts are so complex and significant," states the suit, "yet deliberations on the Home Depot application were so flawed. It constitutes absolute evidence of predisposition, mind-boggling rubber-stamp determinations."

• **Toledo, Ohio: Home Depot Spends Big.** In November of 1998, Home Depot narrowly won a ballot question on rezoning land in Toledo. The Westgate Neighborhood Association, which fought the project, spent $14,297 on their campaign, while Home Depot reported spending $497,549, or just under $12 per vote to win the campaign. Home Depot outspent citizens by a margin of 35 to 1, but won with only 55% of the vote.

• **Brookfield, Wisconsin: When They Don't Want You.** The developer for a Home Depot in this town had very few comments to make when he emerged from a Town Board meeting in Brookfield in June of 1998. "When they don't want you, they don't want you," he said. The Town Board disposed of a Home Depot application in record time.

It took the Board less than five minutes to turn down Home Depot's request to rezone property off Blue Mound road. The rezoning was needed to move forward with plans for a 112,000 square foot store. The Brookfield Planning Commission had recommended several months earlier that the project be rejected because of traffic concerns. Home Depot summoned up a new traffic study to allay town concerns, but the Board wanted none of it. The local press simply reported that Home Depot's plans to locate in Brookfield had "run into speed bumps." "It was a deaf ear," bemoaned Home Depot's development manager.

• **Menomonee Falls, Wisconsin. Home Depot Harassment.** Home Depot admitted publicly to organizing local people in Menomonee Falls to phone village officials who voted against Home Depot's plans to build a store there. Village President Joe Greco and board member Mike McDonald said that a telemarketing firm hired by Home Depot had relayed as many as forty calls a day to their homes. "In my seventeen years in office, I have never seen a tactic like this," Greco said. "It bothered me that they would use those kinds of tactics, I think, to harass public officials." In October 1998, the Village Board took Home Depot off the hook because the site they chose near an existing shopping center would generate too much traffic. Apparently Home Depot then decided to increase the phone traffic into the homes of officials who rejected the company.

"We don't view it as a form of harassment at all," said Home Depot spokeswoman Kelly Hays. "They are elected public officials. The idea was to get factual support to counter the claims of Joe Greco that no one in town supports the project." There is no word on how much money Home Depot spent to hire the telemarketing company that called Menomonee residents.

Home Depot's Future: "A Ton of Stores"

"There are markets in the United States that are so badly undersaturated," explains Home Depot Chairman Bernie Marcus, "that they need to have lots of Home Depots."

"When people ask where are we going to fill in," adds Arthur Blank, Home Depot President, "I say we still have room to add a ton of stores."

The company opened 137 new stores in 1998, and plans to have ribbon cuttings at another 170 new stores in 1999. In 1986, the top three building materials stores controlled 11% of the $56 billion trade market. Ten years later, the top three firms controlled (31%) of a $102 billion market.

Home Depot announced in May of 1998 an ambitious expansion plan. "We're doubling the size of this company," said spokesman Don Harrison. "It took us eighteen years to build the first 500 stores, and we plan to build the next 500 stores in the next three years. That is a growth path."

Most industry analysts predict that any business caught in the line of march of this "growth path" will be crushed. "The smaller regional players are getting squeezed," explained an analyst with Brown Brothers Harriman. "They are banding together or getting out entirely, or shrinking back to a base where they think they can continue to exist." *The Wall Street Journal* predicted in January of 1997 that "regional chains and small independents are likely to feel increasing pressure to merge with rivals or quit." And Citicorp Securities added: "Home Depot and Lowe's are going to make it very difficult for anybody else to get in."

So Home Depot expansion at this point is simply a matter of gaining more market share dominance. Or, as William Blair and Company has stated: "Any company goes through extraordinary growth, and at some point what you're doing is investing in putting other guys out of business."

When Home Depot arrives with its architectural drawings and site plan at your local Planning Board hearing, just remind your local officials that Home Depot is making an investment in your town "in putting other guys out of business."

Good things happen when Home Depot comes to town — but mostly for Home Depot.

Appendix IV

Sprawl-Buster's Toolbox

Other books to help you bust sprawl:

Wal-Mart: A History of Sam Walton's Retail Phenomenon. Vance & Scott, Twayne Publishers, 1994.

Vermont Act 250 Handbook. Argentine, Putney Press, 1993.

How Superstore Sprawl Can Harm Communities, and What Citizens Can Do About It. Beaumont, National Trust for Historic Preservation, 1994.

Made in America: My Story. Walton, Huey. Doubleday, 1992.

Smart States, Better Communities. Beaumont, National Trust for Historic Preservation, 1996.

In Sam We Trust. Ortega, Random House, 1998.

The Sprawl-Busters Alert Newsletter. Norman, Conservation Law Foundation, Boston. 617-350-0990.

On the Internet

There are now literally dozens of hometown websites about Wal-Mart battles. Most have linking sites of interest to sprawl-busters. Here are some samples of these hometown websites:

Friends of Humboldt County: *www.humboldt1.com/friends/*

Gig Harbor, WA: *www.harbornet.com/pna/walmart.htm*
Mesa, AZ: *www.mvna.com*

East Mountain Citizens Against Wal-Mart, NM:
www.nuvo.com/stopthewal/index.htm

Other general websites:

International Council of Shopping Centers: does demographic profiles and publishes white papers on retail market: *www.icsc.org/rsrch/research.html*

Sprawl Resource Guide: *www.webcom.com/~pcj/sprawl.html*

The Bulldozer Brigade: *www.norfolk.county.com/users/*

Institute for Local Self-Reliance: *www.ilsr.org*

Sprawl-Busters: *www.sprawl-busters.com*

Sierra Club Sprawl Materials: *www.sierraclub.org/transportation/*

Wal-Mart lawsuits. Search for personal liability and breach of contract, etc.: *prairielaw.com/findlaw/index.html*

Appendix V

Victorious Secret

Developers have effectively convinced local officials that it is futile to try to stop superstores. They want it to remain a secret that communities can beat sprawl. But the record shows otherwise. Here is just a partial list of nearly 100 communities where sprawl-marts have been defeated — at least once. In some cases, Wal-Mart or Home Depot came back a second or third time to get in, but in the communities listed below, citizens organized to slam-dunk sprawl, and won at least once:

Gilbert, AZ
Grass Valley, CA
North Auburn, CA
Santa Rosa, CA
San Francisco, CA
Santa Maria, CA
Simi Valley, CA
Plainville, CT
Orange, CT
New Milford, CT
Old Saybrook, CT
Tolland, CT
Fort Collins, CO
Jefferson County, CO
Silverthorne, CO
Rehobeth, DE
Clermont, FL
Hallandale, FL
St. Petersburg, FL
Temple Terrace, FL
Hailey, ID
New Albany, IN
Wichita, KS
Barnstable, MA
Billerica, MA
Easthampton, MA
Greenfield, MA
Lee, MA
Northboro, MA
Plymouth, MA
Reading, MA
Saugus, MA

Somerset, MA
Westford, MA
Yarmouth, MA
Gaithersburg, MD
Paradise, MD
Fenton, MI
Burnsville, MN
Warsaw, MO
Lincoln, NB
Durham, NC
Hickory, NC
Claremont, NH
Henniker, NH
Peterborough, NH
Walpole, NH
Hamilton, NJ
Manalapan, NJ
Buffalo, NY
East Aurora, NY
Hornell, NY
Hyde Park, NY
Ithaca, NY
Lake Placid, NY
Leeds, NY
New Paltz, NY
North Greenbush, NY
Saranac Lake, NY
Broadview Heights, OH
Chardon, OH
Cleveland Heights, OH
Granville, OH
Highland Heights, OH

Lorain, OH
North Olmsted, OH
Ottawa, OH
Strongsville, OH
Yellow Springs, OH
Westlake, OH
Mount Joy, PA
Warwick, PA
West Hempfield, PA
Barranquitas, PR
Utuado, PR
Middletown, RI
Layton, UT
Taylorsville, UT
Accomac, VA
Fredericksburg, VA
Roanoke, VA
Warrenton, VA
Williamsburg, VA
Gig Harbor, WA
Port Townsend, WA
Brookfield, WI
Menomonee Falls, WI
Waukesha, WI
St. Albans, VT
St. Johnsbury, VT
Williston, VT
Guelph, Ontario
Waterloo, Ontario
View Royal, British Columbia

Index

Order Form

Raphel Marketing
12 South Virginia Avenue
Atlantic City, NJ 08401
Tel: (609) 348-6646 Fax: (609) 347-2455 e-mail: info@raphel.com

Please send me:
Copies   Total

_____ *Slam-Dunking Wal-Mart* by Al Norman   @ $29.95 _____

_____ *Customer Specific Marketing* by Brian Woolf   @ $29.95 _____
      Increase profits by focusing on your best customers.

_____ *Crowning the Customer* by Feargal Quinn   @ $19.95 _____
      Outstanding customer service ideas.

_____ *Up the Loyalty Ladder* by Murray & Neil Raphel @ $23.00 _____
      Turning customers into full-time advocates.

_____ *Delight Me-10 Commandments of Customer Service* @ $19.95 _____
      by Drs. Richard George and John Stanton

      Shipping and handling $4 first book, $1 each additional book _____

TOTAL DUE $ _____

Please send to:

Name _____

Company _____

Street Address _____

City _____ State _____ Zip _____

Country _____ Telephone: (   ) _____

Credit card: (check one) ❏ Visa ❏ MC ❏ American Express ❏ Discover

Account # _____

Cardholder signature _____

Quantity discounts available: Please call for information.

TOLL-FREE FOR ORDERS   (877) 386-5925